Michel Tournier

PHILOSOPHY AND FICTION

COLIN DAVIS

CLARENDON PRESS · OXFORD
1988

Oxford University Press, Walton Street, Oxford OX2 6DP
Oxford New York Toronto
Delhi Bombay Calcutta Madras Karachi
Petaling Jaya Singapore Hong Kong Tokyo
Nairobi Dar es Salaam Cape Town
Melbourne Auckland
and associated companies in
Beirut Berlin Ibadan Nicosia

Oxford is a trade mark of Oxford University Press

Published in the United States
by Oxford University Press, New York

British Library Cataloguing in Publication Data
Davis, Colin
Michel Tournier: philosophy and fiction.
—(Oxford modern languages and literature monographs).
1. Fiction in French. Tournier, Michel, 1924–
I. Title
843'.914
ISBN 0-19-815152-7

Library of Congress Cataloging in Publication Data
Davis, Colin.
Michel Tournier, philosophy and fiction.
(Oxford modern languages and literature monographs)
Bibliography: p.
Includes index.
1. Tournier, Michel—Criticism and interpretation.
I. Title II. Series
PQ2680.083Z67 1988   843'.914   88-5170
ISBN 0-19-815152-7

Phototypeset by Dobbie Typesetting Service,
Plymouth, Devon
Printed and bound in
Great Britain by Biddles Ltd,
Guildford and King's Lynn

Acknowledgements

THANKS are due to Éditions Gallimard for permission to quote from Tournier's works. I am also grateful to the editors of *Paragraph*, *French Studies*, *French Forum*, and *Neophilologus* for permission to draw on material used in articles for those journals. Of the many people who helped me during the preparation of the D. Phil. on which this book is based, I should like to thank in particular Christopher Robinson, Rhiannon Goldthorpe, Bernard Howells, Christina Howells, Michel Tournier, who was patient enough to tolerate my abstruse questions on two occasions, and, finally, my parents, Wilf Davis and Edith Davis, who have never stood in the way of what I wanted to do.

Contents

Contents

Abbreviations

REFERENCES to Tournier's principal works are given in the text and notes with the following abbreviations:

CB	*Le Coq de bruyère*
G	*La Goutte d'or*
GJ	*Gilles et Jeanne*
GMB	*Gaspard, Melchior et Balthazar*
M	*Les Météores*
RA	*Le Roi des aulnes*
V	*Vendredi ou les limbes du Pacifique*
Vol	*Le Vol du vampire*
VP	*Le Vent Paraclet*

Introduction
Tournier and Philosophy

At the age of seventeen Michel Tournier was introduced to philosophy in the classes of Maurice de Gandillac at the Lycée Pasteur in Neuilly (see *Vol* 379–83). Philosophy became the overriding intellectual passion of his early adulthood, and he pursued his studies in a state of blithe indifference to historical events: 'Je me lançai dans un diplôme sur les idées platoniciennes que l'offensive de la Wehrmacht à Noël dans les Ardennes et le spectre d'un retour de l'Occupation ne purent troubler' (*VP* 84). After the war he went to Tübingen for three weeks and stayed for four years: 'c'était désormais vers la philosophie allemande — Fichte, Schelling, Hegel, Husserl, Heidegger — que ma soif de savoir, de comprendre et de construire me poussait' (*VP* 86). On his return to France, he took the *agrégation* and failed. This failure may be regarded as being responsible for his subsequent turn to literature:

Ainsi donc, s'il fallait dater la naissance de ma vocation littéraire, on pourrait choisir ce mois de juillet 1949 où dans la cour de la Sorbonne Jean Beaufret m'apprit que mon nom ne figurait pas sur la liste des admissibles du concours d'agrégation. Ma révolte fut d'autant plus passionnée que je me jugeais carrément comme le meilleur de ma génération. (*VP* 158)

Tournier has been more successful as a novelist than he was as a philosopher. His first novel, *Vendredi ou les limbes du Pacifique*, was awarded the Grand Prix du Roman de l'Académie Française, and the second, *Le Roi des aulnes*, won the Prix Goncourt by unanimous vote. Although his work has been subject to criticism on both moral and aesthetic grounds, he has been widely acclaimed as the most exciting novelist of his generation.[1] Nevertheless, he has

---

[1] Roger Shattuck describes Tournier as 'the most exciting novelist now writing in French' ('Locating Michel Tournier', p. 218); see also D. G. Bevan, *Michel Tournier*, p. 10. For more ambivalent assessments of Tournier's writing, which acknowledge its quality but express reservations concerning its ethical content, see Robert Poulet, 'Michel Tournier, romancier hors série', and Jean Améry,

not forgotten his years as a student of philosophy. His texts contain a daunting range of references to philosophical influences, extending from Heraclitus and Parmenides (see *CB* 180) to Sartre, whom he described in 1979 as 'pour moi l'homme vivant le plus important de la planète' (*Vol* 301). He regarded the philosophical systems which he encountered in his student days as 'monuments historiques d'une majesté et d'une grandeur supérieures à tout ce que l'humain peut offrir' (*VP* 153–4). This high evaluation of philosophy was accompanied by a dismissive attitude towards literature. Tournier and his student friends distinguished between 'systèmes philosophiques' and 'bandes dessinées': 'Tout ce qui n'était pas système — ou études consacrées à un système — était bande dessinée, et dans cette catégorie méprisable nous jetions pêle-mêle Shakespeare et Ponson du Terrail, Balzac et Saint-John Perse. Nous étions ivres d'absolu et de puissance cérébrale' (*VP* 155). The philosopher who turns to literature and literary studies inevitably adopts an inferior discipline and ceases to practise philosophy 'proper'. Bachelard ('Le seul maître que j'ai approché régulièrement', *VP* 148) is a case in point. In Tournier's view, Bachelard revitalized 'la critique littéraire et plus encore la lecture poétique', but he was not 'un philosophe au sens étroit et un rien intolérant où nous l'entendions' (*VP* 150). Sartre's *L'Être et le Néant* appeared 'tel un météore' (*VP* 155), but his literary and political activity in the post-war period was interpreted as a defection from philosophy. He produced 'bandes dessinées' which were 'Infiniment supérieures à tout ce qui se faisait dans le même genre', but nevertheless 'tout juste bonnes à nous faire pleurer la mort de l'auteur de *L'Être et le Néant*' (*VP* 157). The 'magie du regard philosophique' may relieve 'toute la misère des lettres réduites à elles-mêmes' (*Vol* 383), but literature could never be more than second best for the 'petit Tarzan métaphysicien' (*VP* 175), who judged himself 'carrément comme le meilleur de [sa] génération' (*VP* 158). Tournier shows irony towards his earlier opinions and self-image but does not entirely dismiss them. In this respect, the condemnation of Sartre exemplifies his attitude: 'Jugée avec le recul des ans, cette condamnation m'apparaît dans tout son excès juvénile. Pourtant je ne peux m'empêcher de penser qu'elle contenait une graine de vérité' (*VP* 157).

'Ästhetizismus der Barbarei: Über Michel Tourniers Roman „Der Erlkönig" '. Full details of publication for books and articles cited are given in the Bibliography.

Le Vent Paraclet, an account of some aspects of Tournier's life and works, frequently indicates the author's continuing interest in philosophy. He shows a particular predilection for Leibniz's notion of 'pre-established harmony' (see *VP* 27–31) and the assimilation of life and thought, action and knowledge which he finds in Spinoza's *Ethics* (see *VP* 229 and 277). Sartre, Bachelard, and Lévi-Strauss are the most important of the twentieth-century thinkers to whom he acknowledges a debt. However, Tournier seems to have paid little attention to the French intellectual scene since his failure in the *agrégation*. His use of the word 'métaphysique', for example, suggests his indifference to the problem of metaphysics, which, in the wake of the attacks conducted by Nietzsche and Heidegger, has played a central role in recent continental thinking. In many passages of *Le Vent Paraclet* Tournier apparently uses the words 'philosophie' and 'métaphysique' as if they were interchangeable; and he cheerfully disregards contemporary debate in his definition of metaphysics as 'la rigueur des mathématiques mariée à la richesse de la poésie' (*VP* 60). Moreover, Tournier's conception of 'La grande joie métaphysique' perhaps indicates that the failed philosopher was, after all, better suited to literature than to abstract philosophical speculation:

Le propre de la métaphysique au contraire, c'est toujours de plonger au cœur même du concret, et c'est d'ailleurs ce qui fait sa difficulté propre [. . .] La grande joie métaphysique, c'est le sentiment fort et chaleureux que l'élan cérébral vous mène d'un coup à la racine des choses les plus matériellement palpables, odorantes et rugueuses. Qui n'a jamais senti cela ne sait pas ce qu'est la métaphysique. (*VP* 42–3)

Denied a career in philosophy, Tournier eventually turned to literature and reluctantly undertook the difficult transition from philosophical system to 'bande dessinée': 'Comment faire sortir un roman de Ponson du Terrail de la machine à écrire de Hegel? Pour reprendre une comparaison de Paul Valéry, je prétendais faire des parties de dames avec un jeu d'échecs' (*VP* 175). Tournier describes himself as an outsider in the world of letters, practising what, according to his own value system, must be an inferior discipline. Nevertheless, his fiction will be guided by an unquestioning respect for literary tradition: 'Je prétendais bien sûr devenir un vrai romancier' (*VP* 174). Describing himself as an *émigré* forced to leave his philosophical homeland, Tournier defends the customs of his 'nouvelle patrie': 'Mais bien entendu il ne pouvait être question pour moi que de romans traditionnels. En vrai naturalisé de fraîche date, j'avais le respect scrupuleux des usages de ma nouvelle patrie' (*VP* 189). Tournier compares himself to a Pakistani immigrant to Great Britain, proud of his new homeland and lamenting the loss of the Empire:

Je suis ce naturalisé, romancier au teint quelque peu basané par le soleil métaphysique. A peine ai-je revêtu mon beau costume d'académicien, je m'aperçois que nous avons perdu le personnage, la psychologie, l'intrigue, l'adultère, le crime, les paysages, le dénouement, tous les ingrédients obligés du roman traditionnel. Alors je dis non, comme mon Pakistanais naturalisé dirait non aux étudiants nés et élevés à Oxford qu'il verrait conspuer la reine et le Premier ministre. Non aux romanciers nés dans le sérail qui en profitent pour tenter de casser la baraque. Cette baraque, j'en ai besoin, moi! (*VP* 190)

Tournier continues to value the 'monuments historiques' of philosophy above the 'baraque' of literature. He nevertheless insists on the need to defend literature against those internal dissenters who are 'nés dans le sérail' and who in his view wish to destroy their own art. Elsewhere in *Le Vent Paraclet* Tournier indicates his dislike of what he rather coyly refers to as 'une certaine école moderne' which 's'efforce de faire éclater les limites de la littérature' (*VP* 175). Tournier adopts a polemical stance as he sets himself up in opposition to literary modernism and more specifically to the *Nouveau Roman*. His only detailed criticism lies in the suggestion that the latter has too much form and not enough content (see *VP* 127 and *Vol* 367), whereas, he insists, his own project is to combine traditional form with innovative content: 'Mon propos n'est pas d'innover dans la forme, mais de faire passer au contraire dans une forme aussi traditionnelle, préservée et rassurante que possible une matière ne possédant aucune de ces qualités' (*VP* 190). Tournier's argument depends upon an over-simple opposition between form and content, to which he himself does not adhere in less polemical moments; for example, he greatly admires Bach's *Art of the Fugue* and insists that its formal complexity actually contributes to the 'charge à la fois humaine et cosmique' of the work (*VP* 127). Moreover, some of the formal aspects of Tournier's own novels are less reassuringly traditional than he implies: the use of different narrators in *Les Météores*, for example, unsettles the authority of any single narrative voice and therefore plays a similar role to the perspectival instabilities which characterize some examples of the *Nouveau Roman*. Tournier has more in common with his contemporaries than he would like to admit. He distinguishes between the subversive content of his texts and the subversion of literary form which the *nouveaux romanciers* hope to achieve, but he does not question the value and necessity of subversion in literature (see *VP* 190). He condemns those who seek to 'faire éclater les limites de la littérature' (*VP* 175), but he *also* attempts to transgress the frontiers of literature by introducing philosophy into fiction 'en contrebande':[2]

Donc faire œuvre littéraire. Mais ne jamais oublier que je venais d'ailleurs, et rester dans le monde des lettres un homme d'ailleurs. Il ne fallait pas renoncer aux armes admirables que mes maîtres métaphysiciens avaient mises entre mes mains. Je prétendais bien sûr devenir un vrai romancier, écrire des histoires qui auraient l'odeur du feu de bois, des champignons d'automne ou du poil mouillé des bêtes, mais ces histoires devraient être secrètement mues par les ressorts de l'ontologie et de la logique matérielle [. . .] J'avais l'ambition de fournir à mon lecteur épris d'amours et d'aventures l'équivalent littéraire de ces sublimes inventions métaphysiques que sont le cogito de Descartes, les trois genres de connaissance de Spinoza, l'harmonie préétablie de Leibniz, le schématisme transcendental de Kant, la réduction phénoménologique de Husserl, pour ne citer que quelques modèles majeurs. (*VP* 174–5)

Excluded from his philosophical homeland, Tournier attempts to minimize the discrepancy between the 'monuments historiques' of philosophy and the 'baraque' of literature by making literature a kind—albeit an inferior kind—of philosophy: 'j'ai choisi la littérature comme un autre moyen de faire de la philosophie.'[3]

With his open espousal of metaphysics and his defence of traditional literary forms, Tournier may seem an irrelevant voice in an 'age of suspicion'. However, it is important to read his self-presentation in *Le Vent Paraclet* with a sceptical eye. The characteristic irony and ambiguity of his writing, in *Le Vent Paraclet* and his other non-fictional texts as well as in his novels, invite suspicion towards even the most emphatic statement of intention. In his list of 'quelques modèles majeurs' Tournier cites Descartes, Spinoza, Leibniz, Kant,

---

[2] Tournier uses the phrase 'en contrebande' when he is discussing Sartre's attempt to introduce philosophy into literature, in terms which strongly suggest his own project as novelist; see *Vol* 303.

[3] From 'Je suis comme la pie voleuse', interview with Jean-Louis de Rambures, in *Comment travaillent les écrivains*, p. 165.

and Husserl (*VP* 174–5, quoted above). Elsewhere, he will add Plato and Aristotle to this already imposing list (see *Vol* 382). But he goes too far. The very proliferation of names and philosophies throws doubt upon the seriousness of his declared project. Tournier admits nothing by claiming too much.

Philosophy, for Tournier, is never the disinterested pursuit of knowledge. Ideas are toys to amuse a bored child ('Mes vrais jouets, ceux qui continuent à m'amuser, c'est la philosophie qui me les a donnés', *Vol* 382) or a weapon ('le grand couteau de la dialectique', *VP* 148) with which to exercise his 'volonté de puissance cérébrale' (*VP* 42). Leonardo da Vinci and Pascal may be forgiven for not being familiar with Kant's *Critique of Judgement*, but Paul Valéry has less excuse.[4] Tournier believes he knows better, patronizing and enlightening his benighted reader with his superior understanding. At the same time, he never commits himself unambiguously to any particular philosophical theory or system. Fiction may be another means of practising philosophy, but philosophy, for Tournier, is already to a certain extent an aesthetic phenomenon. The work of Leibniz, 'le penseur baroque par excellence', recalls 'ces gracieuses églises souabes ou autrichiennes'; it describes a universe 'sans contrainte, sans frottements, sans même un seul contact' and characterizes the Creation as 'une sorte de pluie ou une chute de neige douce et continue' (all quotations *VP* 27). Tournier does not believe or disbelieve, agree or disagree, although he insists that he knows no philosophy 'au charme plus convaincant' (*VP* 29): 'Oui, si je devais me déclarer en faveur d'une philosophie, c'est à coup sûr celle-là que je choisirais' (*VP* 29). However, the condition is unfulfilled, and Tournier's commitment remains cautiously hypothetical.

Moreover, Tournier is aware that the novel offers unfavourable ground for the propagation of ideas. In his discussion of the relationship between word and meaning in poetry and philosophy, he adopts what initially seems to be an utterly conventional distinction:

Dans un poème, le mot l'emporte sur l'idée, laquelle suit comme elle peut ou ne suit pas du tout. La musique des rimes est première. L'enchaînement des significations secondaire. Au contraire pour un philosophe l'idée l'emporte absolument sur le mot. Celui-ci n'est jamais assez subordonné à l'idée, au point que le philosophe est constamment amené à créer des termes nouveaux pour mieux exprimer sa pensée. (*VP* 199)

---

[4] See *Vol* 65 and *Canada: Journal de voyage*, pp. 107–8.

This passage seems to indicate Tournier's adherence to what Jacques Derrida has called 'logocentrism':[5] *signifié* and *signifiant*, content and form, meaning and expression, idea and word are kept radically separate, even if Tournier concedes that in poetry at least signifier should take precedence over signified. However, the novel is described as a hybrid form which confuses the relationship between word and meaning:

A mi-chemin entre la philosophie et la poésie, le roman emprunte à la philosophie la propulsion de ses raisonnements et intentions qu'il alourdit il est vrai en lui faisant véhiculer affabulation et évocation. En passant de la philosophie où les concepts jouent sans frottements ni perte d'énergie au roman avec ses personnages et ses paysages, on voit les mots se charger de substance et comme engraisser [. . .] Le mot transparent comme un concept dans la philosophie, opaque comme une chose dans le poème, doit demeurer translucide dans le roman et mêler en lui autant d'intelligence que de couleurs et d'odeurs. (*VP* 200–1)

Tournier hopes that the novel can effect a compromise between the conceptual subtlety of good philosophy and the creative textual freedom of good poetry. However, the difficulty of fulfilling these conflicting requirements may make the novel the locus of confusion and ambiguity rather than synthesis. As Tournier himself insists, the philosophical novel is both 'faux roman' and 'fausse philosophie'.[6]

Tournier's texts, including *Le Vent Paraclet*, are characterized by their combination of dogmatic assertion and uncommitted irony. Tournier's pedagogy invites scepticism when it appears to demand passive acceptance. As one critic has observed, 'Tournier is never closer to facetiousness than when he is at his most sententious.'[7] In *Le Vent Paraclet*, which purports to be non-fictional, this can be simply annoying. In his fictional texts it ensures that what some regard as Tournier's 'bankrupt traditionalism'[8] is less straightforward than it might appear to a hostile reader. The following chapters will attempt to show that Tournier's fictional practice is never the

---

[5] On logocentrism, see particularly Jacques Derrida, *De la grammatologie*.

[6] See 'Dix-huit questions à Michel Tournier', interview with Jean-Jacques Brochier, p. 11.

[7] Geoffrey Strickland, '*Gaspard, Melchior et Balthazar* by Michel Tournier', p. 240.

[8] The phrase is used by Geoffrey Strickland (ibid. 238) in reference to critical remarks about Tournier made by Philippe Sollers in an interview published in *Le Nouvel Observateur*, 19 Jan. 1981, p. 17.

tendentious illustration of philosophical theory. Tournier knows that the language of fiction cannot be the transparent vehicle of unambiguous meanings, and he insists that 'un vrai roman [. . .] n'impose pas au lecteur un "message" fini, bouclé, intouchable' (*Vol* 375). Tournier's texts engage the reader in the quest for understanding, but never arrive at a fully intelligible conclusion.

I

The Philosophical Novel
Vendredi ou les limbes du Pacifique

(i) *Philosophy*

Tournier's first novel, *Vendredi ou les limbes du Pacifique* (1967), brought its author immediate popular and critical acclaim. Shortly after its publication the philosopher Gilles Deleuze established its intellectual and aesthetic credentials in an important article in which he analysed the relationship of *Vendredi* to phenomenological, structuralist, and psychoanalytic theories of *autrui*.[1] Subsequently, critics have developed this line of enquiry by looking for traces of the philosophers who influenced Tournier's text. Spinoza, Leibniz, Nietzsche, Bachelard, and the Stoics have all been suggested;[2] and the relationship between Vendredi and Crusoé has been seen as an illustration of the Hegelian dialectic of master and slave.[3] Tournier himself gives ample support to philosophical readings of *Vendredi*, describing his aim as 'la mise à nu des fondements de l'être et de la vie' (*VP* 223). He characterizes his project as the attempt to combine a classical adventure story with the demanding intellectual speculation of Valéry's *Monsieur Teste* and Descartes's *Discours de la méthode*: 'Fondre l'essai et le roman, la réussite promettant d'être d'autant plus éclatante que l'essai sera plus abstraitement métaphysique et l'affabulation plus aventureusement picaresque' (*VP* 225).

---

[1] See Gilles Deleuze, 'Michel Tournier et le monde sans autrui', in *Logique du sens*, pp. 350–72, first published in *Critique* in 1967 and also published as a postface to the 'Folio' edition of *Vendredi*. On Tournier's friendship with Deleuze, see *VP* 151–2.

[2] See François Stirn, *Tournier: Vendredi ou les limbes du Pacifique*, especially pp. 74–6.

[3] See Jacques Poirier, *Approche de. . . Vendredi ou les limbes du Pacifique (Michel Tournier)*, p. 19; on the 'post-Hegelian' aspect of Tournier's first novel, see also Margaret Sankey, 'Meaning through Intertextuality: Isomorphism of Defoe's *Robinson Crusoe* and Tournier's *Vendredi ou les limbes du Pacifique*', p. 82.

For Tournier, philosophical content has priority over literary form, and writing is the search for an adequate means of expression: 'Mon seul problème littéraire est donc d'ordre pédagogique: comment rendre claires et agréables ces choses subtiles et difficiles que j'ai à dire.'[4] Richness of meaning may be dissipated by the absence of suitable form, and so rigid structure is the indispensable supplement to the plenitude of content: 'La matière amorphe appelle la forme nette' (*VP* 186). The opening pages of Tournier's first novel introduce one of the author's principal concerns as they dramatize the search for a secure form to guard against the threat of chaos. The ship *Virginie* is described as '*un bâtiment à toute épreuve*' (*V* 9); yet within the space of a few pages Crusoé is confronted with the spectacle of its 'silhouette tragique et ridicule', its 'mâts mutilés', and its 'haubans flottant dans le vent' (*V* 15). The island itself is a scene of disorder: 'La grève était jonchée de poissons éventrés, de crustacés fracturés et de touffes de varech brunâtre' (*V* 15). Crusoé surveys the island from the 'sommet du chaos' and eats wild pineapple in order to fill 'un vide nauséeux' (*V* 17). He undertakes the construction of a boat, a rigid structure which proves *too* rigid to fulfil its function since it cannot be moved to the sea. After the failure of this attempt to escape from chaos, Crusoé succumbs for the first time to the temptation of the 'souille', a mud pit in which he wallows like an animal and which marks the lowest point in his spiritual decline.[5]

In Chapter Three the text finally reveals its own solution to the anxiety of formlessness: the act of writing itself. Using the blanched pages of books found in the wreck of the *Virginie*, Crusoé—like Valéry's Monsieur Teste[6]—begins to keep a logbook. His text is literally a palimpsest, written on the top of previous texts,[7] and it marks a new era in his life on the island:

---

[4] From 'Je suis comme la pie voleuse', interview with Jean-Louis de Rambures, in *Comment travaillent les écrivains*, p. 165.

[5] For further discussion of the problem of form and formlessness in the opening pages of *Vendredi*, see Mieke Taat, 'Et si le roi était nu? — Michel Tournier, romancier mythologue', especially pp. 53–5.

[6] For a while Daniel Defoe's Crusoe keeps a journal, but Tournier indicates his debt to Valéry by referring to his protagonist's text as a *logbook*; see 'Extraits du log-book de Monsieur Teste' in Paul Valéry, *Œuvres*, ii. 37–45.

[7] On *Vendredi* itself as a palimpsest, see Gérard Genette, *Palimpsestes*, pp. 418–25.

Il lui semblait soudain s'être à demi arraché à l'abîme de bestialité où il avait sombré et faire sa rentrée dans le monde de l'esprit en accomplissant cet acte sacré: écrire [. . .] Une ère nouvelle débutait pour lui — ou plus précisément, c'était sa vraie vie dans l'île qui commençait après des défaillances dont il avait honte et qu'il s'efforçait d'oublier. (V 39)

Crusoé initially conceives his relationship with Speranza as the struggle between order and chaos: 'Ma victoire, c'est l'ordre moral que je dois imposer à Speranza contre son ordre naturel qui n'est que l'autre nom du désordre absolu' (V 43). Language contributes to this precarious victory. One of Crusoé's first acts is to *name* his island (see V 17). The loss of 'l'usage de la parole' is described as 'cette suprême déchéance' (V 46) because Crusoé believes that language is inseparable from society and the very possibility of knowledge: 'Le langage relève en effet d'une façon fondamentale de cet univers *peuplé* où les autres sont comme autant de phares créant autour d'eux un îlot lumineux à l'intérieur duquel tout est — sinon connu — du moins connaissable' (V 47). However, Crusoé is aware that 'Les phares ont disparu de [son] champ' (V 47). He realizes that language is incapable of communicating an experience which is absolutely individual: 'Je constate d'ailleurs en écrivant ces lignes que l'expérience qu'elles tentent de restituer non seulement est sans précédent, mais contrarie dans leur essence même les mots que j'emploie' (V 47).

Vendredi alternates between a third-person narrative which describes Crusoé's attempts to impose the order of civilization on to the disorder of Speranza and the logbook in which Crusoé endeavours to describe and understand his intellectual and spiritual evolution. Crusoé recognizes that the frantic cultivation and administration of Speranza correspond to an absolute demand to master the unknown:

Je veux, j'exige que tout autour de moi soit dorénavant mesuré, prouvé, certifié, mathématique, rationnel [. . .] Je voudrais que chaque plante fût étiquetée, chaque oiseau bagué, chaque mammifère marqué au feu. Je n'aurai de cesse que cette île opaque, impénétrable, pleine de sourdes fermentations et de remous maléfiques ne soit métamorphosée en une construction abstraite, transparente, intelligible jusqu'à l'os! (V 57)

Crusoé adheres to the Cartesian principle, quoted by Tiffauges in *Le Roi des aulnes*, of making 'des dénombrements si entiers, et des

revues si générales, que je fusse assuré de ne rien omettre'.[8] Yet
Crusoé takes the urge for totality to absurd lengths, warding off
insanity by an activity which is itself insane. The purely practical
difficulties entailed in the Cartesian enterprise seem capable of
preventing its realization. Self-doubt supersedes self-confidence: 'Mais
aurai-je la force de mener à bien cette tâche formidable? Cette
dose massive de rationalité que je veux administrer à Speranza, en
trouverai-je le ressource en moi-même?' (V 57–8).

As a result of his enforced solitude, Crusoé discovers that the
problems involved in the imposition of total rationality are also
philosophical in nature. In the absence of all human company, he
realizes that the possibility of knowledge is severely restricted. Other
people 'constituent des *points de vue possibles* qui ajoutent au point
de vue réel de l'observateur d'indispensables virtualités' (V 46). Before
the breakdown of what Deleuze calls the 'structure Autrui',[9] Crusoé
could believe in the possible completion of his own limited perception
by the potential or imaginary presence of others: 'L'île se trouvait
ainsi quadrillée par un réseau d'interpolations et d'extrapolations qui
la différenciait et la douait d'intelligibilité' (V 47). But solitude
undermines Crusoé's faith in intelligibility: for the solitary subject,
what is unseen ceases to exist. Objects are 'soumis à la loi sommaire
du tout ou rien' (V 32), and knowledge is no longer safeguarded
against the limitations of individual perception: 'Ma vision de l'île
est réduite à elle-même. Ce que je n'en vois pas est un *inconnu absolu*.
Partout où je ne suis pas actuellement règne une nuit insondable' (V
47). *Autrui* is both corrective and normative, completing the partial
perspective of the individual and guarding against the dangers of error
and insanity. Entirely dependent upon the evidence of his own senses,
Crusoé has no means of founding an objective distinction between
the real and the hallucinatory:[10]

Et ma solitude n'attaque pas que l'intelligibilité des choses. Elle mine jusqu'au
fondement même de leur existence. De plus en plus je suis assailli de doutes
sur la véracité du témoignage de mes sens [. . .] Contre l'illusion d'optique,
le mirage, l'hallucination, le rêve éveillé, le fantasme, le délire, le trouble

---

[8]   René Descartes, *Discours de la méthode*, in *Œuvres et lettres*, p. 138, quoted
by Tiffauges in *RA* 100.
[9]   On the 'structure Autrui' and the consequences of its breakdown, see Deleuze,
Logique du sens, especially pp. 369–72.
[10] See also Paul's reference to Crusoé in *M* 364–5.

de l'audition. . . le rampart le plus sûr, c'est notre frère, notre voisin, notre ami ou notre ennemi, mais quelqu'un, grands dieux, quelqu'un! (V 47)

In normal circumstances, and at the beginning of Crusoé's life on Speranza, the accumulation of evidence allows errors in perception to be corrected. What Crusoé initially and mistakenly perceives as a log is *in fact* a goat, and the existence of the log may be disregarded as 'une illusion d'optique, la vue défectueuse de Robinson' (V 84; see also V 16). Later Crusoé sees an ancient Spanish galleon and his sister Lucy (see V 35–6); but the galleon cannot exist, and Lucy is long dead. Retrospectively, Crusoé realizes his mistake and recognizes that he was the victim of an hallucination (see V 83). However, the experience of total solitude gradually removes the normative yardstick of objective reality. In isolation, Crusoé is 'un point de vue sur Speranza — un point, c'est-à-dire rien' (V 59). In the absence of alternative perspectives, he loses the reassuring standard by which the individual normally tests the accuracy of his own perceptions. However, he is unable to accept the chaos of absolute perspectivism. He anxiously insists that a spade should be a spade and, just as importantly, that it should be *called* a spade: 'Il me vient des doutes sur le sens des mots qui ne désignent pas des choses concrètes. Je ne puis plus parler qu'*à la lettre*. La métaphore, la litote et l'hyperbole me demandent un effort d'attention démesuré dont l'effet inattendu est de faire ressortir tout ce qu'il y a d'absurde et de convenu dans ces figures de rhétorique' (V 58). Figurative language is a form of verbal hallucination which obstructs knowledge of the world *as it really is*. Of course, Crusoé's rejection of metaphor only serves to draw attention to the figural quality of his own text.[11] Even so, at least in the early stages of *Vendredi*, the attempt to control figurative language parallels Crusoé's attempt to distinguish between reality and hallucination. Tournier weakens the metaphors used in his own text by attributing them to a momentarily deluded imagination:

La vaste plaine océane légèrement bombée, miroitante et glauque, le fascinait, et il se prit à craindre d'être l'objet d'hallucinations. Il oublia d'abord qu'il n'avait à ses pieds qu'une masse liquide en perpétuel mouvement. Il vit en elle une surface dure et élastique où il n'aurait tenu qu'à lui de s'élancer et de rebondir. Puis, allant plus loin, il se figura qu'il s'agissait du dos de quelque

---

[11] See, for example, the metaphors relating to stone in the lines preceding Crusoé's claim to speak 'à la lettre': 'pierre', 'édifice', 'érosion', 's'effritent', 'choses concrètes' (V 58).

animal fabuleux dont la tête devait se trouver de l'autre côté de l'horizon. Enfin il lui parut tout à coup que l'île, ses rochers, ses forêts n'étaient que la paupière et le sourcil d'un œil immense, bleu et humide, scrutant les profondeurs du ciel. Cette dernière image l'obséda au point qu'il dut renoncer à son attente contemplative. Il se secoua et décida d'entreprendre quelque chose. Pour la première fois, la peur de perdre l'esprit l'avait effleuré de son aile. Elle ne devait plus le quitter. (V 21)

Crusoé frantically resists the disintegration of the structures of reason and intelligbility. However, as he discovers the insufficiency of his own perception when unsupported by the presence of *autrui*, he also learns that *all* perception, however rich the variety of perspectives, is condemned to partiality. The ultimate horizon of Crusoé's intellectual adventure is not the acceptance of a Nietzschean perspectivism which affirms the impossibility of unifying disparate points of view. On the contrary, Crusoé begins to aspire to a higher unity and aims to achieve an intimate familiarity with Speranza which transcends the limitations of perception: 'Robinson n'est infiniment riche que lorsqu'il coïncide avec Speranza tout entière' (V 59). Crusoé's belief that he can attain a more authentic mode of knowledge is confirmed towards the end of the novel, when the arrival of the *Whitebird* provides the occasion for a final consideration of the problem of *autrui*. Using Leibnizian terminology, the narrator describes the members of the crew as 'mondes possibles', each having the discrete self-coherence of a monad:[12] 'Chacun de ces hommes était un monde *possible*, assez cohérent, avec ses valeurs, ses foyers d'attraction et de répulsion, son centre de gravité [. . .] Et chacun de ces mondes possibles proclamait naïvement sa réalité. C'était cela autrui: un possible qui s'acharne à passer pour réel' (V 192). The image the crew members have of Speranza is 'marquée du signe du provisoire, de l'éphémère, condamnée à retourner à bref délai dans le néant d'où l'avait tirée le déroutage accidental du *Whitebird*' (V 192). The variety of new perspectives may correct and complete the subjective partiality of the solitary subject, but at the same time something is irretrievably lost: 'il lui semblait qu'en octroyant à ces hommes la dignité qu'ils revendiquaient, il vouait du même coup Speranza à l'anéantissement' (V 193).

---

[12] For further discussion of this passage and its 'échos leibniziens', see Deleuze, *Logique du sens*, pp. 357–60.

Crusoé will eventually claim to have transcended the partiality inherent in *all* subjective perception as a result of a long period of initiation and discovery, which is accelerated by the arrival of Vendredi on Speranza. In the meantime, Crusoé's logbook indicates a growing awareness of the limitations of discursive speculation. In this respect, Crusoé's longest and most ambitious philosophical discussion, which relates the problem of *autrui* to 'l'antique problème de la connaissance' (V 80), marks an important turning-point in the novel. Crusoé insists that philosophical accounts of knowledge are founded upon a fundamental error: 'Il me semble que la présence d'autrui — et son introduction inaperçue dans toutes les théories — est une source grave de confusion et d'obscurité dans la relation du connaissant et du connu' (V 80). He illustrates the covert introduction of *autrui* into the theory of knowledge through the analogy of a man entering an unknown house: the very description of a stranger — *autrui* — discovering the contents of a previously unseen room presupposes the presence of an observer: 'Le problème général de la connaissance doit être posé à un stade antérieur et plus fondamental, car pour qu'on puisse parler d'un étranger s'introduisant dans ma maison et furetant parmi les choses qui s'y trouvent, il faut que je sois là, embrassant ma chambre du regard et observant le manège de l'intrus' (V 81). Crusoé's discussion develops into a contestation of Cartesian epistemology, which bases the possibility of knowledge on the subject's certainty of its own existence. The most famous expression of the fundamental tenet of Cartesianism is in Descartes's *Discours de la méthode*: 'Et remarquant que cette vérité: *Je pense, donc je suis*, était si ferme et si assurée que toutes les plus extravagantes suppositions des sceptiques n'étaient pas capables de l'ébranler, je jugeai que je pouvais la recevoir sans scrupule pour le premier principe de la philosophie que je cherchais.'[13] Descartes questions everything except the existence of the subject. But Crusoé's argument entails the radicalization of Cartesian doubt, and he now realizes that even the existence of the subject cannot be taken for granted: '[le moi] n'existe que de façon intermittente et somme toute assez rare. Sa présence correspond à un mode de connaissance secondaire et comme réflexif' (V 81–2). The self is described as a secondary construct required as a response to the questions: who knows, feels, observes? Crusoé attempts to describe what perception

---

[13] Descartes, *Discours de la méthode*, pp. 147–8.

and knowledge would be *before* the intervention of the reflexive subject: 'que se passe-t-il en effet de façon primaire et immédiate?' (V 82). The subject is engendered and maintained by an act of reflection. If this 'acte de réflexion qui me fait surgir' (V 82) does not take place, the disjunction between subject and object, observer and thing observed, does not exist. Knowledge coincides with its object: 'Dans l'état primaire de la connaissance, la conscience que j'ai d'un objet est cet objet même, l'objet est connu, senti, etc., sans personne qui connaisse, sente, etc.' (V 82).

The problem of *autrui*, then, arises only after pre-personal consciousness has been surrendered in favour of the reflexive knowledge which occupies a privileged place within the rationalist tradition. The acquisition of individuated consciousness is accompanied by what Crusoé calls a 'déclic': 'Le déclic correspond à un processus de rationalisation du monde. Le monde cherche sa propre rationalité, et ce faisant il évacue ce déchet, le sujet' (V 83). The world loses its pre-reflexive self-sufficiency and becomes the degraded predicate of the individual's senses: 'La lumière devient œil, et elle n'existe plus comme telle: elle n'est plus qu'excitation de la rétine. L'odeur devient narine — et le monde lui-même s'avère inodore. La musique du vent dans les palétuviers est réfutée: ce n'était qu'un ébranlement de tympan' (V 82–3). In the process of rationalization, the original 'virginité des choses' (V 82) is forfeited. The subject takes possession of his environment, but something of the real world, authentically perceived before individuation, is lost. Speranza, transformed into an object of conscious perception, 'se meurt sous mon regard sceptique' (V 83).

Sartrean phenomenology is an important source of Crusoé's attempt to describe a state of consciousness before the appearance of the reflexive subject. In his early essay *La Transcendance de l'ego* Sartre insists upon the necessity of a new Cogito, which would replace the personalized assertion '*j'ai* conscience de cette chaise' with the impersonal '*il y a* conscience de cette chaise'.[14] For Sartre, however, this does not mean that the subject and object of consciousness can ever be identical. On the contrary, in *L'Être et le Néant* he indicates that all intellectual endeavour would be made impossible if we were able to know being 'as it is': 'car pour connaître l'être tel qu'il est, il faudrait être cet être, mais il n'y a de "tel qu'il est" que parce que

---

[14] Sartre, *La Transcendance de l'ego*, p. 37.

je ne suis pas l'être que je connais et si je le devenais le "tel qu'il est" s'évanouirait et ne pourrait même plus être pensé.'[15] On this point, Crusoé diverges significantly from his Sartrean model. He attacks the foundations of rationalist epistemology by denying the absolute validity of the distinction between subject and object: 'Or le sujet et l'objet ne peuvent coexister, puisqu'ils sont la même chose' (V 84). In the process of rationalization, the subject transforms himself into a 'Nœud de contradiction, foyer de discorde', which must be 'éliminé du corps de l'île, éjecté, rebuté' (V 83). Crusoé hopes to restore the original unity of subject and object through his rejection of rationalism. In Sartrean terms, he aspires to be *en soi pour soi*, retaining both the solidity of being (*en soi*) and the freedom of consciousness (*pour soi*). For Sartre, this project will always be frustrated, due to the insuperable non-coincidence of *en soi* and *pour soi*; but Crusoé hopes to achieve the synthesis of consciousness and nature, even if this entails the abandonment of all further philosophical speculation: 'Alors Robinson *est* Speranza. Il n'a conscience de lui-même qu'à travers les frondaisons de myrtes où le soleil darde une poignée de flèches, il ne se connaît que dans l'écume de la vague glissant sur le sable blond' (V 82). Crusoé has now stated what will remain his fundamental ambition: the reversal of individuation and the restoration of what he believes to be the 'virginité des choses' and the 'état primaire de la connaissance' (V 82), an authentic mode of knowledge free from the mediation of language and reflexive consciousness: 'une île féconde et harmonieuse [. . .] sans moi, parce que si proche de moi que, même comme pur regard, c'en serait encore trop de moi et qu'il faudrait me réduire à cette phosphorescence intime qui fait que chaque chose serait connue, sans personne qui connaisse, consciente, sans que personne ait conscience. . .' (V 84).

Tournier's philosophical novel has now turned against philosophy, and Crusoé has become dissatisfied with the form of discursive speculation adopted in his logbook. At the end of his discussion of 'l'antique problème de la connaissance' he is eager to abandon discourse and return to the earth: 'Mais il était impatient de quitter ces rêveries et ces spéculations et de fouler le sol ferme de Speranza' (V 84). Mystical intuition will replace rational analysis, as Crusoé becomes aware of another island, the 'autre île', beneath the structures of the 'île administrée'.

---

[15] Sartre, *L'Être et le Néant*, p. 270.

(ii) 'L'Autre Île'

The first reference to the 'autre île' occurs immediately before Crusoé's discussion of the problem of knowledge and anticipates his rejection of discursive enquiry.[16] Crusoé wakes up one morning to find that his water-clock ('la clepsydre') has stopped. The ordinary sequence of time is interrupted and Crusoé discovers a reality independent of administrative and intellectual superstructures:

> Le temps était suspendu. Robinson était en vacances [. . .] Plus tard, réfléchissant sur cette sorte d'extase qui l'avait saisi et cherchant à lui donner un nom, il l'appela un *moment d'innocence* [. . .] On aurait dit que cessant soudain de s'incliner les unes vers les autres dans le sens de leur usage — et de leur usure — les choses étaient retombées chacune de son essence, épanouissaient tous leurs attributs, existaient pour elles-mêmes, naïvement, sans chercher d'autre justification que leur propre perfection [. . .] Il y avait quelque chose d'heureux suspendu dans l'air, et, pendant un bref instant d'indicible allégresse, Robinson crut découvrir une *autre île* derrière celle où il peinait solitairement depuis si longtemps, plus fraîche, plus chaude, plus fraternelle, et que lui masquait ordinairement la médiocrité de ses préoccupations. (V 79)

The 'autre île' does not belong to the order of language: when the water-clock stops, Crusoé is struck by 'le silence insolite qui régnait dans la pièce' (V 78); he feels an 'indicible allégresse' (V 79). The episode is recounted in the third person, not in Crusoé's first-person logbook: Crusoé himself *experiences* but does not *describe*. Once again, the problem of the text's ambivalence towards language has resurfaced. In only the second entry in his logbook Crusoé observes that the singularity of his experience 'contrarie dans leur essence même les mots [qu'il] emploie' (V 47). Now, describing the *effect* of an experience rather than the experience itself, the narrative can give only an indirect account of the ineffable self-presence to which Crusoé begins to aspire. The inevitable outcome of Crusoé's spiritual evolution would seem to be silence. For the moment, however, Crusoé intuits the plenitude of the 'autre île', but has not yet attained it: 'La larve avait pressenti dans une brève extase qu'elle volerait un jour' (V 79-80). Rather than the 'autre île' itself, the text describes

---

[16] The principal references to the 'autre île' are V 79-80, 105, 117, 149, 177. For the use of the phrase 'autre île' in one of Tournier's source-texts, see Jean Giraudoux, *Suzanne et le Pacifique*, e.g. p. 129. Tournier discusses Giraudoux's novel, as well as other adaptations of the Crusoe story, in *VP* 212-14.

the stages by which Crusoé approaches it. Until the explosion which finally destroys the 'île administrée', Crusoé will be engaged in a phase of quest and initiation. He continues to cultivate and administrate the island, but also begins to explore the possibility of an alternative existence. The logbook is used to elucidate his new relationship with Speranza: 'Speranza n'était plus un domaine à gérer, mais une *personne*, de nature indiscutablement féminine, vers laquelle l'inclinaient aussi bien ses spéculations philosophiques que les besoins nouveaux de son cœur et de sa chair' (V 85).

The first stage of Crusoé's quest for the 'autre île' leads him to the very heart of Speranza, as he discovers a womb-like space in the cave which he had used as a store for provisions. To fit perfectly within the space, Crusoé must assume a foetal posture: 'recroquevillé sur lui-même, les genoux remontés au menton, les mollets croisés, les mains posées sur les pieds' (V 89). In this position he is 'suspendu dans une éternité heureuse' (V 89) and he achieves 'un retour vers l'innocence perdue que chaque homme pleure secrètement' (V 94). Tournier self-consciously underlines the psychoanalytic implications of Crusoé's experience in the cave. Crusoé becomes a foetus in the womb of his surrogate mother Speranza: 'A ce degré de profondeur le nature féminine de Speranza se chargeait de tous les attributs de la maternité' (V 90). The drought which afflicts Speranza (V 94) is equated with the interruption of the mother's menstrual cycle caused by pregnancy: 'Enceinte de moi-même, Speranza ne pouvait plus produire, comme le flux menstruel se tarit chez la future mère' (V 95).

Crusoé's descent to the heart—or the womb—of Speranza represents the fantasy of an incestuous return to the origins of life. But maternal incest is not the solution to Crusoé's quest. His rediscovery of what he calls the 'sources mêmes de la sexualité' (V 108) does not come to rest in the rigid structures of Œdipal desire. When Crusoé later considers the stages of his sexual development (or regression), first in a cave, then with a tree (see V 100–2), and finally with the 'combe rose', he recognizes their shortcomings: 'Mes amours avec Speranza s'inspiraient encore fortement des modèles humains. En somme, je fécondais cette terre comme j'aurais fait une épouse' (V 185).[17] The

---

[17] Paul Valéry's 'Robinson' tentatively suggests the possibility of a sexual aspect to the Crusoe story which is absent from Defoe's novel; see Valéry, Œuvres, ii. 412: 'Il eût presque inventé l'amour, s'il n'eût pas été si sage et puis si seul.' For a brief

residual influence of social conditioning is still a decisive element in Crusoé's experiments with non-human sexual partners, since the latter are imagined as possessing human attributes. To return to what he believes to be the true, pre-human sources of his sexuality, Crusoé must isolate desire in its pure form, before and beyond maternal incest and the impregnation of an island–wife–mother:

Ainsi le désir. C'est un torrent que la nature et la société ont emprisonné dans un bief, dans un moulin, dans une machine pour l'asservir à une fin dont par lui-même il n'a cure: la perpétuation de l'espèce.

J'ai perdu mon bief, mon moulin, ma machine. En même temps que toute la construction sociale, tombée en ruine en moi d'année en année, a disparu l'échafaudage d'institutions et de mythes qui permet au désir de *prendre corps*, au double sens du mot, c'est-à-dire de se donner une forme définie et de fondre sur un corps féminin. (*V* 98–9)

Desire, in Crusoé's account, is distinct from the ends it is made to serve. Rather than an attribute of the individual, it acts as a pre-personal force independent of human volition, seeking liberation from the social and intellectual superstructures, the 'échafaudage d'institutions et de mythes' (*V* 99), which subjugate it to the ends of propagation:

Or c'est trop peu dire que mon désir n'est plus canalisé vers les fins de l'espèce. Il ne sait même plus à qui s'en prendre! Longtemps ma mémoire était assez nourrie pour fournir à mon imagination des créatures désirables bien qu'inexistantes. Maintenant, c'est fini. Mes souvenirs sont exsangues. Ce ne sont plus que cosses vides et desséchées. Je prononce: femme, seins, cuisses, cuisses écartelées par mon désir. Rien. La magie de ces mots ne joue plus. Des sons, *flatus vocis*. Est-ce à dire que mon désir est mort lui-même d'inanition? Tant s'en faut! Je sens toujours murmurer en moi cette fontaine de vie, mais elle est devenue totalement disponible. Au lieu de s'engager docilement dans le lit préparé à l'avance par la société, elle déborde de tous côtés et ruisselle en étoile, cherchant comme à tâtons une voie, la bonne voie où elle se rassemblera et roulera unanime vers un objet. (*V* 99)

The 'bonne voie', when it is found, will not lead towards a human object, nor towards an object deemed to act as a surrogate human. Crusoé's experiment with the tree ends on a note of comic demystification when he is bitten on the penis by a spider: 'Il y vit le signe

comparison of the problem of *autrui* in *Vendredi* and 'Robinson', see Régine Pietra, 'Génétique et modèles culturels du Robinson valéryen', pp. 86–9.

que la voie végétale n'était peut-être qu'une dangereuse impasse' (*V* 102). Later, when he copulates with the 'combe rose', Crusoé's sexuality is still restricted to the genital functions, and Speranza is still described in human terms as the 'wife' of Crusoé (see, for example, *V* 112). Nevertheless, the direct copulation with the earth is an important step beyond the restriction of desire to human objects:

Privé de femme, je suis réduit à des amours *immédiates*. Frustré du détour fécond qui emprunte les voies féminines, je me retrouve sans délai dans cette terre qui sera aussi mon dernier séjour [. . .] Quand j'ai été jeté sur ces bords, je sortais des moules de la société. Le mécanisme qui détourne la vocation naturellement géotropique du sexe pour l'engager dans le circuit utérin était en place dans mon ventre. C'était la femme ou rien. Mais peu à peu la solitude m'a simplifié. Le détour n'avait plus d'objet, le mécanisme est tombé en floche. Pour la première fois dans la combe rose, mon sexe a retrouvé son élément originel, la terre. (*V* 111)

In the course of his meditation upon sexuality, Crusoé discovers the Freudian 'instinct de mort' and its link with the sexual urge.[18] Through procreation, the individual guarantees the continuation of the species, but also wills his own disappearance:

Procréer, c'est susciter la génération suivante qui innocemment, mais inexorablement, repousse la précédente vers le néant. A peine les parents ont-ils cessé d'être indispensables qu'ils deviennent importuns [. . .] Dès lors il est bien vrai que l'instinct qui incline les sexes l'un vers l'autre est un instinct de mort [. . .] C'est apparemment un plaisir égoïste que poursuivent les amants, alors même qu'ils marchent dans la voie de l'abnégation la plus folle. (*V* 109)

Sexuality offers Crusoé a release from selfhood:

Le jour, l'individu tendu, monté, lucide refoule l'indésirable, le réduit, l'humilie. Mais à la faveur des ténèbres, d'une langeur, de la chaleur, de la torpeur, de cette torpeur localisée, le désir, l'ennemi terrassé se relève, darde son glaive, simplifie l'homme, en fait un amant qu'il plonge dans une agonie passagère, puis il lui ferme les yeux — et l'amant devient ce petit mort, un dormeur, couché sur la terre, flottant dans les délices de l'abandon, du renoncement à soi-même, de l'abnégation. (*V* 110)

[18] For discussion of how the death instincts (*Todestriebe*) are antagonistic to but intertwined with the sexual instincts, see Freud, *Beyond the Pleasure Principle*, in *The Standard Edition of the Complete Psychological Works of Sigmund Freud* (henceforth referred to as *The Standard Edition*), xviii. See also Jean Laplanche and J.-B. Pontalis, *Vocabulaire de la psychanalyse*, entry under 'Pulsions de mort', pp. 371–8.

At first, Crusoé observes with dismay how the structures of thought and identity begin to collapse in the absence of all human company. Subsequently, he realizes that the 'complexe et fragile échafaudage' (V 46) which constitutes selfhood and the 'citadelle verbale dans laquelle notre pensée s'abrite et se meut familièrement' (V 58) are by no means indispensable. He abandons his early speculations in favour of a *poetic* meditation (and this section of the novel contains some of the best writing to be found in *Vendredi*) on love and death, 'ces deux aspects d'une même défaite de l'individu' (V 111). Through his experiments with elemental and eventually non-genital sexuality, Crusoé deliberately seeks the freedom from individuation which he had earlier feared: 'Qu'ai-je fait dans la combe rose? J'ai creusé ma tombe avec mon sexe et je suis mort de cette mort passagère qui a nom volupté' (V 111).[19]

Tournier's first novel has much in common with Sartre's *La Nausée*. Like Crusoé, Roquentin experiences the collapse of the structures imposed by man on reality. Even Crusoé's logbook is often strongly reminiscent of Roquentin's journal.[20] Where the two novels differ is in the conception of what is disclosed through the collapse of structure. In *La Nausée* the world is revealed to be without order and without meaning: 'une effrayante et obscène nudité'.[21] Ultimately, for Sartre, it is necessary to accept the anthropocentric meaning which domesticates the chaos of reality. Like Roquentin, Crusoé retreats from the terrifying absence of structure; but the rejection of discursive reason and the self-abnegation facilitated by the exploration of sensual experience allow the genesis of a new, dehumanized order. The chaos which initially terrifies Crusoé is revealed to be 'un cosmos en gestation' (V 98). As we saw in the comparison with Sartre's phenomenological writings, Tournier's novel indicates the belief in a fully authentic mode of being, which Sartre considers to be unattainable.

---

[19] The slang expression *petite mort* (orgasm) may be at the back of Tournier's mind here. See also V 110 (quoted in text), where Crusoé refers to the lover as 'ce petit mort'.

[20] See, for example, Jean-Paul Sartre, *La Nausée*, in *Œuvres romanesques*, p. 150, which prefigures the enquiry into the breakdown of language in *Vendredi*: 'Les mots s'étaient évanouis et, avec eux, la signification des choses, leurs modes d'emploi, les faibles repères que les hommes ont tracés à leur surface.' For further similarities between *La Nausée* and *Vendredi*, compare, for example, the two mirror scenes, *Œuvres romanesques*, pp. 22–4, and V 75–6.

[21] Sartre, *La Nausée*, in *Œuvres romanesques*, p. 151.

Crusoé's spiritual Odyssey is a return to origins: not the (albeit rectified) social origins of the individual, as in Defoe's *Robinson Crusoe*, but rather a state which precedes individuation. The ambiguity of this and of every return to origins is that the original state must be restored *in the future*, and hence can be achieved only through a further distancing from origins. Crusoé construes the problem of construction/reconstruction in terms of the *donné* and the *construit*, one of the dichotomies which occur most frequently in Tournier's work: 'Remplacer du *donné* par du *construit*, problème général, problème humain par excellence, s'il est vrai que ce qui distingue l'homme de l'animal, c'est qu'il ne peut attendre que de sa propre industrie tout ce que la nature donne à l'animal — sa robe, ses armes, sa pitance' (*V* 97). Man must *make* what the animal is *given*. As in existentialist thought, even the self is regarded as a precarious construct: 'Je ne sais où va me mener cette création continuée de moi-même. Si je le savais, c'est qu'elle serait achevée, accomplie et définitive' (*V* 98). Crusoé's self-creation is both a *progression* away from his original self and a circular *regression* towards a pre-social state: creation is also re-creation and regeneration; the *construit* is the *re*construction of the *donné* forfeited by man in society.[22] Crusoé suggests the ambiguity of this construction/reconstruction when he uses the word 'original' in his attempt to describe the changes which he is undergoing: 'je me sens le théâtre d'une évolution plus radicale qui substitue aux ruines que la solitude crée en moi des solutions originales' (*V* 97). The word 'original' confronts the reader with the undecidable choice between contrary meanings: 'des solutions originales' are both absolutely old (*originaire, originel*) and absolutely new (*inédit, neuf, bizarre, étrange*).[23]

In his important article on *Vendredi* Gilles Deleuze plays down and even denies the extent to which Tournier's novel can be seen as a return to sources. For Deleuze, *Vendredi* is prospective and heuristic: 'Ce n'est donc pas l'origine qui compte ici, mais au contraire l'issue, le but final [. . .] Le Robinson de Tournier [. . .] est rapporté

---

[22] For a brief but useful account of the circular structure of Tournier's fiction, and of *Vendredi* in particular, see François Stirn, *Tournier: Vendredi ou les limbes du Pacifique*, pp. 60-2, and 69-70.
[23] Synonyms given by the *Petit Robert* (1978 edn.), entry under *original*. The *originaire/originel* alternative is given as old or literary.

à des fins, à des buts, au lieu de l'être à une origine.'[24] Deleuze completely overlooks the persistent rhetoric of regression and return which Crusoé uses to describe his experiences in the 'autre île' and his rediscovery of the pre-social sources of life and sexuality (see, for example, V 108, 111). Deleuze sees Tournier's novel as a form of psychoanalytic study contributing to contemporary attempts to redefine the concept of perversion.[25] Even so, Deleuze does suggest—without exploring the suggestion—that 'perversion' may also be restoration: 'La conjugaison de la libido avec les éléments, telle est la déviation de Robinson; mais toute l'histoire de cette déviation quant aux buts, c'est aussi bien le "redressement" des choses, de la terre et du désir.'[26] Here, Deleuze suggests the simultaneity of 'déviation' and 'redressement', one of the key terms in his essay. Crusoé 'sets right' (redresser) by deviating and deviates in order to set right. In Chapters Nine and Ten of Vendredi Crusoé rediscovers the (perverse) possibilities normally obscured by the 'structure Autrui':

Mais il découvre (lentement) que c'est plutôt autrui qui troublait le monde. C'était lui, le trouble. Autrui disparu, ce ne sont pas seulement les journées qui se redressent. Ce sont les choses aussi n'étant plus par autrui rabattues les unes sur les autres. C'est le désir aussi, n'étant plus rabattu sur un objet ou un monde possible exprimé par autrui. L'île déserte entre dans un redressement, dans une érection généralisée.[27]

The arrival of Vendredi on Speranza initially retards but ultimately accelerates Crusoé's exploration of the 'autre île'. With Vendredi's help, Crusoé still attempts to cultivate and administrate his island, but he has lost faith in the structures of the 'île administrée': 'quoi que fît Robinson, il y avait toujours quelqu'un en lui qui attendait un événement décisif, bouleversant, un commencement radicalement nouveau qui frapperait de nullité toute entreprise passée ou future' (V 149–50). An explosion accidentally caused by Vendredi eventually

---

[24] Deleuze, Logique du sens, pp. 351–2. Tournier gives some support to this view in Le Vent Paraclet when he is discussing the differences between his novel and Defoe's Robinson Crusoe: 'Ainsi donc mon roman se veut inventif et prospectif, alors que celui de Defoe, purement rétrospectif, se borne à décrire la restauration de la civilisation perdue avec les moyens du bord' (VP 223).

[25] See Deleuze, Logique du sens, p. 371.

[26] Ibid. 364. The notion of 'redressement' is suggested by V 176: 'On dirait, par suite, que mes journées se sont redressées' (quoted by Deleuze, Logique du sens, p. 361).

[27] Deleuze, Logique du sens, p. 362.

inaugurates a new age of discovery, in which Vendredi plays the role of initiator to his former master. He shows Crusoé how laughter undermines the totalitarian seriousness of the administrator, and Crusoé attempts to emulate his ignorance of 'toute notion de passé et de futur' (V 156). At the end of Chapter Nine of the novel Crusoé and Vendredi seem fully installed within the 'autre île'. Tournier shows this and also emphasizes the Romantic affiliation of his text when Vendredi transforms the skull of the old goat Andoar into an Aeolian harp, the instrument which became closely associated with the Romantic movement and which is probably best known to modern readers through Coleridge's celebrated poem.[28] Vendredi's harp plays an elemental music which facilitates the dissolution of selfhood and communion with nature: 'Serrés l'un contre l'autre à l'abri d'une roche en surplomb, Robinson et Vendredi perdirent bientôt conscience d'eux-mêmes dans la grandeur du mystère où communiaient les éléments bruts. La terre, l'arbre et le vent célébraient à l'unisson l'apothéose nocturne d'Andoar' (V 171; see also V 183).

Crusoé's use of the word 'mystique' suggests that his quest for enlightenment has been successfully concluded, as he describes the moments before sunrise at the beginning of Chapter Ten: 'J'ai mis un genou à terre et je me suis recueilli, attentif à la métamorphose de la nausée qui m'habitait en une attente mystique à laquelle participaient les animaux, les plantes et même les pierres' (V 173). In an essay on Sartre Tournier defines nausea as 'l'émergence terrible et menaçant de l'Être' and 'cette chose impensable et innommable qui réduit à néant nos projets, notre passé, notre présent' (Vol 308).[29] Even if the word 'nausée' in Crusoé's text is not a deliberate allusion to Sartre, its use illustrates the principal difference between Crusoé and Roquentin: the protagonist of La Nausée can overcome nausea only by retreating into the structures of language and art; Crusoé surpasses nausea and claims to achieve a state of mystical communion in which animal ('les animaux'), vegetable ('les plantes') and mineral ('les pierres') are united. By this point Tournier's novel seems to have reached its natural conclusion. In accordance with the teleology of the roman d'initiation, which promises the promotion

---

[28] See 'The Aeolian Harp', in Samuel Taylor Coleridge, pp. 27-9.
[29] For other uses of 'nausée' and 'nauséeux' in Vendredi, see V 17, 93, 103, 200.

from ignorance to understanding,[30] Crusoé claims to have 'avancé sur le chemin d'une longue et douloureuse métamorphose' before winning his 'salut dans la communion avec les éléments' (*V* 182). The eighteenth-century rationalist and moralist has completed his mystical conversion to the authentic life of the 'autre île'.

(iii) *Writing*

In *Vendredi ou la vie sauvage*, the children's version of Tournier's first novel, Vendredi warns Crusoé about their use of language: 'Nous parlons trop. Il n'est pas toujours bon de parler.'[31] However, the text does not heed its own warning and both *Vendredi ou la vie sauvage* and *Vendredi ou les limbes du Pacifique* continue beyond the destruction of the 'île administrée'. Tournier does not curtail his narrative and allow his text to succumb to the silence which seems to be the logical conclusion of Crusoé's evolution.[32] Despite his tendency to view ordinary language as a fallen and inauthentic medium, Tournier never attempts anything along the lines of Georges Bataille's 'holocauste des mots', a deliberate and strategic destruction of language which aims to clear a space for non-linguistic experience.[33] Tournier remains committed to narrative, and the final three chapters of *Vendredi* contravene the mystical inclinations of the novel by extending Crusoé's story beyond the apparent conclusion of his spiritual adventure. Moreover, after a space of thirty pages, Crusoé himself resumes his activity as author.

[30] On *Vendredi* and the *roman d'initiation* in general, see Simone Vierne, *Rite, roman, initiation*, especially pp. 119–23. For pertinent criticisms of Vierne's reading of *Vendredi*, see Mieke Taat, 'Et si le roi était nu? — Michel Tournier, romancier mythologue', pp. 53–5.

[31] Tournier, *Vendredi ou la vie sauvage*, p. 114. Tournier himself has often insisted that *Vendredi ou la vie sauvage* is a 'rewriting' of *Vendredi ou les limbes du Pacifique* and not specifically a 'version for children'; see, for example, 'Vers la concision et la limpidité', interview with Jean-Marie Magnan, p. 16. On the whole, however, the second version adds little to the first and loses a lot. For unenthusiastic assessments, see Daniel Bougnoux, 'Des métaphores à la phorie', p. 543, and Gérard Genette, *Palimpsestes*, pp. 424–5.

[32] Tournier even lengthened the 'Folio' edition of *Vendredi ou les limbes du Pacifique* (published in 1972) by adding episodes from *Vendredi ou la vie sauvage*. For additions to the original Gallimard edition, see *Vendredi* (Folio 959), pp. 172–3, 209–13.

[33] On the 'holocauste des mots', see, for example, Georges Bataille, *L'Expérience intérieure*, p. 158, and Sartre's discussion in *Situations*, i. 136–42. Anthony Purdy makes some interesting comparisons between Tournier and Bataille in 'Les Météores de Michel Tournier: Une perspective hétérologique'.

Chapter Ten of *Vendredi* consists of the final long series of extracts from Crusoé's logbook. Vendredi is 'enfermé dans l'instant présent' (*V* 183), and Crusoé now seeks to emulate this refusal of historical time. The art-form which best represents the absolute privilege of the present moment is the '*symphonie instantanée*' of the Aeolian harp, 'le seul instrument dont la musique au lieu de se développer dans le temps s'inscrit tout entière dans l'instant' (*V* 183). Writing, requiring the inscription of experience into a framework of past, present, and future, is clearly *not* such an art-form. Time cannot be abstracted from language; and so writing is by its very nature a hostile medium for the presentation of a state which has transcended sequential temporality. Crusoé's endeavour as author is, then, made problematic by the potential incompatibility of his experience and the language he uses. Moreover, internal inconsistencies begin to appear in the novel. In the opening section of *Vendredi*, when Van Deyssel predicts Crusoé's future with the aid of Tarot cards, he seems to promise that, before Vendredi's departure, Crusoé will achieve '*le zénith de la perfection humaine*' (*V* 11). However, as we shall see with Tournier's subsequent fiction, *Vendredi* does not fulfil its own teleological programme. The first and last sentences of Chapter Ten indicate that Crusoé has not attained the perfection promised by Van Deyssel because he has not yet learned to abolish time and need:

Ce matin, debout avant le jour, chassé de ma couche par une angoisse lancinante, j'ai erré parmi les choses désolées par la trop longue absence du soleil. (*V* 173)

Vénus, le Cygne, Léda, les Dioscures. . . je tâtonne à la recherche de moi-même dans une forêt d'allégories. (*V* 187)

Important changes can nevertheless be seen in the practice of writing adopted by Crusoé.[34] In his prayer to the sun, for example, the use of language as exclamation and imprecation begins to replace the speculative or descriptive modes which dominate the rest of the text (see *V* 180-1). Significantly also, Crusoé begins to use a form of highly metaphoric description. This can be seen, for example, in his account of the rising sun, in which metaphor describes and encourages a creative transformation of reality: 'Ensuite deux épées

---

[34] These changes are suggested by the blue ink and albatross feather with which Crusoé now writes and which replace the red ink and vulture feather used earlier: '— Maintenant, lui dit-il [Vendredi] simplement, l'albatros est mieux que le vautour, et le bleu est mieux que le rouge' (*V* 172).

de feu ayant touché mes épaules, je me suis relevé, chevalier solaire'. Aussitôt une volée de flèches brûlantes ont percé ma face, ma poitrine et mes mains, et la pompe grandiose de mon sacre s'est achevée tandis que mille diadèmes et mille sceptres de lumière couvraient ma statue surhumaine' (V 174; see also V 204–5). Earlier in the text metaphor was rejected on the grounds that, like hallucination, it obstructed the accurate perception and literal description of reality (V 21). Claiming to speak 'à la lettre', Crusoé rejected figurative language as a lure into error and absurdity (V 58–9). Now, however, the text accepts and flourishes in its own metaphoric mode, even if its intelligibility is partially impaired.[35]

Tournier's most sustained experiment (to date) in a non-representational narrative is in the final chapter of Les Météores, which will be discussed in Chapter 3. Vendredi anticipates some elements of that experiment—but with caution. Textual play in Tournier's first novel is tentative and on the whole carefully controlled.[36] In Chapter Ten, however, the primacy of the signified over the signifier is brought into question for the first time. Crusoé begins to allow linguistic resonances, private and cultural, to direct his meditation. This becomes most clear towards the end of Chapter Ten, when Crusoé discusses 'La vénusté de Vendredi':

Je le regarde s'arracher en riant à l'écume des vagues qui le baignent, et un mot me vient à l'esprit: la vénusté. La vénusté de Vendredi. Je ne sais pas exactement ce que signifie ce substantif assez rare, mais cette chair luisante et ferme, ces gestes de danse alentis par l'étreinte de l'eau, cette grâce naturelle et gaie l'appellent irrésistiblement sur mes lèvres. (V 183)

The rest of the logbook entry introduced by these words consists of a series of reflections in which Crusoé explores the 'écheveau de significations dont Vendredi est le centre' (V 183). 'Vendredi' is the title of the novel, a character in that novel, and the name of a day, the day of Venus, which also evokes Good Friday, the day on which Christ was crucified. Crusoé is reminded of Van Deyssel and

---

[35] Compare Vendredi ou la vie sauvage, where this change is made explicit. Before the explosion which destroys the 'île administrée', Crusoé 'aurait obligé Vendredi à reconnaître qu'une fleur est une fleur, et un papillon un papillon' (p. 109). After the explosion, he learns to appreciate Vendredi's verbal games: 'Il acceptait [. . .] que les mots volent d'une chose à une autre, même si ça devait un peu embrouiller les idées' (p. 110).

[36] For representative examples of tentative wordplay, see V 11 ('Jupiter'/'terre'), 106 ('combe'/'lombes'), and 142 ('torture'/'tortue').

his references to Venus at the beginning of the novel, and this leads directly to an account of his own elemental sexuality. As he explores the resonances of a single word, his text, like all Tournier's fiction, enters into a potentially endless spiral of commentary and self-commentary, generating itself through its own labour of self-explanation. At the same time, Crusoé denies the referential authority of 'literal' language which seeks simultaneously to name and confine an experience which is essentially unique and non-linguistic. For Crusoé and Vendredi, 'la différence de sexe est dépassée' (V 185), and sexual identity cannot be defined in a language which relies upon the crude dualism of male and female. Human language can only disclose its own limitations, and Crusoé acknowledges the inability of his text to pursue its enquiry into the specific nature of his experience: 'S'il fallait nécessairement traduire en termes humains ce coït solaire, c'est sous les espèces féminines, et comme l'épouse du ciel qu'il conviendrait de me définir. Mais cet anthropomorphisme est un contresens' (V 185).

As we have seen, Tournier seems to believe that the absolute primacy of the signified is a necessary feature of good philosophy, but not of literature (see VP 199–201). Tournier himself writes novels, not philosophy; and now Crusoé also has adopted a form of writing which is literary rather than philosophical (at least in terms of Tournier's distinction in Le Vent Paraclet) in as far as it celebrates language at the expense of meaning. At the end of Chapter Ten Crusoé begins his mytho-poetic description of the night sky by disclosing the ethereal nature of his own meditation:

La pleine lune répand une lumière si vive que je puis écrire ces lignes sans le secours d'une lampe. Vendredi dort, couché en boule à mes pieds. L'atmosphère irréelle, l'abolition de toutes choses familières autour de moi, tout ce dénuement, donnent à mes idées une légèreté, une gratuité qu'elles rachètent par leur fugacité. Cette méditation ne sera qu'un souper de lune. Ave spiritu, les idées qui vont mourir te saluent! (V 185)

Denied the qualities of seriousness, necessity and permanence, Crusoé's reflections—'les idées qui vont mourir'—are characterized by 'légèreté', 'gratuité', and 'fugacité'. Turning away from a representational narrative, Crusoé adopts a metaphoric mode without claim to referential seriousness. The questions of mystical silence and linguistic falsification are simply set aside, and for the first time the text seems entirely reconciled to its inevitable reliance upon language.

Even so, this section of the novel is no more than tentative. In the last two chapters of *Vendredi* the text returns to a representational narrative and Tournier withdraws from an experiment which might take him too close to the literary avant-garde.

(iv) *Repetition*

As we shall see in subsequent chapters, the endings of Tournier's novels consistently raise more problems than they solve. In Chapter Eleven of *Vendredi* a British ship, the *Whitebird*, visits Speranza. Crusoé refuses the possibility of returning to human society, but Vendredi chooses to leave on the *Whitebird* and thereby jeopardizes the serenity of Crusoé's life on Speranza. Tournier's original text leaves this desertion unexplained: '[Crusoé] ne comprenait pas comment Vendredi avait pu le trahir' (V 201). *Vendredi ou la vie sauvage* is more comprehensive, evoking Vendredi's admiration for the *Whitebird*: 'C'était cela: Vendredi avait été séduit par ce nouveau jouet, plus magnifique que tous ceux qu'il avait construits lui-même dans l'île.'[37] In *Le Vent Paraclet* Tournier repeats this interpretation (see VP 228). Critics, on the other hand, have attempted to explain Vendredi's departure in terms of the internal development of the novel by describing it as a prelude to Crusoé's final apotheosis and his ultimate release from the structures of time and language.[38] Such a reading, however, cannot offer a convincing explanation of why the novel does not end with either Chapter Nine or Chapter Ten. In an interview, Tournier himself admitted that the final pages of *Vendredi* are not entirely in keeping with the logic of the preceding narrative: 'Si vous voulez, dans ma première idée, il n'était pas question du mousse que j'ai rajouté pour faire plus romanesque, pour surprendre. Dans ma conception initiale, qui était plus rigoureuse, Robinson devenait une sorte de stylite, immobilisé debout sur une colonne au soleil.'[39] Here, Tournier acknowledges that the logical conclusion of his novel is a silence which precludes further action and further narrative. Such a conclusion, however appropriate it may seem to the rest of the novel, would contravene Tournier's only

---

[37] Tournier, *Vendredi ou la vie sauvage*, p. 148.
[38] See, for example, Sankey, 'Meaning through Intertextuality', pp. 87–8, and Poirier, *Approche de. . . Vendredi ou les limbes du Pacifique (Michel Tournier)*, p. 25.
[39] From 'Entretien avec Michel Tournier', interview with Daniel Bougnoux and André Clavel, p. 14.

unambiguous commitment, which is to the act of narration itself. In his first novel he preserves the possibility of continuation within the narrative even at the expense of the internal coherence of his text: Vendredi's unexpected departure finally enables the novel to overcome its inclination towards mystical silence without recourse to the (for Tournier) unacceptable solution of non-referential, or only incidentally referential, textual play.

The beginning of Chapter Eleven marks an abrupt return to a mimetic narrative: 'Vendredi récoltait des fleurs de myrte pour en faire de l'eau d'ange, lorsqu'il aperçut un point blanc à l'horizon, du côté du levant' (V 188). Crusoé himself rejects the sequential temporality of human history, preferring Speranza and its 'présent perpétuel, sans passé ni avenir': 'Il n'allait pas s'arracher à cet éternel instant, posé en équilibre à la pointe d'un paroxysme de perfection, pour choir dans un monde d'usure, de poussière et de ruines!' (V 198). However, by allowing the departure of Vendredi, the text confronts Crusoé with the effects of time: 'il était devenu tout à coup un vieil homme' (V 202). For Crusoé, it seems, 'il n'y avait plus d'alternative qu'entre le temps et l'éternité' (V 202). From the context, it is clear that in this instance 'eternity' means death. Crusoé seems obliged to choose between ageing and suicide, human time and the *stasis* of eternity. However, the conclusion of the novel allows him to avoid this choice. Jaan, the ship's boy from the *Whitebird* has escaped from the ship in order to join Crusoé on Speranza and in a sense to replace Vendredi. When Crusoé discovers Jaan emerging from the cave-womb of Speranza, the text describes a symbolic rebirth and promises a new beginning: 'Une pierre roula à l'intérieur et un corps obstrua le faible espace noir. Quelques contorsions le libérèrent de l'étroit orifice, et voici qu'un enfant se tenait devant Robinson, le bras droit replié sur son front, pour se protéger de la lumière ou en prévision d'une gifle' (V 203). The new beginning involves both a return to something familiar and the discovery of something unknown. Crusoé has already been made aware of this entanglement of repetition and strangeness through his experience of time. He describes each morning as 'un premier commencement, le commencement absolu de l'histoire du monde' (V 198); at the same time, each day is indistinguishable from the day before: '[mes journées] se ressemblent au point qu'elles se superposent exactement dans ma mémoire et qu'il me semble revivre sans cesse la même journée' (V 176). Vendredi and Speranza are utterly familiar, yet nothing can impair their 'magique nouveauté' (V 178). The sunrise is 'une fête qui, pour être quotidienne, n'en gardait pas moins chaque fois une intense nouveauté' (V 165). For Crusoé, then, repetition and familiarity are entirely compatible with a sense of intense, inaugural newness. The final page of Vendredi describes a sunrise and Crusoé's 'extase solaire': refusing the choice between time and eternity, Crusoé experiences the eternal recurrence of an event which perpetually recaptures the freshness of a new beginning.

In an episode added to the 'Folio' edition of Vendredi, Crusoé and Vendredi invent a game in which they reverse roles and re-enact episodes from their own past: repetition is playful, creative, and even therapeutic.[40] The end of Vendredi looks forward to a new version of that game, in which Crusoé will assume Vendredi's role as initiator to his own younger double (Jaan, like Crusoé, is redhaired; see V 195), whilst Vendredi himself will perhaps replace Jaan on the Whitebird or become a slave again as during the first period of his life on Speranza. Rather than being 'beyond language, beyond writing, beyond history', as one critic argues,[41] Crusoé is firmly ensconced within the structures of time and language. The final paragraph begins with the word 'Désormais', followed by a future tense: ' — Désormais, lui dit Robinson, tu t'appelleras Jeudi' (V 205). The text looks beyond its own inconclusive ending to a new phase of initiation and discovery, creation and play, in which Crusoé and Jaan will repeat and renew the experiences of Crusoé and Vendredi.

This attempt to combine the familiar and the new and to achieve what Tiffauges describes in Le Roi des aulnes as 'une répétition sans monotonie' (RA 124) also illuminates Tournier's relationship to literary and philosophical forerunners in his first novel. Tournier acknowledges that Vendredi is indebted to Defoe's Robinson Crusoe, as well as to Descartes's Discours de la méthode and Valéry's Monsieur Teste. Writing, for Tournier, is always rewriting, and the new always contains the old.[42] But Tournier's self-professed

---

[40] On the therapeutic effects of role-play and repetition, see Vendredi (Folio), p. 213: 'Robinson avait compris que ce jeu faisait du bien à Vendredi parce qu'il le libérait du mauvais souvenir qu'il gardait de sa vie d'esclave.'

[41] Sankey, 'Meaning through Intertextuality', p. 87. Sankey is misled by phrases such as 'un présent perpétuel', 'cet éternel instant' (both V 198) and 'l'éternité sereine des Dioscures' (V 199), which in fact refer to the experience of time as circular rather than to the total escape from temporality.

[42] On the importance of rewriting in Tournier's work, see Michael J. Worton, 'Écrire et ré-écrire: Le projet de Tournier'.

traditionalism involves both fidelity and infidelity to his source-texts. His aesthetic wager is that imitation and repetition can be made to play an essential role in the process of original creation. The end of *Vendredi* foretells the continuation of Crusoé's story into a future which repeats and renews his own past; and, in his first novel, Tournier looks backwards to the canonical texts from which he draws his inspiration and forwards to his future rewritings of them.

2

Interpretation and Violence
Le Roi des aulnes

(i) The Recovery of Truth

Le Roi des aulnes (1970), Tournier's second novel, recounts the search for truth of an outsized garage mechanic. Abel Tiffauges inhabits a medieval world of signs, symbols, and hieroglyphs, which incite his hermeneutic frenzy to extravagant intellectual constructions. Here, fiction is already interpretation and self-commentary. Even the novel's playful scatology is drawn into the search for hidden meanings: Göring, one of Tiffauges's masters in ogritude, exercises his gift for 'la lecture des laissés du gibier' (RA 227); he is able to 'déchiffrer tous les messages inscrits dans les déjections des bêtes' (RA 227); and all manner of animal excreta, even 'les modestes crottes des lapins', seem 'également intéressantes et dignes de commentaires' (RA 228).

Tiffauges's own urge to interpret is introduced in the opening sentences of the novel: 'Tu es un ogre, me disait parfois Rachel. Un Ogre? C'est-à-dire un monstre féerique, émergeant de la nuit des temps?' (RA 11). The following paragraphs exceed by far the length of Rachel's original statement, as Tiffauges attempts to analyse the implications of what she has said. The individual utterance offers a rich source of hidden meanings, which the hermeneut attempts to raise to the clarity of consciousness. For Tiffauges, the aim of interpretation is to recover a truth which has been obscured or forgotten. Dissatisfied with his own present, he believes that the key to the future lies in the past: 'J'ai toujours été scandalisé de la légèreté des hommes qui s'inquiètent passionnément de ce qui les attend après leur mort, et se soucient comme d'une guigne de ce qu'il en était d'eux avant leur naissance. L'en deçà vaut bien l'au-delà, d'autant plus qu'il en détient probablement la clé' (RA 11).

Le Roi des aulnes promises a teleological progression towards the rediscovery and reconstruction of an original state. 'Il est bien caractéristique de notre temps que le progrès se fasse désormais *à rebours*' (*RA* 73), writes Tiffauges. On a trivial level, this is illustrated by the different modes of transport which Tiffauges uses. Motorized transport is replaced by a horse and cart as he enters the Rominten Heide ('Ainsi évitait-on autant que possible de violer la pureté de la nature en introduisant des engins motorisés dans l'enceinte de Rominten', *RA* 209); later Tiffauges learns to ride a horse; and the final pages of the novel see him *walking* into the Prussian marsh where he will (presumably) die. Tiffauges's journey to East Prussia as a prisoner of war is described in terms which suggest a return to the sources of light ('*Ex Oriente Lux*', *RA* 172) and Tiffauges imagines a connection between his voyage to the East and the backwards progression in time: 'Il songeait que cette longue migration vers le levant [. . .] s'accompagnait d'un pèlerinage dans le passé' (*RA* 215). Tiffauges looks backwards to the source of truth and forwards to its imminent recovery. As Professor Keil, called from Königsberg to examine the exhumed 'Roi des aulnes', suggests in his account of the ancient Germans, the future tends towards the rediscovery of the past: 'Mais plus nous avançons dans le temps, plus le passé se rapproche de nous' (*RA* 202).

Through interpretation, Tiffauges attempts to understand and recover his own origins in 'la nuit des temps' (*RA* 11). Like a paranoiac (which he perhaps is), he sees reality as a profusion of signs which urgently require analysis.[1] Claudel's 'Tout est symbole ou parabole' (quoted as the epigraph to the second section of the novel, *RA* 170)[2] is echoed in Tiffauges's search for the meaning of reality:

Tout est signe. Mais il faut une lumière ou un cri éclatants pour percer notre myopie ou notre surdité. Depuis mes années d'initiation au collège Saint-Christophe, je n'ai cessé d'observer des hiéroglyphes tracés sur mon chemin ou d'entendre des paroles confuses murmurées à mes oreilles, sans rien comprendre, sans pouvoir en tirer autre chose qu'un doute supplémentaire sur la conduite de ma vie, mais aussi, il est vrai, la preuve réitérée que le ciel n'est pas vide. (*RA* 13)

Meaning proceeds from a transcendent source, but remains inscrutable: 'tout est signe ici, comme ailleurs, davantage qu'ailleurs. Mais

---

[1] On paranoia and the interpretation of signs, see Jean-Jacques Lecercle, *Philosophy through the Looking Glass*, especially p. 130: 'We all live in a world of signs, but for the paranoiac everything is a sign, and signs take on a new importance and urgency.'

[2] The passage quoted in *RA* 170 is taken from 'Du sens figuré de l'Écriture', in *Œuvres complètes de Paul Claudel*, xxi. 42.

signe de quoi? C'est mon éternelle question dans ce monde semé d'hiéroglyphes dont je n'ai pas la clé' (*RA* 103). The black and white landscapes of East Prussia provide particularly fertile ground for the untutored hermeneut: 'C'est que je me trouve ici constamment confronté à une *réalité signifiante* presque toujours claire et distincte, ou alors quand elle devient difficile à lire, c'est qu'elle s'approfondit et gagne en richesse ce qu'elle perd en évidence' (*RA* 276). Reality tantalizes Tiffauges with the promise of meaning; the sign demands interpretation, obliging the hermeneut to reconstruct an originally coherent message that has been fragmented and dispersed on the surface of the world. Meaning is given, understanding is a task and a necessity.[3]

Tiffauges's destiny is influenced by a series of apparently chance occurrences: the explosion of the cigarette lighter in church when he is a child (*RA* 62), the accusation of the rape of Martine (*RA* 133), the meeting with the Oberforstmeister of Rominten (*RA* 194), the discovery of Kaltenborn (*RA* 244–6), and so on. Yet Tiffauges insists that the course of his destiny (and hence the course of *Le Roi des aulnes* itself) is 'rectiligne, imperturbable, inflexible', and he maintains 'une lucidité sans indulgence à l'égard de l'accidentel, de l'anecdotique, de toutes ces menues babioles auxquelles le commun des mortels s'attache et laisse des lambeaux de son cœur quand il faut partir' (*RA* 171). Tiffauges must distinguish between the necessary and the accidental and make full use of the former whilst disregarding the latter. He places his trust in an obscure guiding force: when nursing a sickly pigeon, as in the major events of his life, he is 'Averti par un instinct confus mais infaillible' (*RA* 158). He leaves his short-term companion Étienne at the door of the Louvre, 'non sans un petit sanglot silencieux dans la gorge', but, he adds, 'je sais de source sûre, de source infaillible et impérative qu'il ne me sied pas de nouer des relations individuelles avec tel ou tel enfant' (*RA* 97–8).

One of the keywords in *Le Roi des aulnes* is 'certitude', which is used for the first time in the second entry of Tiffauges's 'Écrits sinistres': 'j'ai la certitude que je me trouve, comme on dit, à un

---

[3] For a *mise en abyme* of this model of interpretation, see the game played by the Jungmannen on a lake near the Napola: 'Cent petits voiliers occupés chacun par quatre Jungmannen croisaient d'une rive à l'autre à la recherche des messages dispersés dans des bouteilles numérotées qui flottaient sur plusieurs kilomètres carrés. Il fallait glaner le plus de bouteilles possible, puis reconstituer le texte chiffré du message à travers les fragments qu'elles contenaient' (*RA* 310).

tournant de mon existence' (RA 12–13). Later, Tiffauges will claim to be 'conforté par la seule certitude qu'un fil invisible guide [ses] pas vers un accomplissement mystérieux' (RA 100). Frequent other uses indicate that Tiffauges's wilful certainty precedes and predetermines all subsequent understanding, whilst also guaranteeing the coherence and intelligibility of his existence.[4] In a sense he already knows what he seeks to discover. The importance of foreknowledge in the process of understanding has frequently been underlined by hermeneutic theorists. The German philosopher Hans-Georg Gadamer insists that all interpretation is influenced by the *Vorverständnis* (pre-understanding) of the hermeneut.[5] This pre-understanding is an essential element in the so-called hermeneutic circle, of which Paul Ricoeur gives a succinct explanation in *La Symbolique du mal*: 'Tel est le cercle: l'herméneutique procède de la précomprehension de cela même qu'en interprétant elle tâche à comprendre.'[6] For both Gadamer and Ricoeur, the aim of philosophical reflection on interpretation is to blunt the teeth of the potentially vicious hermeneutic circle. This may be achieved through a direct inter-rogation of the interpreter's pre-understanding;[7] and, although both Gadamer and Ricoeur acknowledge that understanding can never be definitive, their theoretically sophisticated hermeneutics attempt to ensure the viability of the interpretative act and thereby to transform the vicious hermeneutic circle into a relatively benign spiral.

Tiffauges never engages in the liberating reflection upon his own pre-understanding. Eschewing common sense and relying on his unquestioning 'certitude', he believes that the coherence of his destiny is guaranteed by his mythical origins and his immemorial familiarity with being:

Je crois, oui, à ma nature féerique, je veux dire à cette connivence secrète qui mêle en profondeur mon aventure personnelle au cours des choses, et lui permet de l'incliner dans son sens.

---

[4] For the most significant uses of the word 'certitude', see RA 13, 100 (twice), 108, 168, 179, 190, 222, 245, 307, and, for Éphraïm's 'certitude', 384.

[5] On *Vorverständnis*, see Hans-Georg Gadamer, *Wahrheit und Methode*, e.g. pp. 250–75.

[6] Paul Ricoeur, *La Symbolique du mal*, p. 327.

[7] See, for example, Hans-Georg Gadamer, 'Rhetorik, Hermeneutik und Ideologie-kritik', in *Kleine Schriften*, i. 127, and Paul Ricoeur, *La Symbolique du mal*, p. 327.

Je crois aussi que je suis issu de la nuit des temps [. . .] Or moi, j'étais là déjà, il y a mille ans, il y a cent mille ans. Quand la terre n'était encore qu'une boule de feu tournoyant dans un ciel d'hélium, l'âme qui la faisait flamber, qui la faisait tourner, c'était la mienne. Et d'ailleurs l'antiquité vertigineuse de mes origines suffit à expliquer mon pouvoir surnaturel: l'être et moi, nous cheminons depuis si longtemps côte à côte, nous sommes de si anciens compagnons que, sans nous affectionner particulièrement, mais en vertu d'une accoutumance réciproque aussi vieille que le monde, nous nous comprenons, nous n'avons rien à nous refuser. (RA 11)

Tiffauges claims absolute seriousness: 'ce que je viens d'écrire doit être envisagé avec un sérieux total' (RA 12). However, from the opening pages of Le Roi des aulnes his credibility and even his sanity are brought into question by the incongruity of what he claims to be his mythical origins with his actual profession: 'Je crois, oui, à ma nature féerique [. . .] Je crois aussi que je suis issu de la nuit des temps [. . .] Je m'appelle Abel Tiffauges, je tiens un garage place de la Porte-des-Ternes, et je ne suis pas fou' (RA 11–12). The playful quality of Tournier's text draws the ground from under Tiffauges's mythologizing fantasies, and Tournier is careful to dissociate himself from the extravagant claims of his protagonist.[8] However, the force and significance of Le Roi des aulnes are not in what Tiffauges says, but in the transition from his early benign playfulness to the violent scenes at the end of the novel. Motivated by a deep-rooted dissatisfaction with himself and with his life, Tiffauges enters the war convinced that it is no more than 'un affrontement de chiffres et de signes, une pure mêlée audio-visuelle sans autre risque que des obscurités ou des erreurs d'interprétation' (RA 148). As he becomes more and more entangled with the violence of war and the crimes of Nazism, Tiffauges learns the shattering consequences of misinterpretation which masquerades as truth.

(ii) Theories of the Sign: 1. Truth and Performance

A long tradition in linguistic and poetic theory distinguishes carefully between sign and symbol. Hegel and Saussure, for example, both contrast the arbitrariness of the sign with the at least partial motivation of the symbol.[9] Saussure explains this distinction in his

---

[8] For Tournier's refusal to corroborate the claims of his characters, see VP 113.
[9] See Jacques Derrida, Marges de la philosophie, pp. 97–100.

Cours de linguistique générale: 'Le symbole a pour caractère de n'être jamais tout à fait arbitraire; il n'est pas vide, il y a un rudiment de lien naturel entre le signifiant et le signifié. Le symbole de la justice, la balance, ne pourrait pas être remplacé par n'importe quoi, un char, par exemple.'[10] *Le Roi des aulnes* breaks with this tradition by making no distinction between *signe* and *symbole*. Appropriating Claudel's 'Tout est symbole ou parabole' (quoted *RA* 170), Tiffauges asserts variously that 'Tout est signe' or 'tout est symbole' without indicating any clear difference between these different formulations (see *RA* 13, 103, 113, 320). Rather than distinguishing between sign and symbol, Tournier's text suggests a strict distinction between different *kinds* of sign. In the army, Tiffauges proves incapable of learning Morse code, since it uses 'des signes conventionnels, abstraits, futiles, sans charge fatale' (*RA* 146); they are 'dépourvus de l'élément vivant, chaleureux et sanguin qui était pour lui comme la signature de l'être' (*RA* 148). For Tiffauges, '*les signes ont besoin de la chair pour se manifester*' (*RA* 109); and he lives in expectation of 'cette union du signe et de la chair qui était pour lui la fin dernière des choses' (*RA* 148). In other words, the abstract sign must have a direct organic relationship with its living referent. The arbitrary sign is of no interest, since it is caught within a differential system from which truth, or what Derrida calls the 'signifié transcendantal',[11] is excluded. Tiffauges may state that 'Tout est signe', but his whole endeavour is to uncover the 'plan général' (*RA* 152) which governs the proliferation of signs and so to save truth from the operation of infinite deferment.[12] However, in *Le Roi des aulnes*, as in Spinoza's *Ethics*, the sign solicits the imagination but never guarantees knowledge; it does not teach the interpreter how to distinguish

[10] Quoted by Derrida, ibid. 100 n, from Ferdinand de Saussure, *Cours de linguistique générale*, p. 101.

[11] On the 'signifié transcendantal', see, for example, Jacques Derrida, *Positions*, p. 30.

[12] A much more literal reading of the dictum 'Tout est signe' is suggested by C. S. Peirce's classic definition of the sign as 'anything which determines something else (its *interpretant*) to refer to an object to which itself [*sic*] refers (its *object*) in the same way, the interpretant becoming in turn a sign and so on *ad infinitum*' (C. S. Peirce, *Elements of Logic*, p. 169). For discussion of *Le Roi des aulnes* in relation to Saussure, Peirce, and Barthes, and comparison of Tiffauges's belief that 'Tout est signe' with German Romantic literature, see J. J. White, 'Signs of Disturbance: The Semiological Import of some Recent Fiction by Michel Tournier and Peter Handke'.

between truth and falsehood, and so it may promote error when it seems to promise enlightenment.[13]

For Tiffauges, the world, and especially East Prussia, is a text waiting to be read:

'Un pays noir et blanc, pensa Tiffauges. Peu de gris, peu de couleurs, une page blanche couverte de signes noirs.' (*RA* 180)

Dès les premiers pas qu'il fit en enfonçant profondément dans la neige, il en trouva la confirmation — infime certes, mais significative — dans les traces d'oiseaux, de rongeurs et de petits carnassiers qui entrecroisaient leur délicate sténographie sur la grande page blanche ouverte à ses pieds. (*RA* 190)

Mais pour Tiffauges dont le ciel clouté d'allégories et d'hiéroglyphes retentissait sans cesse de voix indistinctes et de cris énigmatiques, l'Allemagne se dévoilait comme une terre promise, comme le *pays des essences pures*. Il la voyait à travers les récits du fermier et telle que la circonscrivait le petit carreau de la fenêtre avec ses villages vernis comme des jouets, étiquetés d'enseignes totémiques, mis en page dans un paysage noir et blanc. (*RA* 192–3)

Tiffauges's 'ciel clouté d'allégories et d'hiéroglyphes' recalls the medieval and Renaissance belief in correspondences and analogies,[14] or the 'confuses paroles' and 'forêt de symboles' of Baudelaire's poem 'Correspondances'.[15] Tiffauges attempts to make sense of a world deemed to be meaningful. In his endeavour, language is essential both as the vehicle and as an object of interpretation. Like all Tournier's characters, Tiffauges shows a great concern for language and particularly for etymology. He locates the truth of language in the origin of the signifier: 'Et d'abord qu'est-ce qu'un monstre? L'étymologie réserve déjà une surprise un peu effrayante: *monstre* vient de *montrer*. Le monstre est ce que l'on montre — du doigt, dans les fêtes foraines, etc.' (*RA* 11–12; see also *M* 143). The two meanings of the French word *inspiration* (inspiration and respiration) coincide, and Tiffauges insists that this is no idle pun: 'Ici, je ne joue pas sur les mots. Il est logique qu'à ce niveau, le sens propre et le

---

[13] See Spinoza, *Éthique*, Part Two, Proposition XL (Scolie II) and Propositions XLI and XLII. For an account of the sign in Spinoza's philosophy, see Gilles Deleuze, *Spinoza: Philosophie pratique*, pp. 143–5.

[14] On the medieval and Renaissance notion of the world as a text inscribed with signs and hieroglyphs, see Michel Foucault, *Les Mots et les choses*, pp. 32–59.

[15] See Charles Baudelaire, 'Correspondances', in *Œuvres complètes*, i. 11 and note on pp. 839–47. Compare also Tiffauges's references to 'paroles confuses' (*RA* 13) and Crusoé's 'forêt d'allégories' (*V* 187).

sens figuré se confondent' (*RA* 327; see also *RA* 364). Tiffauges may seem to be reverting to a naïve faith in the *etymon*, or 'true meaning', of language, which Socrates had already ridiculed in Plato's *Cratylus*.[16] At moments, however, the playfulness of his analysis of language evidently disqualifies any serious heuristic purpose (even if *he* is not fully aware of the playful quality of his text); for example, when he visits les Halles (in a scene reminiscent of Zola's *Le Ventre de Paris*),[17] he describes the porters ('les forts') who practise a form of *phorie* (carrying): 'Mais c'est une *phorie* trivialisée, abaissée à des utilités mercantiles et subalternes. Et sans doute est-ce pourquoi on écrit grossièrement *forts* des Halles, au lieu de *phores* des Halles. Le fort est la forme vulgaire du phore' (*RA* 92).

Tiffauges's notion of *phorie*, which functions as a leitmotiv and principle of cohesion throughout *Le Roi des aulnes*, is itself derived from the etymology of the word *euphorie*: 'Sensation de bien-être, dit platement le dictionnaire. Mais l'étymologie est plus instructive' (*RA* 90). Etymology teaches Tiffauges the essential link between carrying and euphoria. However, what is more revealing than Tiffauges's faith in the truth of the signifier is the way in which the word *euphorie* appears in the 'Écrits sinistres'. Significantly, it does not occur in the account of his first experience of carrying, when the boy Jeannot is injured in an accident at the garage. Only later, when Tiffauges considers the incident in his 'Écrits sinistres', is the word used: 'Le premier mot qui se présente sous ma plume est apparemment banal et faible, mais il se révèle d'une grande ressource: l'*euphorie*' (*RA* 89–90). The reflexive construction ('se présente', 'se révèle') is used for a third time at the end of this entry in the 'Écrits sinistres': 'Le mot *inversion* se présente aussitôt sous ma plume' (*RA* 91). These reflexive constructions imply that the notion of *phorie* and the principle of inversions are suggested to Tiffauges from some external source which is independent of his conscious volition. As he writes and speaks, Tiffauges surrenders his autonomy as subject to a force which surpasses him.

On an immediate level, this force is attributed to the continuing influence of Nestor, Tiffauges's childhood protector, who is directly responsible for his ability to write with his left hand:

[16] See Plato's *Cratylus*, 437 A–D.
[17] The most specific allusion to Zola's *Le Ventre de Paris* is in Tiffauges's description of 'une charmante poissonnière' (*RA* 91), which recalls Louise Méhudin, the 'belle poissonnière' of Zola's novel.

Car cette main, Nestor l'a longuement tenue dans la sienne, il a couvé dans sa grande main pesante et moite mon faible poing, ce petit œuf osseux et translucide qui s'abandonnait à cette chaude étreinte sans savoir de quelles énergies il se chargeait alors. Toute la force de Nestor, tout son esprit dominateur et dissolvant sont passés dans cette main, celle dont procèdent jour après jour ces écrits sinistres qui sont ainsi notre œuvre commune. (*RA* 38–9)

Tiffauges's 'écriture sinistre' is 'déformée par toutes les *gaucheries du génie*, pleine d'éclairs et de cris, habitée en un mot par l'esprit de Nestor' (*RA* 39). Tiffauges believes that Nestor has been revived as part of his own identity: 'car d'une certaine façon il revit en moi, je suis Nestor' (*RA* 138). The survival of Nestor within Tiffauges is suggested through verbal resonances, as Tiffauges relives the experience of his dead friend and quotes him almost verbatim (compare *RA* 54 with *RA* 89, and *RA* 53 with *RA* 391). Tiffauges's '*euphorie*' itself echoes Nestor's reference to the '*euphorie cadente*' discovered by the baron des Adrets (see *RA* 57). Nestor's influence reveals itself through, and is also inseparable from, an experience of language. Rachel's phrase, 'Tu es un ogre', quoted in the first line of the novel and again a few pages later, provokes Tiffauges's reminiscences of his childhood:

— Tu n'es pas un amant, tu es un ogre.
    Ô saisons, ô châteaux! En prononçant cette simple phrase, Rachel a fait surgir le fantôme d'un enfant monstrueux, d'une précocité effrayante, d'une puérilité déconcertante dont le souvenir prend possession de moi avec une impérieuse souveraineté. Nestor. (*RA* 17)

Rimbaud quotes his poem 'Ô saisons, ô châteaux' in 'Délires II: Alchimie du verbe', a critical account of his former belief in the magical force of language.[18] Tiffauges continues to believe in what Rimbaud ultimately rejected. Rather than the continuity of sensuous impressions, as for Proust or in *Vendredi ou les limbes du Pacifique*,[19] for Tiffauges it is language which seems to possess an autonomous force capable of both unlocking the past and anticipating the future course of the novel. The reflexive construction already seen in Tiffauges's discovery of *phorie* also occurs in his

---

[18] See Arthur Rimbaud, 'Délires II: Alchimie du verbe', in *Une saison en enfer*. For Tiffauges's predilection for Rimbaud's poetry, see *RA* 73: 'j'ignorais superbement Corneille et Racine, mais je me récitais en secret Lautréamont et Rimbaud.'
[19] For a passage with strong Proustian echoes, see *V* 47–8.

attempt to characterize Nestor: 'Au milieu de ces incertitudes, un mot s'impose que je ne retiendrai pas davantage dans ma plume: intemporel' (RA 27). Later, Tiffauges's horse acquires its name through the combination of a pun and an allusion to Perrault's story 'La Barbe bleue'. The barbe ('horse' in the masculine, 'beard' in the feminine) appears to have a blue sheen in the sunlight: 'Ce barbe était ainsi un barbe bleu, et le nom qu'il convenait de lui donner s'imposait de lui-même' (RA 238). The repeated use of the reflexive construction suggests that Tiffauges has no control over the web of intertextuality and punning with which Tournier constructs his novel. For Tiffauges as for Heidegger, language speaks,[20] using the human voice and the author's pen to explore its own resonances. The human subject is within language, but claims no mastery over it.

Nowhere is this more clear in Le Roi des aulnes than in Tiffauges's characterization of his own text, the 'Écrits sinistres'. Tournier's second novel shows a fundamental change in his conception of the relationship between life and writing. In Vendredi ou les limbes du Pacifique Crusoé's logbook is described as 'le reflet superficiel d'une métamorphose de son être profond' (V 96), or as a 'témoin intéressant de son cheminement' (V 172). In Vendredi, then, writing is still conceived in conventional terms as the linguistic representation of a non-linguistic hors-texte, in this case Crusoé's spiritual evolution. In Le Roi des aulnes Tiffauges's journal ceases to be a neutral transposition of a given reality:

Pour un homme aussi naturellement secret que moi, répandre ses viscères sur papier, c'est bien rebutant au début, mais ma main m'entraîne, et il me semble qu'ayant commencé à me raconter, je ne pourrai plus m'arrêter avant d'être arrivé au bout de mon rouleau. Peut-être aussi les événements de ma vie ne peuvent-ils plus se succéder désormais sans ce reflet verbal qu'on appelle un journal? (RA 14)

Tiffauges's vocabulary still suggests that writing is the record either of a personal history or of external events ('répandre ses viscères sur du papier', 'ayant commencé à me raconter', 'ce reflet verbal'). But he adopts the rhetoric of writing as representation in order to suggest something quite different. Writing is no longer the passive ancillary to life: it has overturned its subordination to the task of representation

---

[20] For Heidegger's assertion that 'language speaks' ('Die Sprache spricht'), see Martin Heidegger, 'Die Sprache', in Unterwegs zur Sprache, p. 12.

and actively participates in the reality it was deemed to transcribe ('ayant commencé à me raconter, je ne pourrai plus m'arrêter'). The extra-textual event can no longer be separated from the language in which it is constituted ('Peut-être aussi les événements de ma vie ne peuvent-ils plus se succéder désormais sans ce reflet verbal qu'on appelle un journal?'). In *Vendredi* the distrust of linguistic mediation leads in the direction of (without ever fully embracing) a quasi-mystical renunciation of language. In *Le Roi des aulnes* Tiffauges rejoins Roquentin at the end of *La Nausée* as he positively welcomes the possibility that writing confers meaning and coherence on the apparent chaos of reality: 'Cette manière de journal–souvenir que je tiens sinistrement depuis plus de deux mois a l'étrange pouvoir de situer les faits et les gestes qu'il relate — mes faits et mes gestes — dans une perspective qui les éclaire et leur donne une dimension nouvelle' (*RA* 51).

Tiffauges disclaims all responsibility for his 'écriture sinistre'. He believes that truth is *revealed* by an external agency rather than *discovered* by a conscious human subject. He perceives the presence of a force which surpasses him and which he obeys without question: 'Tiffauges se sentait pris en main, orienté, commandé, et il obéissait avec un sombre bonheur' (*RA* 244). He is 'à demi consentant' and even 'passionnément soumis' when he recognizes the dictates of destiny (*RA* 86–7). Tiffauges is no Jansenist: for him, where there is no free will, none can be held responsible and so all are innocent. Ernest, the man who causes the death of his beloved pigeons, is forgiven because his actions can be interpreted as evidence that reality is coherent and meaningful: 'Il avait au demeurant pardonné à Ernest sa responsabilité dans le sacrifice des pigeons auquel il avait reconnu, comme à presque tous les événements de sa vie, un caractère de fatalité qui le douait d'innocence et d'intelligibilité' (*RA* 173).

Tiffauges finds it hard to cope with what he calls 'la pestilence de l'adultat' (*RA* 107). Significantly, he recounts the breakdown of his relationship with Rachel immediately before embarking on his childhood reminiscences, as if the latter were a direct response to his failure in adult life. He refers wistfully to 'ce paradis perdu que je n'ai pas fini de pleurer, l'esclavage' (*RA* 114) and seeks refuge from the disturbing possibility of freedom by retreating into the past or by accepting various forms of self-imposed slavery in the present. In Nazi Germany he finds the fulfilment of his own most fundamental urge for enslavement and hence absolution from individual responsibility. He becomes the active supporter of a system which makes him a slave amongst slaves, and, showing his profound complicity with Fascist ideology, he justifies his own aberrations from received morality through his faith in a 'plan général' (RA 152): a transcendent necessity which surpasses—and ultimately annihilates— the individual. The racial theories of Blättchen, the Nazi geneticist at Kaltenborn, depend upon a normative concept of truth, which Tiffauges perceives to be disturbingly close to his own (see RA 286–8 and 292–4). Subjecting all forms of life to a totalizing and totalitarian cult of heredity, Blättchen uses what he believes to be a biological fact as the basis for a moral imperative: 'Le mauvais sang n'est ni améliorable ni éducable, le seul traitement dont il est justiciable est une destruction pure et simple' (RA 293).

The urge for totalization, presented in Le Roi des aulnes as common to both Tiffauges and Nazism, entails a potentially violent imposition of order on to disorder. Tiffauges realizes that 'le vaste monde est une réserve de chasse inépuisable — et qui désespère l'exhaustion' (RA 120). He lives 'en milieu ouvert, exilé loin de la citadelle nestorienne et de ses sujets dénombrés' (RA 100). Through photography, Tiffauges finds a benign means of domesticating the 'infini sauvage' of reality (RA 120). But he realizes that his rejection of 'gestes vagues' and 'totalités inachevées' puts him in conflict with the flux and complexity of the living (RA 192). He becomes aware of a struggle within himself between human uncertainty and his inhuman aspirations: 'je vais par le monde mi-chair, mi-pierre, c'est-à-dire avec un cœur, une main droite et un souvenir avenants, mais aussi en moi quelque chose de dur, d'impitoyable et de glacé sur quoi se brisera inexorablement tout l'humain qui s'y heurtera' (RA 86). Tiffauges's desire for the restoration of unity can be fulfilled only in death: 'Je sais maintenant ce que sera ma fin: elle sera la victoire définitive de l'homme de pierre qui est en moi sur ce qui me reste de chair et de sang' (RA 102). Tiffauges's death is not necessary: at the end of Le Roi des aulnes the Russian invaders of Kaltenborn seem prepared to allow safe passage to the French prisoner-of-war (see RA 391). But Tiffauges insists on suicidal flight, finding the fulfilment of his thinly-disguised death-wish as he sinks deeper into the Prussian marsh, 'sachant que tout était bien ainsi' (RA 393).

Throughout Le Roi des aulnes an elaborate system of prefigurations indicates the future course of Tiffauges's destiny. His demise in the Prussian marsh, for example, is prefigured in the first section of the novel by his 'rêves de noyade et d'ensevelissement sous le sable, sous la terre, dans la boue' (*RA* 98); and the slaughter of his three favourite pigeons anticipates the deaths of the children Haïo, Haro, and Lothar. Tiffauges attributes such correspondences to the coherence of the 'plan général' (*RA* 152) which governs his destiny. The external world conforms to his innermost thoughts and desires, and he is convinced that 'ses pensées avaient le pouvoir redoutable de faire surgir des êtres réels à leur semblance' (*RA* 215; see also *RA* 297). His wishes and questions are never left unanswered: 'L'une des plus lourdes fatalités qui pèsent sur moi — mais ne faudrait-il pas dire plutôt: l'une des plus lumineuses bénédictions qui planent sur ma tête? — c'est que je ne puis formuler une question ou un vœu sans que tôt ou tard le destin ne se charge de lui donner une réponse' (*RA* 366).

The correspondences and improbable coincidences which strengthen Tiffauges's belief in the coherence of his destiny are of course formal strategies adopted by Tournier to ensure the aesthetic unity of his novel, which he has compared in this respect to Bach's *Art of the Fugue*.[21] At the same time, however, *Le Roi des aulnes* is not just a hermetically sealed artefact, since it constantly refers to real historical circumstances in its depiction of Nazi Germany and the Second World War. The notes added to the end of the novel reveal the sources of Tournier's information and attest the accuracy of historical details (see *RA* 395–6 and *VP* 108–9). *Le Roi des aulnes* combines a self-regarding formalism with a closely documented realism and attempts to reconcile the conflicting demands of reference and self-reference. Tournier's realism (and perhaps all realism) is characterized by the refusal to choose between *mimesis* and creation, truth and performance. Reference to an extra-textual 'real' may be illusory, but what Barthes calles the 'illusion référentielle'[22] is carefully maintained and profoundly desired—as much by the reader as by the author, perhaps. In structuralist terms, the codes of realism

[21] See Tournier's discussion of Bach's *Art of the Fugue* in *VP* 125–7. Gide's *Les Faux-Monnayeurs* is an important source of this discussion; see *Les Faux-Monnayeurs*, in *Romanz, récits et soties, oeuvres lyriques*, p. 1084.

[22] On the 'illusion référentielle', see Roland Barthes, 'L'Effet de réel', in *Le Bruissement de la langue*, p. 174. Tournier illustrates the conflict between the formal and the referential aspects of *Le Roi des aulnes* by claiming, on the one hand, that *phorie* is 'le seul véritable sujet' of his novel (*VP* 120) and, on the other hand, that his novel is 'un document historique' ('Tournier face aux lycéens', p. 24).

may lack any genuine referential authority, but the desire to refer remains a fundamental characteristic of the realist text. The tension within a practice of language which wants to be both truthful and creative is perhaps what makes *Le Roi des aulnes* (in opposition to more avant-garde texts in which *écriture* has excluded all claims to reference) so eminently but deceptively readable: sense and reference lure the reader into a confrontation with the vicious inversions which will shatter the coherence of Tiffauges's world.

Tiffauges believes that interpretation and the reading of signs ('la grande affaire de ma vie', *RA* 34) are stages in the process of truth. At the same time, as we shall see in the following section, interpretation is the performative speech act *par excellence*, dynamically altering its object, the life of the hermeneut, and even the course of history: 'Les signes, le déchiffrement des signes. . . De quels signes s'agissait-il? Que révélait leur déchiffrement? Si je pouvais répondre à cette question, toute ma vie serait changée, et non seulement ma vie mais — j'ose l'écrire assuré que personne ne lira jamais ces lignes — le cours même de l'histoire' (*RA* 29).

(iii) *Intervention and Appropriation*

Tiffauges distinguishes between two tools of interpretation, the key ('clé') and the grid ('grille de déchiffrement'). He explains the distinction by reference to his obsession with *phorie*: 'Différence d'ordre phorique, puisque la clé est portée par son essence — comme la serrure porte sa clé — tandis que c'est la grille qui porte son essence, comme les barreaux de fer incandescents portent le corps du martyr' (*RA* 335). The key is less powerful than the grid because it can reveal only 'un sens particulier de l'essence' (*RA* 335). But the grid does not give neutral elucidation of its object. The image of the 'barreaux de fer incandescents' suggests a scarcely hidden violence which operates within the act of interpretation itself. This can be illustrated briefly by Tiffauges's own application of the 'grille de déchiffrement' provided by mythology. When he is told about the murder of gypsies and Jews by the Nazis, Tournier's protagonist 'recognizes' the repetition of an archetypal antagonism: 'Ainsi, il retrouvait ici poussée à son paroxysme la haine millénaire des races sédentaires contre les races nomades. Juifs et gitans, peuples errants, fils d'Abel, ces frères dont il se sentait solidaire par le cœur et par l'âme, tombaient en masse à Auschwitz sous les coups d'un Caïn botté, casqué et scientifiquement organisé' (*RA* 379). Tiffauges's interpretation of the Nazi death camps provides a revealing example of the distortions involved in his mythological interpretation of history. The assertion of mythical fraternity between Jew and gypsy is at best problematic, at worst nonsense; and the invocation of Cain and Abel is of little help in explaining the historical circumstances which made the death camps possible. Nor is it certain that Tiffauges himself belongs to the nomadic type. Despite his first name (Abel), his attraction to self-enclosed communities such as Saint-Christophe and Kaltenborn gives an indication of the strong sedentary side to his character. Myth provides a powerful means of making sense; but here, as elsewhere, Tiffauges's mythological grid seems inadequate to his historical material.[23]

Tiffauges refers to Descartes's demand for totality as 'cette règle fondamentale', which is best satisfied by 'un monde clos sur lui-même, sans ouverture sur le dehors, obéissant aux seules lois internes qu'il s'est données' (*RA* 100). Self-coherence usurps truth as an absolute value, and the imperious rejection of fragmentation justifies the violence of interpretation. Tiffauges views reality through a distorting lens; as he sits in a Prussian farmhouse, he observes how the window mediates his vision of the outside world and gives it the appearance of art:

Il était assis près d'une fenêtre double à petits carreaux, entre les deux châssis de laquelle rampaient des tiges de misère. L'un des petits carreaux encadrait exactement le bas du village de Wildhorst, ses maisons chaulées jusqu'aux fenêtres de l'étage, lambrissées ensuite jusqu'au toit, la mignonne église au clocher de bois, une boucle de chemin où il vit passer une vieille femme remorquant un bébé sur une luge, une fillette chassant du bout d'une badine un troupeau d'oies indignées, un traîneau de billes de sapins tiré par deux chevaux. Et tout cela, enfermé dans un carré de trente centimètres de côté,

---

[23] Tournier himself underlines, and even overemphasizes, the importance of myth in his attempt to combine philosophy and literature: 'Le passage de la métaphysique au roman devait m'être fourni par le mythe' (*VP* 183). Nevertheless, his definitions of myth are sufficiently vague and broad to leave him uncommitted to any particular theory (see *VP* 183–8), and in *Le Vol du vampire* he acknowledges the ambiguity of his fictional use of myth: 'Il reste que la notion même de mythe est frappée d'équivoque: un mythe, c'est à la fois une belle et profonde histoire incarnant l'une des aventures essentielles de l'homme, et un misérable mensonge débité par un débile mental, un "mythomane" justement' (*Vol* 12). For further discussion, see Michael J. Worton, 'Myth Reference in *Le Roi des aulnes*', and Mieke Taat, 'Et si le roi était nu? — Michel Tournier, romancier mythologue'.

était si net, si bien dessiné, posé à une si juste place, qu'il lui semblait avoir vu toutes choses auparavant dans un flou incertain qu'une mise au point plus rigoureuse venait de corriger pour la première fois. (*RA* 191–2)

The frame of the window seems to endow the scene with the finality and intentionality which are normally absent from life and nature ('si bien dessiné, posé à une si juste place'). The 'flou incertain' of the lived seems to have been corrected by 'une mise au point plus rigoureuse'. The absurd and the contingent, the essentially unrelated and the haphazard, are made meaningful and necessary when enframed and reinterpreted as art.[24]

During his visit to the Louvre Tiffauges describes how art offers 'un peu d'éternité' and a 'havre de paix' in a world prey to the corrosion of time (see *RA* 95).[25] Guido Reni's painting of David, like the portraits of the bourgeois in Sartre's *La Nausée*,[26] exemplifies the fascination of art and of those people whose bad faith allows them to live as if life had the coherence of an aesthetic object. Reni's David belongs to what Tiffauges describes as 'la race très fascinante de *ceux qui n'ont jamais douté de rien*':

Il y a des êtres limités, d'une beauté éclatante mais sans prolongement et, soyons francs, qu'on aurait tout lieu de mépriser s'ils ne nous offraient le spectacle d'une adaptation sans défaut à l'existence, d'une adéquation miraculeuse de leurs désirs et des choses à leur portée, de leurs paroles et des questions qu'on leur pose, de leurs capacités et de la profession qu'ils exercent. Ils naissent, vivent et meurent, comme si le monde avait été fait pour eux et eux-mêmes pour le monde, et les autres — les douteurs, les troublés, les indignés, les curieux, Étienne, moi — les regardent passer et s'émerveillent de leur *naturel*. (*RA* 96)

Tiffauges both scorns and envies the form of bad faith epitomized by Reni's David; and he fails to recognize that he is describing his own most fundamental delusion when he refers to people who live 'comme si le monde avait été fait pour eux et eux-mêmes pour le monde'. In the first paragraph of the novel Tiffauges refers to the

---

[24] For a good description of the desire for coherence and unity, see Albert Camus, *L'Homme révolté*, p. 314: 'Il ne suffit pas de vivre, il faut une destinée, et sans attendre la mort. Il est donc juste de dire que l'homme a l'idée d'un monde meilleur que celui-ci. Mais meilleur ne veut pas dire alors différent, meilleur veut dire unifié. Cette fièvre qui soulève le cœur au-dessus d'un monde éparpillé, dont il ne peut cependant se déprendre, est la fièvre de l'unité.'

[25] For further discussion of this passage, see ch. 5, sec. (iii).

[26] See Sartre, *La Nausée*, in *Œuvres romanesques*, pp. 98–113.

'connivence secrète qui mêle en profondeur [son] aventure personnelle au cours des choses, et lui permet de l'incliner dans son sens' (*RA* 11). Tiffauges believes that he occupies a privileged position within a coherent universe. He aims to suppress his own doubt and anxiety and become the inhuman 'homme de pierre' which he describes shortly after his visit to the Louvre (*RA* 102). Certainty triumphs over incoherence as Tiffauges allows life to become art.

The formal structure of *Le Roi des aulnes* and its internal system of correspondences and prefigurations seem to support Tiffauges's desire to correct the world's disorder and perhaps indicate that his revolt against incoherence is, to some extent at least, shared by Tournier himself. Tiffauges's intuitions and predictions are almost systematically proved accurate: the school *does* burn down and save him from punishment, the war *does* cause the rape charge to be dropped. Tiffauges may be mystified and deluded, but the novel apparently justifies his mystification and encourages his delusions. More disturbingly, the demand for coherence makes Tiffauges blind to the moral implications of his actions. Despite his realization that Nazism is 'toujours à la limite du sadisme et du crime' (*RA* 267), Tiffauges co-operates with the Nazi regime because the 'cohérence de son évolution' proves that 'il marchait dans la voie de sa vocation' (*RA* 267–8). Moreover, the search for mythological models is not restricted to Tiffauges's individual perspective. Even a Russian tank can be given a mythical significance: the Jungmannen of Kaltenborn imagine the tank to be a form of mechanical ogre, 'une bête fabuleuse, d'une force redoutable, mais lente, bruyante, maladroite, myope et sourde' (*RA* 362–3). The children laugh with pleasure as they think of 'les bonnes parties de chasse qui se préparaient' (*RA* 363). But Tournier's novel *also* indicates the discrepancy between this mythological vision and the reality of war: 'Le tir réel au Panzerfaust [. . .] les rappela à une réalité plus rude' (*RA* 363). A boy is accidentally decapitated; and, as the novel approaches its conclusion, the closure of Tiffauges's mythical world is shattered by the violent intrusion of history. Tiffauges demands an *aesthetic* unity which Tournier's novel supplies, but which it also reveals to be *merely* aesthetic, involving the potentially murderous imposition of order on to refractory material.[27]

---

[27] The critic Jean Améry condemns *Le Roi des aulnes* on the grounds that it 'aestheticizes' Nazism; see Jean Améry, 'Ästhetizismus der Barbarei: Über Michel

At moments Tiffauges realizes that his hermeneutic endeavour involves the distortion and transformation of what he attempts to understand. In the account of his childhood at Saint-Christophe he admits that he is forced to transcribe Nestor's gnomic utterances with 'des mots qui ne sont à coup sûr pas les siens' (RA 38). Later, he concedes that his recollections of Nestor are influenced by his own tendentious interpretation of the facts: 'Certes je mets dans ses propos plus de clarté et de force qu'ils n'en pouvaient contenir, obéissant en cela à ma vocation fondamentale' (RA 59). Just as the presence of the photographer alters the reality which he records (see RA 122–3), the interpreter actively transforms the object of interpretation. The use of the adjective 'tiffaugéen' underlines Tiffauges's urge to make his mark on reality. An 'interprétation dérivée' reveals the 'sens tiffaugéen' of baptism (i.e. its phoric and paedophile aspects; see RA 118). Rominten yields 'des fruits imprévus et purement tiffaugéens' (RA 268), and Tiffauges recognizes the 'vocation tiffaugéenne' of Kaltenborn (RA 246). Interpretation is a mode of active participation in the world; and the labour of understanding, for Tiffauges, contributes to the more fundamental process of appropriation and celebration: 'Car il n'avait pas seulement vocation de déchiffrer les essences, mais aussi de les exalter, de porter toutes leurs vertus à incandescence. Il allait livrer cette terre à une interprétation tiffaugéenne, et en même temps, il l'élèverait à une puissance supérieure, encore jamais atteinte' (RA 193).

In L'Écriture et la différence Derrida describes what he calls 'deux interprétations de l'interprétation': 'L'une cherche à déchiffrer, rêve de déchiffrer une vérité ou une origine échappant au jeu et à l'ordre du signe, et vit comme un exil la nécessité de l'interprétation'; the other entails 'l'affirmation nietzschéenne, l'affirmation joyeuse du jeu du monde et de l'innocence du devenir, l'affirmation d'un monde de signes sans faute, sans vérité, sans origine, offert à une interprétation active'.[28] Tiffauges's hermeneutic activity can be characterized as

---

Tourniers Roman „Der Erlkönig" '. It is easy to understand Améry's moral distrust of Tournier's novel; but Tournier's point, of course, is that the moral problem posed by Nazism is made all the more acute by its powerful aesthetic appeal. For Tournier's defence of his novel against Améry's criticisms, see 'Tournier face aux lycéens', p. 24, and 'Michel Tournier en questions', interview with Serge Koster, p. 155.

[28] See Derrida, L'Écriture et la différence, p. 427. Derrida continues: 'Je ne crois pas pour ma part, bien que ces deux interprétations doivent accuser leur différence et aiguiser leur irréductibilité, qu'il y ait aujourd'hui à choisir' (pp. 427–8).

the oscillation between these different interpretations of interpretation: on the one hand, he attempts to restore a coherent message inscribed in the world; on the other hand, his 'interprétation tiffaugéenne' (*RA* 193) involves the appropriation and the creative transformation of reality. The problem of certainty in interpretation is raised by Nestor's gyroscope, the 'absolu de poche' which indicates that truth may not be what it seems: 'Car vois-tu, Mabel, ce mouvement que tu suis des yeux, eh bien, il n'existe pas! C'est toi, c'est Saint-Christophe, c'est la France entière qui dansent! Le gyroscope a le don d'échapper au mouvement terrestre, et c'est pourquoi il paraît tourner. En vérité, c'est nous qui tournons autour de lui' (*RA* 42). Nestor uses the gyroscope to suggest a reversal of perspectives equivalent to the Copernican revolution in physics. His warning to Tiffauges haunts the rest of the novel and lies at the centre of its epistemological anxiety: 'Tu t'accroches à un point fixe, mais la terre veut tourner, et tu ne l'empêcheras pas de tourner' (*RA* 42). The quest for certainty, particularly moral certainty, must prove treacherous if, as Tiffauges realizes at an early stage of the novel, 'Satan [. . .] présente un miroir à la face de Dieu', so that 'la droite devient gauche, la gauche devient droite, le bien est appelé mal et le mal est appelé bien' (*RA* 84). There may be no ultimate guarantee of truth, but the notion of error cannot be simply discarded in a gesture of pseudo-Nietzschean affirmation. As Tiffauges is drawn further into the service of the Nazi regime, he glimpses the potential consequences of his failure to make an adequate distinction between Good and Evil (see *RA* 292–3). He begins to fear the possibility of an inversion which will be all the more shattering because he has refused to consider the ethical consequences of his actions. The *inversion maligne* is made possible *precisely because* he has abandoned any normative standard of truth or morality in his joyful appropriation of the Napola at Kaltenborn:

Après le joyeux tumulte de la soirée, ce spectacle de massacre m'a cruellement rappelé un certain tour de mon destin, toujours menaçant, et qui s'appelle: l'inversion maligne [. . .] Toutes les essences que j'ai dévoilées et portées à l'incandescence peuvent demain, ce soir même, *changer de signe* et brûler d'un feu d'autant plus infernal que je les aurai plus magnifiquement exaltées. (*RA* 351–2)

As we shall see in the next section, Tiffauges's encounter with the Commander of Kaltenborn prepares the apocalyptic conclusion of

Le Roi des aulnes by undermining his hope of achieving, except in death, 'cette union du signe et de la chair qui était pour lui la fin dernière des choses' (*RA* 148).

(iv) *Theories of the Sign:*
2. *Proliferation and Autonomy*

Professor Essig, Göring's unwelcome academic guest at Rominten, suggests that the potency of the symbol may be independent of its practical function, when he refers to 'le bâton d'un maréchal qui serait une bien médiocre arme de combat, mais qui le rend physiquement intouchable par la dignité qu'il lui confère' (*RA* 230). Later, during a ceremony marking the winter solstice at Kaltenborn, the SS officer Stefan Raufeisen indicates the importance of symbols within Fascist ideology: 'Enfin, d'une voix calme, il expliqua que chaque type d'homme se réalise par un outil privilégié qui est aussi un symbole [. . .] Les Jungmannen de Kaltenborn eux étaient doublement voués à l'épée, comme jeunes guerriers du Reich, d'abord, et par la vertu du blason du château ensuite' (*RA* 280). The Jungmannen are 'voués à l'épée': promised, dedicated, and even doomed to the sword, like sacrificial victims. Tiffauges's use of coercive tactics in his attempts to recruit new candidates for the Napola proves that the children have no more choice in their destiny than their parents (see *RA* 302–3, 314–15, and 317–18); and, once integrated into the Nazi machine, the Jungmannen owe absolute and exclusive obedience to the tyrannical order of symbols: 'Tout ce qui ne relevait pas de l'épée devait leur être étranger. Tout autre recours que celui de l'épée était lâche et traître' (*RA* 280).

The reclusive Commander of Kaltenborn, in his most important appearance in *Le Roi des aulnes*, attempts to explain the potency of the symbol within Nazi Germany (see *RA* 320–4). In the early parts of the novel Tiffauges believes that the 'obscurités' or 'erreurs d'interprétation' to which the sign may give rise are relatively harmless (*RA* 148). The Commander warns that this is not the case:

Jusqu'ici vous avez découvert des signes sur les choses, comme les lettres et les chiffres qu'on lit sur une borne. Ce n'est que la forme faible de l'existence symbolique. Mais n'allez pas croire que les signes soient toujours d'inoffensives et faibles abstractions. Les signes sont forts, Tiffauges, ce sont eux qui vous ont amené ici. Les signes sont irritables. Le *symbole* bafoué devient *diabole*. Centre de lumière et de concorde, il se fait puissance de ténèbres et de déchirement. (*RA* 320–1)

The symbol disunifies[29] by reversing the ordinary relationship with its referent; it asserts its supremacy and then its independence from any need to signify: 'Car il y a un moment effrayant où le signe n'accepte plus d'être porté par une créature, comme un étendard est porté par un soldat. Il acquiert son autonomie, il échappe à la chose symbolisée, et, ce qui est redoutable, *il la prend lui-même en charge.* Alors malheur à elle!' (*RA* 321). The symbol seizes its autonomy, and the free proliferation of meaning is equivalent to no meaning at all: 'Parce qu'alors, le symbole n'étant plus lesté par rien devient maître du ciel. Il prolifère, envahit tout, se brise en mille significations qui ne signifient plus rien du tout' (*RA* 321). Explicitly referring to the Apocalypse ('Avez-vous lu l'Apocalypse de saint Jean?', *RA* 321), the Commander makes a dark prophecy which will be fulfilled in the final pages of *Le Roi des aulnes*: 'Dans le ciel saturé de figures se prépare un orage qui aura la violence d'une apocalypse, et qui nous engloutira tous!' (*RA* 324).

The Commander's account of the symbol bears an important resemblance to Tournier's discussion of poetic language in *Le Vent Paraclet*. Tournier believes that in a poem the word becomes 'opaque comme une chose' (*VP* 201) and that purely verbal criteria take precedence over any signifying intention: 'Dans un poème, le mot l'emporte sur l'idée, laquelle suit comme elle peut ou ne suit pas du tout' (*VP* 199). Tournier describes poetry as 'le plus éminent des arts' because it demands a high degree of participation from the reader (*VP* 169), but he is clearly not prepared to abandon his own texts to the play of the signifier. In the most densely self-referential passage of *Le Roi des aulnes* the Commander warns against the dissolution of reference within the self-engendering order of signs and attempts to re-establish the primacy of intentional meaning. The sign which does not signify, or which signifies too much, is regarded as catastrophic for the human search for meaning.

The Commander underlines his own insistence upon the referential function of language by illustrating his discussion with the *historical* example of Nazi Germany, described as 'le produit des symboles eux-mêmes qui mènent souverainement le jeu' (*RA* 322). The potent

---

[29] According to the *Petit Robert*, the word *diable*, and hence also the neologism *diabole*, are derived from the Greek word *diabolos*, meaning 'qui désunit'.

symbolic pantheon of Nazism is deployed independently of all human signification: 'Dans tout ce qui touche désormais à l'Allemagne, l'homme est accessoire' (RA 323). By invoking the historical situation, the Commander attempts to control the reference and intelligibility of his own discourse, and this is undoubtedly a reflection of Tournier's desire to maintain mastery over his own text.[30] Both Tournier and the Commander are aware, however, that apocalypse is on the horizon. Nazism has liberated the sign from all ethical and referential obligation. The sacrifice of the human in favour of the symbolic is also reflected in Tiffauges's preference for signs over people and in the surrender of his humanity after the discovery of his 'écriture sinistre'.[31] And the Commander's vision of apocalypse serves as a characterization of the text in which Tiffauges finds himself. Whilst attempting to maintain a historically referential and conceptually coherent use of language, the Commander describes the autonomy of the symbol and the threat which it poses to the intelligibility of both world and text: 'Et tout cela est symbole, tout cela est chiffre, indiscutablement. Mais ne cherchez pas à comprendre, c'est-à-dire à trouver pour chaque signe la chose à laquelle il renvoie. Car ces symboles sont diaboles: ils ne symbolisent plus rien. Et de leur saturation naît la fin du monde' (RA 321).

The Commander's discussion of signs and symbols marks an important turning-point in Le Roi des aulnes. Tournier's novel begins to question and undermine Tiffauges's presumption of unity and coherence. In the final continuous series of entries from the 'Écrits sinistres', which concludes the fifth section of the novel, Tiffauges finally becomes the master of Kaltenborn and seems to have achieved his apotheosis (see RA 337–53). This period corresponds to Chapters Nine and Ten of Vendredi ou les limbes du Pacifique. But, like Vendredi, Le Roi des aulnes continues beyond its 'age of play'. Tiffauges wants to have the hair of the Jungmannen woven into a cape: 'Ce serait en somme ma toison d'or, une chlamyde d'amour

---

[30] For further discussion of Tournier's desire to maintain control over his own texts, see ch. 4.

[31] For an illustration of this, see RA 157. Madame Unruh attempts to prevent Tiffauges from taking a bird which symbolizes her love for her dead husband, but Tiffauges ignores her plea: 'Elle comprit alors que si le pigeon platiné était un symbole pour elle, il était bien davantage encore pour Tiffauges, et que toutes ses supplications se briseraient sur un impératif prédateur qui était ce qu'il y avait en lui de plus inflexible et de moins humain.'

et d'apparat à la fois, satisfaisant ma passion en dedans et manifestant mon pouvoir au-dehors' (RA 345). However, this Golden Fleece, the ultimate symbol of power and satisfaction, is refused as Frau Dorn, the weaver, runs away in horror when she hears Tiffauges's request (RA 345). Tiffauges's incomplete apotheosis does not mark the final point of his destiny, and it precedes a series of shattering inversions. Le Roi des aulnes will have six sections, not five. Earlier in the novel, the description of Göring's activity as a hunter prefigures this addition of a final section: 'Forcer un cerf, le tuer, l'émasculer, manger sa chair, lui voler ses bois pour s'en glorifier comme d'un trophée, telle était donc la geste en cinq actes de l'ogre de Rominten [. . .] Il en existait un sixième, plus fondamental encore, que Tiffauges devait découvrir quelques mois plus tard' (RA 226). The text suggests a five-act structure, but then transgresses the teleological closure of the classical scene. Tiffauges's near-apotheosis will be transformed into apocalypse, as Tournier's protagonist finds himself amidst signs which signify too little, or too much, to satisfy the quest for meaning.

(v) The Over-determined Symbol

In the opening pages of Section Six of Le Roi des aulnes reality makes an unwelcome intrusion into the self-coherent world of the novel. Administrative and commercial structures collapse, and the German people is 'confronté à la réalité brute' (RA 361). Tiffauges discovers a human corpse, flattened by the retreating German troops, which is 'dépourvu de toute aura symbolique' and which reveals only 'l'horreur la plus nue' (RA 358). Tournier's novel acquires a vicious realism in its final pages, as Tiffauges's latent sadistic fantasies become progressively more manifest. Tiffauges is fascinated by the headless corpse of one of the Jungmannen; and when he lifts it, the sound of Russian cannons in the background seems to participate in a great cosmic orgasm: 'Quant à l'extase phorique, elle m'a emporté dans un ciel noir qu'ébranlait de seconde en seconde la pulsation des canons de l'Apocalypse' (RA 365). Shortly afterwards a landmine explodes in the arms of Arnim, another of the Jungmannen, and Tiffauges is bathed in the dead boy's blood. Tiffauges's account of the incident takes the form of an ecstatic and intensely disturbing litany of death:

Venant après ma veillée auprès d'Hellmut, ce farouche baptême a fait de moi un autre homme.

Un grand soleil rouge s'est levé tout à coup devant ma face. Et ce soleil était un enfant.

Un ouragan vermeil m'a jeté dans la poussière, comme Saul sur le chemin de Damas, foudroyé par la lumière. Et cet ouragan était un jeune garçon.

Un cyclone écarlate a enfoncé ma figure dans la terre, comme la majesté de la grâce ordinante cloue au sol le jeune lévite. Et ce cyclone était un petit homme de Kaltenborn.

Un manteau de pourpre a pesé d'un poids intolérable sur mes épaules, attestant ma dignité de Roi des Aulnes. Et ce manteau était Arnim le Souabe.
(*RA* 368)

After this experience Tiffauges remains in the infirmary 'sans raison avouable', prey to 'd'étranges transports' (*RA* 369). He remembers his own illness after he was forced to clean Pelsenaire's wounded knee with his mouth. He finally confronts the implications of 'cet épisode malheureux, mais de si vaste portée' (*RA* 369). In the penultimate entry in the 'Écrits sinistres', Tiffauges illustrates how his own attempts to penetrate the obscure have been impeded by a fundamental blindness to the obvious. The sexual and sado-masochistic aspects of his relationship with Pelsenaire are already evident within his original account 350 pages earlier:

Ma langue fit le tour de la blessure qu'elle entoura d'une auréole grise [. . .] J'y passai la langue rapidement une première fois, pas assez légèrement cependant pour ne pas provoquer un tressaillement qui souleva en rictus le bourrelet de muscle arrondi coiffant la rotule. Puis une seconde fois plus longuement. Enfin mes lèvres se posèrent sur les lèvres de la blessure et y demeurèrent un temps que je ne mesurai pas.

Je ne saurais dire exactement ce qui se passa ensuite. Je crois que je fus pris de frissons, de convulsions même, et qu'on dut m'emporter à l'infirmerie. (*RA* 23)

The 'convulsions' and 'frissons' which he describes suggest the erotic force of his experience. Tiffauges claims to have been blind to the blatant eroticism with which he invests the suffering of others. Now, at the end of his 'Écrits sinistres', he has finally achieved a degree of insight into his own nature. He promises to shed 'toute la lumière [. . .] sur cet épisode malheureux' and to give 'l'aveu de la vérité':

Aujourd'hui donc, aujourd'hui seulement, je suis en mesure d'écrire la vérité sur cette crise, et je le fais avec le minimum de mots: ce qui m'a devasté au moment où mes lèvres ont rencontré les lèvres de la blessure de Pelsenaire, ce n'est rien d'autre qu'un excès de joie, une joie d'une insupportable violence, une brûlure plus cruelle et plus profonde que toutes celles que j'avais subies précédemment et que j'ai endurées depuis, mais une brûlure de plaisir. Il était tout à fait exclu que mon organisme vierge, et tout clos encore sur sa propre tendresse, supportât une pareille fulguration. (*RA* 369–70)

Tiffauges discovers the coincidence of pain and pleasure, eroticism and suffering. At the same time, he finally assumes the full implications of his own mythological fantasies: he may be Abel, the eternal victim, but he is also Gilles de Rais (who had a castle at a village named Tiffauges and who is the subject of Tournier's *Gilles et Jeanne*), or the ogre who feasts upon the flesh of his victims, or the *Erlkönig* who attempts to steal a dying child from the arms of his father.

The duality of 'Abel Tiffauges', combining victim and victimizer, innocence and guilt, within one subject, reflects the cult of ambiguity which can be seen throughout *Le Roi des aulnes*. *Phorie*, for example, is both mastery and servitude, possession and abnegation: 'Admirable ambiguïté de la phorie qui veut qu'on possède et maîtrise dans la mesure où l'on sert et s'abnie!' (*RA* 348). The child is both 'possédé' and 'servi', 'porté' and 'emporté' (*RA* 59; see also *RA* 341). Nestor, Tiffauges's childhood mentor, is 'd'une précocité effrayante', but also 'd'une puérilité déconcertante' (*RA* 17); Tiffauges cannot tell if his friend was an 'adulte nain' or a 'bébé géant' (*RA* 27); what he says is 'd'une stupéfiante précocité', but he may be no more than 'un attardé, un demeuré, un installé à demeure dans l'enfance' (*RA* 27). At different moments Tiffauges feels 'une angoisse voluptueuse' (*RA* 215), or 'une joie douloureuse' (*RA* 343); joy and sadness are united 'sans peine' (*RA* 352). In the infirmary Tiffauges is sensitive to the 'atmosphère mêlée d'angoisse et d'extase (*RA* 369); he recalls the 'odeur [. . .] pleine d'équivoque' and the sensation of 'une ivresse légère, à la fois heureuse et inquiète' (*RA* 370). The Napola is designed to 'soumettre' and to 'exalter' the innocent flesh of the Jungmannen (*RA* 267), and Nazism gives rise to 'une fascination exquise et vénéneuse' (*RA* 269). The cry which Tiffauges hears on several occasions in the course of *Le Roi des aulnes* and which he believes to be 'le son fondamental de son destin' (*RA* 389) epitomizes the ambiguity which permeates the novel. It is a 'plainte heureuse' (*RA* 106), characterized by 'rigueur' and 'plénitude', 'équilibre' and 'débordement' (*RA* 105). At the end of the novel, when Tiffauges hears the cry 'dans son absolue pureté' (*RA* 388), it is described as 'Cette longue plainte gutturale et modulée, pleine d'harmoniques, certains d'une étrange allégresse, d'autres exhalant la plus intolérable douleur' (*RA* 388). The 'état originel' (*RA* 389) of the cry is already the complex coexistence of apparently irreconcilable qualities.

The interrelation of opposites has a direct bearing on the ethical dilemma presented in and by *Le Roi des aulnes*. From the first section of the novel, Tiffauges is aware of a balance between Good and Evil: 'Ce premier jour du printemps a été marqué pour moi d'une pierre noire et d'une pierre blanche, comme si désormais le faste et le néfaste devaient sans cesse s'équilibrer de part et d'autre de mon chemin' (*RA* iii). The reversal of moral values ('le bien est appelé mal et le mal est appelé bien', *RA* 84) confounds moral certainty, but Tiffauges still hopes to maintain his own form of Blättchen's 'vigoureux manichéisme' (*RA* 266) by distinguishing between *inversion bénigne* and *inversion maligne*. The distinction proves indispensable but treacherous, as Tiffauges realizes when he glimpses his own complicity with the Nazi machine. He begins to doubt his ability to distinguish between moral opposites: 'Mais ce Blättchen — qui sent le crime à plein nez — me fait entrevoir l'éventualité d'une immense et déchirante révélation: qui sait si tout, absolument tout ce qui ici répond — ou paraît répondre — à mes faims et à mes aspirations, n'est pas en vérité leur *inversion maligne*?' (*RA* 292-3). The profound resemblance between the malign and the benign fills Tiffauges with anxiety and doubt on even the most joyous occasion (see *RA* 351-2). In a world of correspondence and ambiguity, the benign act is necessarily shadowed by its *inversion maligne*. Tiffauges is made aware of this when he encounters Éphraïm and discovers the horror of the concentration camps which reflect and invert his own private obsessions:

Abreuvé d'horreur, Tiffauges voyait ainsi s'édifier impitoyablement, à travers les longues confessions d'Éphraïm, une Cité infernale qui répondait pierre par pierre à la Cité phorique dont il avait rêvé à Kaltenborn. Le Canada, le tissage des cheveux, les appels, les chiens dobermans, les recherches sur la gémellité et les densités atmosphériques, et surtout, surtout, les fausses salles de douche, toutes ses inventions, toutes ses découvertes se reflétaient dans l'horrible miroir, inversées et portées à une incandescence d'enfer. (*RA* 378-9)

The abrupt revelations of Section Six contrast sharply with the joyful scenes which conclude Section Five. But Tournier has carefully prepared this 'déduction tiffaugéenne des camps de mort' (*RA* 379) in the first 350 pages of the novel. Tiffauges's playful search for meaning gives way to sadistic fantasy, and *Le Roi des aulnes* turns out to be a much more vicious novel than the reader might have expected. Tiffauges and the Nazis share a potentially criminal will-to-power, towards which Tournier's text shows a discomforting mixture of revulsion and fascination.

Like Jaan at the end of *Vendredi ou les limbes du Pacifique*, Éphraïm appears in the final stages of *Le Roi des aulnes* as a possible agent of salvation.[32] After revealing the extent to which Tiffauges's actions reflect the crimes of Nazism, he promises deliverance from the hands of the oppressors: 'Les soldats de l'Éternel vont venir délivrer le peuple d'Israël' (*RA* 383); 'Les temps étaient mûrs, répétait-il, et la délivrance approchait' (*RA* 384). The Russian invasion of Prussia is equated with the deliverance of the Jews from Egypt. Here, however, the tension between historical reality and the mythological interpretation of history is at its most acute. The Soviet troops are hardly 'Les soldats de l'Éternel' and it is by now too late to save the 'peuple d'Israël' killed in the Nazi death camps. Éphraïm promises deliverance from the oppressor, but Tiffauges is both oppressor and oppressed, seeking an apocalyptic deliverance from *himself* which brings salvation only through destruction. Earlier in the novel Prussia was described as 'une terre promise' (*RA* 192); but the promise of Tiffauges's promised land has turned sour. In the final pages of the novel, as the Russians attack Kaltenborn, the text alludes to or quotes Exodus, Montaigne, Nestor, the Commander of Kaltenborn, and the Apocalypse of Saint John. Tiffauges hears the 'son fondamental de son destin' (*RA* 389), and alpha and omega are finally united, in cruel and grotesque fashion, when Haïo, Haro, and Lothar are impaled on the swords of Kaltenborn. Biblical and literary allusion, self-quotation, and thematic repetition combine with a vivid depiction of war. The novel fulfils its prophecies of apocalypse, but there is no joy here for the expatriate hermeneut. Earlier Tiffauges's journey to the East was presented as a return to the sources of light and truth (see *RA* 172). Now he takes Éphraïm on his shoulders and turns his back on the East, symbolically renouncing his own deluded quest for

---

[32] The parallels between Jaan and Éphraïm include, for example, a common link with Estonia; see *RA* 377 and *V* 205.

knowledge: 'il s'engagea sur la route de Schlangenfliess, vaguement orienté en direction de l'ouest sauveur' (*RA* 391).

For Hans-Georg Gadamer, even though ultimate verification is never possible, interpretation is preserved from the anarchy of absolute relativism by the continuing debate with tradition and the dialectic of question and answer.[33] Paul Ricoeur also endeavours to save interpretation from arbitrariness by his hopeful dialectic between the donation and the creation of meaning: the symbol, characterized as 'cette région du double sens',[34] provokes interpretation by its very ambiguity; it is by nature *generous*: 'Le symbole donne à penser', it elicits reflection but does not entirely command the activity of the thinker, meaning is both *given* in the symbol and *created* by the hermeneut.[35] The emphasis on meaning as both given and created bears an important relationship to Tournier's theory of reading and his account of the interaction of text and reader.[36] But *Le Roi des aulnes* does not seem to share the measured confidence of Gadamer and Ricoeur, nor does it allow the generous exchange implied in Tournier's own theories, as it dramatizes the guilt and impotence of the hermeneut and the devastation of the scene of interpretation. In its final pages the text frustrates Tiffauges's presumption of intelligibility and succumbs to its own most-feared prophecy: '[Le symbole] prolifère, envahit tout, se brise en mille significations qui ne signifient plus rien du tout [. . .] Mais ne cherchez pas à comprendre [. . .] Car ces symboles sont diaboles: ils ne symbolisent plus rien' (*RA* 321). Interpretation may be an indispensable human activity, but is also proves to be, as Paul de Man suggests, 'nothing but the possibility of error'.[37]

At the end of *Le Roi des aulnes* Tournier reproduces the ambiguous conclusion of Flaubert's 'Un cœur simple'. On her death bed Félicité is afforded a final consolation for her uneventful life as she sees her stuffed parrot soaring into the heavens: 'et, quand elle exhala son dernier souffle, elle crut voir, dans les cieux entr'ouverts,

---

[33] On the dialectic of question and answer, see Gadamer, *Wahrheit und Methode*, e.g. pp. 344–60.

[34] See Ricoeur, *De l'interprétation*, pp. 16–18.

[35] On the phrase 'Le symbole donne à penser', see the final chapter of *La Symbolique du mal*, especially pp. 324–5, and *Le Conflit des interprétations*, p. 284.

[36] For discussion of Tournier's conception of the creative role of the reader, see ch. 4, sec. (i).

[37] Paul de Man, *Blindness and Insight*, p. 141.

un perroquet gigantesque, planant au-dessus de sa tête.'[38] Is this
confirmation of her sainthood or the final proof of her senility?
Flaubert refuses to intervene in his text to privilege either interpretation. The closing words of Le Roi des aulnes recall the ambiguity
of this conclusion as Tiffauges sinks deeper into a Prussian marsh:
'Quand il leva pour la dernière fois la tête vers Éphraïm, il ne vit
qu'une étoile d'or à six branches qui tournait lentement dans le ciel
noir' (RA 393). Salvation through Éphraïm or the final consequences
of Tiffauges's will-to-death; sublime apotheosis or the banality of
accidental death; the fulfilment of destiny or its ultimate frustration:
Tournier, like Flaubert, allows no clear choice between incompatible
readings.

Throughout Le Roi des aulnes truth is conceived in visual terms
and suggested through metaphors of light: 'il faut une lumière
[. . .] pour percer notre myopie', writes Tiffauges (RA 13); he
refers to 'l'incroyable cécité des autres au signe fatidique qui me
distingue entre tous' (RA 70); in Church he hopes to find 'un rai
de lumière' or the 'faible lueur' which sometimes penetrates the
'forêt de mensonges et de crimes' (RA 80); in Germany he anticipates 'révélations d'une éblouissante soudaineté' (RA 172) and later
he promises to shed 'toute la lumière' on his own past (RA 369).[39]
But Tiffauges is prey to the simultaneous urge for light and for
darkness, to see the truth and to be preserved from it. As he flees
from Kaltenborn 'sans espoir de salut' (RA 391), he is 'doublement
aveugle' (RA 392), wandering through the dark night without his
glasses: '— Éphraïm, dit Tiffauges, je n'ai plus mes lunettes. Je
ne vois presque plus rien. Guide-moi!' (RA 391). The 'nuit des
temps' to which he refers in the first paragraph of the novel (RA 11)
prefigures the 'ciel noir' described in the final words of Le Roi des
aulnes. Tiffauges advances into darkness: 'Puis l'obscurité se referma
sur lui [. . .] il avança dès lors, les bras tendus en avant, comme
un aveugle' (RA 392). He believes he sees the redemptive light of
a golden star; yet, without his glasses, he is short-sighted to the point

---

[38] Gustave Flaubert, 'Un cœur simple', in Trois Contes, p. 61. Compare also the
final lines of Tournier's story 'Que ma joie demeure', in CB 91. For Tournier's own
discussion of Flaubert's Trois Contes, see 'Nécessité et liberté dans les Trois Contes
de Flaubert', in Vol 161–8.
[39] For further discussion of the visual conception of truth in Tournier's fiction,
see ch. 5, sec. (ii).

of blindness. Even this final vision may be, like the transcendence of Félicité's parrot, the ultimate delusion of an enfeebled mind. The light of truth appears as an uncertain glimmer, and Tournier's novel about interpretation ends in ambiguous darkness.

3

Identity and Imitation
Les Météores

Les Météores is a long and ambitious work, and since its publication
in 1975 Tournier has not attempted anything which approaches it
in either length or scope. It tells the stories of the brothers Alexandre
and Edouard Surin, of Edouard's wife Maria-Barbara, and of their
children Jean and Paul, twins whose blissful childhood ends with
the loss of their parents and their inevitable separation from one
another. The theme of twinship, already present in Tournier's earlier
fiction, dominates the novel, and, in so far as the twin can be seen
as a modern version of the *Doppelgänger*, gives evidence of an
important relationship between Tournier's writing and Romantic
fiction. The word *Doppelgänger* (originally spelt 'Doppeltgänger')
was first used by the German Romantic novelist Jean Paul, to whom
Tournier alludes when he gives the collective name 'Jean-Paul' to the
twins in his novel. In works by Jean Paul, Hoffmann, Tieck, Achim
von Arnim, Brentano, and more recently in Robert Musil's *The Man
without Qualities*, the *Doppelgänger* appears as a duplication and
completion of the original self, but also reveals a fatal division within
identity.[1] Tournier is well aware of his literary ancestry, and in *Les
Météores* he adopts a Romantic rhetoric of presence and absence,
unity and duality, harmony and dislocation. A tempting schematic
account of the novel would show how the original perfection of the
'cellule gémellaire' is fractured by contact with the world; we see a
series of imperfect approximations to the perfection of twinhood—
the relationships of Edouard and Maria-Barbara, Ralph and Deborah,
or the homosexuality of Alexandre—until Paul's long initiation is
completed and he is readmitted to the original plenitude of his
childhood. The incursion of alterity into selfhood, made possible

---

[1] On the *Doppelgänger* in Romantic literature, see Wilhelmine Krauss, *Das
Doppelgängermotif in der Romantik*, and Ralph Tymms, *Doubles in Literary
Psychology*. For the theme of twins in Tournier's earlier fiction, see, e.g., V 186,
and *RA* 303-7.

by the contact of the absolute (represented by the twins) with the fallen world of relativity, is finally reversed.

Although this reading of *Les Météores* receives significant support from the text itself, and from Tournier's account of his novel in *Le Vent Paraclet* (see VP 233–70), it remains partial because it overlooks complexities and tensions introduced into the work by Tournier's use of different narrative viewpoints. At least six narrators are used in the course of *Les Météores*, but two are of particular importance: the flamboyant homosexual Alexandre Surin and his nephew Paul. After the death of Alexandre, the final third of the novel concentrates exclusively on Paul's search for his twin, which ends with a crippling accident under the Berlin Wall in 1961. In his essay on *Les Météores* Tournier insists that the principal subject of his text is Paul's gradual understanding and acceptance of his destiny (see VP 233–4); Alexandre should be regarded simply as one of the novel's 'personnages secondaires' (*VP* 250). At the same time it is significant that Tournier devotes more space to Alexandre than to Paul in both *Le Vent Paraclet* and the first two-thirds of *Les Météores*; and his attempt to underplay Alexandre's importance reveals a deep ambivalence towards the character whom he clearly finds most fascinating. Tournier's mistrust may be explained by the way Alexandre diverts attention away from Paul and undermines the authority of the novel's principal speaker. Referring to Balzac's Vautrin, Proust's Charlus, and a character in Modiano's novel *Villa Triste*, Tournier acknowledges the danger presented by the flamboyant homosexual: 'Tout romancier doit savoir que s'il lâche dans son œuvre le personnage d'un grand homosexuel flamboyant, il devra renoncer à le contenir dans les limites congrues' (*VP* 251). Alexandre escapes authorial control and assumes for many readers what is, in Tournier's view, an unwarranted importance.

In the early stages of the text the respective journals of Alexandre and Paul suggest thematically related but ultimately incompatible viewpoints. Paul claims that his powers of understanding, which he attributes to what he calls his 'intuition gémellaire', give him a privileged insight into the lives and experiences of others and assure his ability to comprehend his personal evolution. He seeks the restoration of his childhood happiness and the original plenitude of identity and self-knowledge. However, his fantasy of return is directly opposed by Alexandre's experience of uncertain self-creation. At the same time Alexandre gives an insight into important aspects of

Tournier's thought and aesthetics. Moreover, the initial opposition between Alexandre and Paul is superseded by an unacknowledged identification. Alexandre dies less than two-thirds of the way into the text, but Paul is destined to re-enact his uncle's experience of solitude and dispossession.

(i) *The Model and the Copy*

At the beginning of *Les Météores* Jean and Paul are described as being 'murés dans un refus unanime de ce qui n'est pas l'autre' (*M* 10). The embrace of identical twins represents the rejection of alterity and the perfect retention of what Paul calls the 'identité éternelle, immobile, inaltérable qui est notre statut originel' (*M* 366). For him, Christ's entreaty '*Tu aimeras ton prochain comme toi-même*' (*M* 171) is fully realizable only between twins:[2] 'Rien n'est retenu, tout est donné, et pourtant rien n'est perdu, tout est gardé, dans un admirable équilibre entre l'autre et le même. Aimer son prochain comme soi-même? Cette impossible gageure exprime le fond de notre cœur et la loi de ses battements' (*M* 172). The identical twin is literally an *alter ego*, a second self. Loving one's twin involves loving onself in the twin, with no loss of vital energy ('rien n'est perdu, tout est gardé'). Paul's defence of the 'cellule gémellaire' is, then, the attempt to preserve the unity and continuity of identity against the fragmentation caused by contact with time and society.

This preservation of identity depends upon the refusal to acknowledge the existence of *autrui*. As Sister Béatrice realizes in regard of her wards, the 'débiles mentaux' of Sainte-Brigitte, the rejection of the other precludes all possibility of enrichment through human relationships: 'Leur grande infirmité, c'était leur solitude, leur incapacité à nouer avec autrui — fût-il infirme comme eux — des relations entraînant un enrichissement réciproque' (*M* 46). On the other hand, this rejection of *autrui* seems essential to the state of grace in which the children live:

Mais il y avait plus. Sœur Béatrice s'était convaincue que ses innocents étaient plus proches de Dieu et des anges que les autres humains — à commencer par elle-même — non seulement parce qu'ils ignoraient la duplicité et les

---

[2] For discussion of this phrase in one of the important sources of *Les Météores*, see Robert Musil, 'Liebe deinen Nächsten wie dich selbst', in *Der Mann ohne Eigenschaften*, iv. 1211–19.

fausses valeurs de la vie sociale, mais aussi parce que le péché n'avait pour ainsi dire aucune prise sur leur âme. Elle subissait une manière de fascination devant ces êtres auxquels avait été donnée — en même temps qu'une très cruelle malédiction leur était infligée — une sainteté en quelque sorte originelle [. . .] Sa foi était confortée par le rayonnement de leur présence. (M 47–8)

Here, as elsewhere in the novel, Tournier is playing on the word *innocent*, which can be used in French to mean both mentally retarded and innocent in the theological sense. The 'sainteté en quelque sorte originelle' of the innocents is the state *before* original sin ('le péché n'avait pour ainsi dire aucune prise sur leur âme'). If this sainthood is conferred 'en même temps qu'une très cruelle malédiction', the coincidence of sainthood and debility is clearly no pure chance. Freedom from original sin is the corollary of the incapacity to form social relationships. 'Duplicité', both falsehood and duality, is the condition of society and the social self; and it can be avoided only if the child is kept in Edenic ignorance of 'les fausses valeurs de la vie sociale'. The 'débiles mentaux', and the twins during their childhood, remain immune from duality in as far as they resist the influence of *autrui*.

The 'sans-pareil' is forced into social relationships in search of the comfort and companionship which the twin finds in the presence of his *alter ego*. Paul dismisses the relationships of the 'sans-pareil' as unsatisfactory copies of the original perfection of twinship; and Jean fully accepts his brother's views:

Car il faut être juste et reconnaître que Paul n'a pas toujours tort: sous cet angle, oui, les sans-pareil sont les pâles imitateurs des frères-pareils. Ils connaissent bien eux aussi un principe exogamique, une prohibition de l'inceste, mais de quel inceste s'agit-il? De celui qui accouple un père et sa fille, une mère et son fils, un frère et sa sœur. Cette variété suffirait à trahir la médiocrité de cette sorte d'inceste sans-pareil, et qu'il s'agit en vérité de trois pauvres contrefaçons. Car le véritable inceste, l'union insurpassablement incestueuse, c'est évidemment la nôtre, oui, celle des amours ovales qui nouent le même au même et suscitent par entente cryptophasique une brûlure de volupté qui se multiplie par elle-même au lieu de se juxtaposer pauvrement comme dans les amours sans-pareil — et encore, au mieux de leur réussite! (M 239–40)

According to Jean and Paul, the authentic relationship, the model of all incestuous and non-incestuous relationships, is the alliance of 'le même au même' achieved by twins. The 'sans-pareil' are 'imitateurs', their relationships are mere 'contrefaçons' of 'le véritable inceste'. The hierarchical opposition of model and copy is used throughout *Les Météores*: the narrator of the opening chapter implies that the marriage of Edouard and Maria-Barbara is only 'une reprise triviale et superficielle' of the twins' 'amours sublimes' (*M* 11); Thomas Koussek, drawing an analogy with Molière's *Le Bourgeois Gentilhomme* describes the 'roturier' heterosexual trying to copy the life-style of the aristocratic homosexual (*M* 126); also referring to Molière's play, Paul in turn describes the homosexual as an imitator of the true aristocrat of nature, trying to reproduce twinship 'en contrefaçon' (*M* 335–6); sexual relations between the 'sans-pareil' are a 'simulacre' of the coupling of twins (*M* 340); and homosexuality is described as a 'contrefaçon sans-pareil de la gémellité' (*M* 360).

The perfection of twinship is copied, but never equalled, in homosexual relations, which are in turn copied by the heterosexual couple. Tournier himself, in his discussion of twins in *Le Vent Paraclet* affirms the priority of the original over the 'contrefaçon' or 'copie':

l'homosexualité et l'inceste pratiqués par des singuliers ne sont que deux approches grossières et imparfaites de la gémellité. On ne rend pas compte d'un fait original par sa contrefaçon, on rend compte d'une contrefaçon par l'original qu'elle imite [. . .] En fait d'inceste et d'homosexualité, la gémellité apparaît comme un absolu inaccessible. C'est l'original d'une authenticité indiscutable dont l'inceste et l'homosexualité tirent des copies maladroites. (*VP* 247)

Tournier seems to foreclose any dispute of the scheme which he describes ('C'est l'original d'une authenticité *indiscutable*'). But, as we have already seen, *Le Vent Paraclet* cannot be taken at face value because of a pervasive irony which makes even the most dogmatic assertion subject to an element of doubt. In the present instance Tournier contrives to overlook those aspects of his text, initially contained within Alexandre's narrative, which dispute Paul's rigid categories of self and other, model and copy.

Alexandre is certainly not immune from nostalgia for twinship and the sexual alliance of the same to the same (see especially *M* 213 and 218). But for him sexuality is primarily a relationship with the other ('Le sexe, c'est la force centrifuge', *M* 73; see also *M* 76 and 288) and he rejects the 'coup sec' (orgasm without ejaculation) because of its self-enclosed nature:

Cet orgasme sans éjaculation s'enferme dans une sorte de circuit fermé qui me paraît impliquer le refus d'autrui [. . .] C'est la réaction d'un être ayant profondément opté pour la cellule fermée, pour la réclusion gémellaire. Je suis trop loin — faut-il ajouter: hélas? — du couple absolu, j'aime trop les autres, en un mot je suis trop instinctivement chasseur pour m'enfermer ainsi en moi-même. (M 41)

Alexandre's hesitation between nostalgia for twinship and the affirmation of homosexual desire is suggested by the unanswered question: 'faut-il ajouter: hélas?' He rejects the closed cell of twinship with a twinge of regret. But sexuality is not, for Alexandre, the intimate fusion of complementary halves, like the reunification of the dislocated hermaphrodite in Plato's *Symposium* or the coupling of twins in *Les Météores*; and Alexandre's desire for the other cannot be understood in terms of Paul's attempt to conserve libidinal energy within the closed circuit of fraternal incest. He does not share his nephew's faith in the original autonomy and plenitude of the self which must be protected from the corrupting influence of *autrui*. And this denial of the primacy of origins also influences his aesthetic preferences. In the section of his journal entitled 'Esthétique du dandy des gadoues' (M 86–9), Alexandre proposes an aesthetic which directly reverses Paul's rigid hierarchy of model and copy:

L'idée est plus que la chose, et l'idée de l'idée plus que l'idée. En vertu de quoi l'imitation est plus que la chose imitée, car elle est cette chose plus l'effort d'imitation, lequel contient en lui-même la possibilité de se reproduire, et donc d'ajouter la quantité à la qualité.

C'est pourquoi en fait de meubles et d'objets d'art, je préfère toujours les imitations aux originaux, l'imitation étant l'original cerné, possédé, intégré, éventuellement multiplié, bref pensé, spiritualisé. (M 86–7)

Alexandre describes the collection of original works as 'absolument réactionnaire, intempestif' (M 88) and he prefers 'la puissance infinie de ces objets produits en masse — et donc copies de copies de copies de copies de copies de copies, etc.' (M 89). Far from being less than the original because further removed from some atemporal model, the copy is *more* than the original because it combines imitation with the possibility of creative innovation. Alexandre's first encounter with the dog Sam provides an illustration of this aesthetic in practice. By sodomizing an already copulating dog, Sam copies the activity of the first dog, but also supplements and surpasses it in an act of exemplary and comic *cynisme* (see M 193–5). Similarly,

Thomas Koussek observes that, when the homosexual is conditioned by social forces to behave like a woman, he both copies and surpasses his model: 'son génie créateur l'emporte au-delà de son modèle dérisoire, et il bat la femme sur son propre terrain [. . .] il devient une femme si brillante, élégante, fine et racée — une superfemme — qu'il éclipse sans peine les femmes — les vraies — qui commettent l'imprudence de l'approcher' (M 128).

Baudelaire's 'Éloge du maquillage', which describes how artifice improves nature, and Des Esseintes's belief, described in Huysmans's *A Rebours*, that artifice is 'la marque distinctive du génie de l'homme',[3] are evident literary precursors of Alexandre's aesthetic. Moreover, Alexandre's subversion of the authority of the model has important parallels in the work of contemporary philosophers such as Gilles Deleuze and Jacques Derrida. Deleuze, for example, describes a Nietzschean reversal of Platonism which subverts the hierarchy of model, copy, and simulacrum: 'Renverser le platonisme signifie dès lors: faire monter les simulacres, affirmer leurs droits entre les icônes ou les copies [. . .] Le simulacre n'est pas une copie dégradée, il recèle une puissance positive qui nie *et l'original et la copie, et le modèle et la reproduction* [. . .] Il n'y a pas d'hiérarchie possible.'[4]

The opposition between Paul and Alexandre illustrates a hesitation in Tournier's aesthetics between, on the one hand, a respect for origins, sources, and tradition, and, on the other hand, an iconoclastic tendency to parody established hierarchies. Tournier refuses any simple choice between these options. Through his characters he gives voice to the conflicting but simultaneous attractions of imitation and creation, tradition and innovation. Paul gazes backwards nostalgically to an origin-in-plenitude, whereas Alexandre, more reconciled to history and to adult consciousness, attempts to realize his latent potential for creative self-construction and infinite self-surpassing. And, despite Tournier's misgivings, it is the experience of Alexandre which dominates the first two-thirds of the novel.

[3] Huysmans, *A Rebours/Le Drageoir aux épices*, p. 75. For Baudelaire's 'Éloge du maquillage' and his description of the dandy, who is evidently another of Alexandre's important literary ancestors, see Charles Baudelaire, *Le Peintre de la vie moderne*, in *Œuvres complètes*, ii.

[4] Gilles Deleuze, *Logique du sens*, pp. 302–3. See also ch. 5 n. 38.

(ii) *Self-creation*

In Tourner's short story 'La Jeune Fille et la mort', Coquebin interprets Mélanie's combination of *ennui* and fascination with death in terms of a fundamental philosophical experience. Internal psychological conflict is subsumed within the immemorial antagonism of two currents of thought, which Coquebin associates with the names of Parmenides and Heraclitus: 'Pour Parménide la réalité et la vérité se fondent dans l'Être immobile, massif et identitaire. Cette vision figée fait horreur à l'autre penseur, Héraclite, qui voit dans le feu tremblant et grondant le modèle de toutes les choses, et dans le courant limpide d'une eau chantante le symbole de la vie perpétuellement créatrice' (*CB* 180). Coquebin summarizes the two philosophies as 'le repos en l'Être et le dépassement de l'Être' (*CB* 180): on the one hand, immobility, identity, *stasis*; on the other hand, creativity, movement, alteration. In *Les Météores* Alexandre represents the latter pole of this opposition. He discovers his homosexuality and his vocation for self-exceeding at the 'collège du Thabor'. Although the allusion is not explained, Mount Tabor is the traditional location of Christ's Transfiguration.[5] Alexandre is sensitive to the sacred resonances of the name of his school: 'Le Thabor! nom mystérieux, environné d'un prestige magique, nom sacré où il y a de l'or et du tabernacle!' (*M* 35). The very name contains 'des promesses d'extases et de transfiguration' (*M* 35). Ecstasy and transfiguration are the opposite of the *stasis* to which Paul aspires, and they become, for Alexandre, a moral imperative (he refers to his '*devoir de transfiguration*', *M* 30) and a principle of life itself: 'Car le verdict de mort tombera au moment où mes instants cesseront d'être autant d'attributs nouveaux venant enrichir ma substance pour n'être plus que les point successifs d'une translation sans altération' (*M* 91).

Les Météores constantly returns to the theme of transfiguration. Thomas Koussek's theological speculations, which are derived in part from the Trinitarian doctrine of the medieval theologian Joachim of Fiore,[6] translate the necessity of becoming into the religious

---

[5] On the significance of the Transfiguration for Tournier, see *Le Vagabond immobile*, p. 109, and *VP* 62.

[6] In *Le Vent Paraclet* Tournier indicates the principal sources of Koussek's speculations when he refers to the 'études que j'ai pu faire sur Joachim de Flore, le millénarisme et la place du Saint-Esprit dans la théologie orthodoxe' (*VP* 253). On

sphere. Koussek compares sacred history to individual psychology and sees in both the need for development and change: 'La psychiatrie et la psychanalyse décrivent certaines névroses comme une fixation plus ou moins définitive du sujet à un stade d'évolution qui est normal et même indispensable, mais qui doit être dépassé vers un autre état plus proche de la maturité' (M 132). The consequences of this for the Western Church is that, as Koussek puts it, 'Le Christ doit être dépassé' (M 133).[7] The *filioque* controversy split the Eastern Church from Rome in the eighth century because, in Koussek's view, Orthodox theologians could not accept the fixation of the Catholic Church on Christ.[8] Koussek describes John the Baptist and the prophets as the precursors of Christ (M 133 and 135); and Christ Himself precedes and announces the advent of the Paraclete.

Koussek's belief in the coming Age of the Paraclete suggests the possibility of a definitive conclusion to the history of the Spirit. But it is uncertain whether any such conclusion will ever be reached. The sacred history recounted by Koussek is the story of prophets and precursors who announce an ill-defined future. The present is a provisional stage in a process of transformation which may be identified with time itself. Alexandre realizes that the only end to the order of the provisional is death. He describes how the youth Eustache lives 'provisoirement' in a seedy hotel:

Provisoirement, comme tout ce qu'il fait, tout ce qu'il est. Tout est provisoire pour lui — et depuis toujours — en fonction d'un avenir vague, mal défini où les choses étant à leur place et lui à la sienne, tout deviendrait enfin définitif. Je n'ai pas eu la cruauté de lui demander si ce définitif ne revêtirait pas finalement les espèces d'un rectangle de terre dans un cimetière, mais je l'ai pensé. (M 94)

For Alexandre, there is no definitive resting place other than death. Although Koussek seems to envisage the possibility of an end to the

Joachim of Fiore and his influence, see Marjorie Reeves, *The Influence of Prophecy in the Later Middle Ages: A Study in Joachimism*; on Joachim's conception of history and the problems of interpretation which it poses, see especially pp. 17–27, 126–32.

[7] For discussion of Tournier's use of the word *dépassement*, see 'Concluding Remarks: Between Synthesis and Scarcity'.

[8] On the Orthodox repudiation of the 'double procession' of the Spirit (i.e. from the Father and from the Son—'filioque'), and for discussion of the Orthodox conception of the relationship between Christ and the Holy Spirit, see Father Kallistos Ware, *The Orthodox Way*, pp. 40, 44–6, 122–6. On the *filioque* controversy and its importance for Tournier, see Susan Petit, 'Salvation, the Flesh and God in Michel Tournier's *Gaspard, Melchior et Balthazar*', pp. 60–1, and 65 n. 14.

series of sacred transformations which he describes, such an end does not seem imminent; and, revealingly, Koussek displays a marked ambivalence towards the coming of the Paraclete. He may be 'converti sans réserve à l'Esprit' (M 139), but Christianity, with all its attendant errors and mystifications, remains a vital transitional phase: 'L'Esprit avant de devenir lumière doit se faire chaleur' (M 139). Moreover, Koussek indicates that the coming of the Paraclete will involve significant losses. The Old Testament banned the making of images and the Age of the Paraclete will make them valueless; on the other hand, as Tournier will show in Gaspard, Melchior et Balthazar, art flourishes in the era inaugurated by the birth of Christ. Koussek believes that Christianity is destined to be surpassed, but he also values the indispensable enrichment brought by art and seems to regret the fact that the coming of the Paraclete will dry up the sources of aesthetic creativity:

Mais comment ne pas voir l'immense enrichissement que constituent pour la foi les icônes, les vitraux, les statues, les cathédrales elles-mêmes fourmillant d'œuvres d'art? Or cette floraison géniale, maudite par le Premier Testament et stérilisée par le Troisième Testament — celui de l'Esprit-Saint, les Acts des Apôtres — , c'est dans le Testament du Fils qu'elle trouve toutes ses semences, et surtout le climat dont elle a besoin. (M 139)

For Alexandre, the process of change obeys a necessary but mysterious logic. He is constantly surprised by the unexpectedness of his own decisions and choices:

Ce qui fait le charme de ma vie, c'est qu'arrivé à l'âge mûr, je continue à me surprendre moi-même par les décisions ou les options que je prends, et ce d'autant plus qu'il ne s'agit pas de caprices ou de tours de girouette, mais bien au contraire de fruits longuement cultivés dans le secret de mon cœur, un secret si bien gardé que je suis le premier étonné de leur forme, substance et saveur. (M 192)

Alexandre seems to believe in the existence of an unconscious agency within the human mind; but, far from being a dark threat to the hegemony of consciousness (like the Freudian unconscious) or a tyrannical master to the ego (like the id and the super-ego in Freud's later structural topology of the mind), the unconscious in Alexandre's account aids and supplements the development of identity. Metamorphosis—feared by Paul, profoundly desired by Alexandre—is not something which takes place in silence and isolation. The essential condition for change is the readiness to interact with that which potentially jeopardizes the integrity of identity. The transfigurations of the self are made possible by the collusion of an internal propensity and the chance encounter of external circumstances: 'Il faut bien sûr que les circonstances se prêtent à l'éclosion', says Alexandre (M 192); and the 'beau et lourd mot de *destin*' is, according to him, appropriate when external circumstances seem uncannily propitious for the direction of his labour of self-creation.

For Alexandre, friendship is a privileged relationship with the other which contributes to the construction and modification of the self: 'Or donc il me semble que des relations amicales ne sont supportables que si elles s'accompagnent d'une certaine *surestime* réciproque, tellement que chacun ne cesse de choquer l'autre, l'obligeant par là même à s'élever à un degré d'éminence supérieur' (M 193). The first encounter with the dog Sam, seen sodomizing another copulating dog, reminds Alexandre of the derivation of the word 'cynisme' from the Greek *kunos* (dog's); and Sam provides an exemplary case of the *cynisme* essential to the reciprocal enrichment through friendship:

Car cynisme il y a! Mais de la bonne espèce, un cynisme qui va dans mon sens, et qui y va plus vite et plus loin que je n'aurais su le faire, de telle sorte que comblé je suis aussi dépassé, un peu bousculé, exalté par conséquent [. . .] il m'a *édifié*, au double sens du mot, augmentant ma vertu, ma moralité, mais aussi ajoutant comme un étage au château de mes rêves par cet acte d'amour en seconde position [. . .] J'ai un chien, un ami *cynique* qui me scandalise en allant plus loin que moi dans mon propre sens, qui m'*édifie*. . . (M 194–5)

In a comic vein, Sam demonstrates the possibility of *dépassement* which Koussek advocated in his account of sacred history. The metaphors of vertical elevation ('exalté', 'édifié', 'ajoutant comme un étage au château de mes rêves') suggest an image of the self as something which can always be supplemented through the addition of an extra layer. Self-surpassing is achieved through continuous self-construction; and, since the construction is vertical, it is never complete, another storey can always be added, until perhaps the precarious edifice collapses under its own weight due to the inevitable absence of secure foundation (see M 34–5).

Identification is an essential and surprising feature of the process of self-creation. When it is suggested that Alexandre should take over his dead brother's refuse business, his initial reaction is horrified rejection: 'Moi? Me glisser dans les pantoufles encore chaudes de ce pisse-vinaigre qui conduisait chaque dimanche son dragon d'épouse et ses quatre filles laides à la grand-messe de la cathédrale Saint-Pierre? Moi? Prendre la direction de cette entreprise ridicule et malodorante? Cette inénarrable bouffonnerie me suffoquait' (M 29). However, after a night spent reading about his brother's business, he experiences a dramatic conversion: 'Mais que n'ai-je pas appris dans cette nuit du 26 au 27 septembre 1934 qui ne peut se comparer qu'à celle de l'extase nocturne du grand Pascal!' (M 29). External circumstance has given Alexandre a unique opportunity to take possession of society through sovereignty over what it rejects. He perceives the call of the 'devoir de transfiguration': 'J'entrevoyais aussi la métamorphose que cette souveraineté diabolique pourrait opérer sur moi' (M 30). He returns to Rennes, the town where he was brought up, to assume the position of his brother Gustave, who seems the diametrical opposite of his homosexual and impious sibling: 'D'abord, marche arrière, retour à Rennes, remise de mes pas dans leurs traces enfantines, adolescentes, etc. Cela s'appelle communément reculer pour mieux sauter. Ensuite identification brutale à celui de mes deux frères qui était le plus éloigné de moi, qui était au monde l'homme auquel je me croyais le plus étranger' (M 31). Paul envisages the self as an autonomous monadic unit which must be anxiously defended against external interference (see M 172); Alexandre, on the other hand, allows for the incursion of alterity into the constitution of the subject through his identification with and internalization of what seemed most alien.

Les Météores shows how the radical insecurity of identity can be affirmed with a certain perverse jubilation, as by Alexandre, or experienced as a source of fear and anxiety, as in the life of Alexandre's brother Edouard. Alexandre describes Edouard's charm as 'celui [. . .] des hommes faibles et sans caractère' (M 33). This absence of character, coupled with the inability to construct an identity when none is given, will cause Edouard's downfall (see M 34 and 334–5). Edouard is characterized by contradictory qualities: he shares Alexandre's 'goût de la vie et même de l'aventure, l'amour des choses et des êtres' (M 20); but he also has Gustave's 'respect inné du cours des choses, qu'il considérait comme normal, partant sain, souhaitable, béni' (M 20). These characteristics make Edouard the universal mediator, the 'intermédiaire familial avec tous' (M 19), but they are not successfully synthesized in the unity of a single subject. Like Gustave, Edouard fulfils his duties as husband and father in Brittany; like Alexandre, he enjoys the thrill of sexual conquest in Paris. At first this 'vie partagée' seems 'un chef-d'œuvre d'organisation heureuse' (M 20): 'cette double appartenance [. . .] l'avait longtemps comblé comme un surcroît de richesse' (M 21). With age, however, Edouard's double life assumes 'l'aspect d'un double exil, d'un double déracinement' (M 21). As his sexual desire becomes distinct from his need for tenderness (a dissociation which is later characterized as a prefiguration of death; see M 279), he becomes aware of 'une certaine fêlure de son être' and feels 'déchiré, doublement traître et défaillant' (M 24). His awareness of duality leads to the nostalgia for a unity which he projects on to an imagined past: 'Il avait été fort, équilibré, sûr de lui et des siens aussi longtemps que cette faim [sexuelle] et cette soif [de tendresse] étroitement mêlées s'étaient confondues avec son goût de la vie, son assentiment passionné à l'existence [. . .] Il rêvait d'une rupture, d'une fuite qui restaureraient son ancien bon cœur tout d'une pièce' (M 24).[9] Edouard searches in vain for an action or gesture by which he can acquire a secure sense of his own existence. Like his son Paul, he longs for the restoration of a lost unity, but he is forced to realize that his double life is a play of masks, superimposed on to the real absence at the core of his being: 'Mais avec des années, cet homme peu porté à l'analyse intérieure dut cependant s'avouer que chacune de ces vies servait de masque à l'autre et l'aveuglait sur le vide et l'incurable mélancolie qui constituaient leur commune vérité' (M 20).

Elsewhere in Les Météores it will be suggested, insistently even, that duality originates in the conflict between an authentic and a social self. This Romantic conception, articulated in different voices throughout Tournier's novel, locates the sources of dissension, duplicity, and difference outside the original identity of the individual. This is illustrated in the opening pages of the novel, when the twins are described sleeping: 'Ils dorment, et, rendus au plus intime d'eux-mêmes, ramenés à ce qu'il y a en eux de plus profond et de plus immuable — ramenés à leur fonds-commun — ils sont indiscernables' (M 9–10). Sleep restores 'cette innocence originelle dans laquelle ils

[9] For another statement of the desire for a 'rupture' which paradoxically restores a former state, see RA 74, where Tiffauges refers to 'une rupture qui me libérera et me permettra d'être enfin moi-même'.

se confondent' (*M* 10). When the twins awake, however, the external world introduces difference within this perfect harmony: 'Ils se dénouent. L'environnement reprend possession de leurs sens' (*M* 10). Their two faces respond 'différemment à la vie extérieure' (*M* 10), and, at least to the experienced eye of Maria-Barbara, they can now be distinguished from one another.

In a passage which foreshadows the twins' 'chute dans le temps' (*M* 366), Edouard imagines that the love of Romeo and Juliet— 'absolu, éternel, immuable'—is brought to grief through contact with time and society: 'Mais ils baignent dans un milieu voué à toutes les vicissitudes de la société et de l'histoire. L'absolu est la proie de la corruption, l'éternité de l'altération. Leur mort découle fatalement de cette contradiction' (*M* 274). This passage suggests, then, that the separation of Jean and Paul, like the deaths of Romeo and Juliet, is caused by contact with the fallen world of relativity. Nostalgia for immobile absolutes is coupled with the interpretation of history as degradation and exile. Nevertheless, as we shall see, the absolutist rhetoric adopted in parts of *Les Météores* never entirely succeeds in dominating the novel and cannot account for its more dangerous and frightening insights into the presence of alterity within the human subject.

(iii) *Self and Other*

After the death of Alexandre, Paul explains narcissistic object choice amongst homosexuals as the attempt to reproduce the fraternal love of twins with imperfect means: 'le couple homosexuel s'efforce de former une cellule gémellaire, mais avec des éléments sans-pareil, c'est-à-dire en contrefaçon' (*M* 335). However, Paul also perceives an aspect of homosexuality which makes it irreducible to the values of twinship:

L'homosexuel est un comédien [. . .] Il joue et il perd, mais non sans d'heureux coups [. . .] L'homosexuel est artiste, inventeur, créateur. En se débattant contre un malheur inéluctable, il produit parfois des chefs-d'œuvres dans tous les domaines. Le couple gémellaire est tout à l'opposé de cette liberté errante et créatrice [. . .] Couple soudé, il ne saurait bouger, souffrir, ni créer. (*M* 336)

The homosexual, by dint of his or her very mortality, is doomed to failure in the absolute, as Alexandre is aware: 'Je suis un condamné

en sursis d'exécution' (*M* 34). Even so, the homosexual might achieve
a kind of success withheld from the twin. As in Proust's *A la recherche
du temps perdu*, homosexuality is equated with art and creativity;
and, although at this stage Paul excludes these from the supposed
perfection of twinship, phrases such as 'chefs-d'œuvre' and 'cette
liberté errante et créatrice' inevitably retain their positive connotations.
For Paul, the homosexual is a frustrated twin hopelessly searching
for his identical double. Nevertheless, what *Les Météores* actually
describes is more complex than Paul's account allows, and Alexandre's
homosexual narcissism is not recuperable to his nephew's experience
of twinship.

Alexandre is the gay deconstructor of *Les Météores*. He explains
the contradictory imperatives of endogamy and exogamy in order
to show how the homosexual confounds both of them. Alexandre
chooses his sexual partner beyond the limit prescribed by the
endogamic principle, preferring 'des jeunes hommes dont les charmes
agissaient d'autant plus fortement sur moi qu'ils étaient d'origine et
d'étoffes plus grossières, plus éloignés de mes eaux familiales' (*M*
287). At the same time he transgresses the exogamic principle,
because what he looks for in his partner is the reflection of his own
image: 'Car cette virilité joyeuse et cabrée, c'est d'abord l'image de
la mienne, quand même je l'adore chez mes complices. A la source
de l'homosexualité il y a le narcissisme' (*M* 288). In violation of the
prohibitions of heterosexual society ('mes amours [. . .] réussissent
à bafouer doublement les interdits hétérosexuels', *M* 288), the homosexual attempts to establish 'des relations fraternelles, identitaires,
narcissiques' (*M* 288). The principal illustration of this in *Les
Météores* is Alexandre's relationship with Daniel. Alexandre dreams
of making the boy into his own 'copie conforme' (*M* 213); Daniel
will be an 'étrange sosie', a 'fils-jumeau', and together they will form
a 'couple identitaire' (*M* 216).

There is clearly a strong narcissistic element in Alexandre's fantasy.
But, contrary to what Paul suggests, Alexandre is not looking for
an exact copy of his *present* self. He sees Daniel as a potential '*fils-*
jumeau', not a twin brother for the man he now is, but a copy of
the child he once was: 'moi-même trente ans plus tôt' (*M* 216). In
his important essay on narcissism Freud observes that homosexuals
do not conform to anaclitic object choice ('der Anlehnungstypus der
Objektwahl'), that is, the form of object choice which takes the
mother or the person who cared for them as infants as the model of

subsequent sexual partners.[10] Instead, the homosexual chooses himself, or more precisely his *former* self, as the prototype of the sexual object. He attempts to reproduce his relationship with his mother by undergoing a strong identification with her and choosing the image of his childhood self as his later sexual partner. Love for the other may be an expression of self-love, but this form of narcissistic object choice *also* involves a complex process of substitution and identification which inevitably alters the constitution of the self.[11] Alexandre's experience corresponds closely to the Freudian scheme. He describes his mother as 'ma petite chérie à laquelle je ressemble' (*M* 27); and her death leaves him with what he calls 'mon petit chagrin': 'La mort de maman ressemble à une plaie ulcéreuse, limitée, dont on finit par s'accommoder jour et nuit, mais qui suppure indéfiniment et sans espoir de cicatrisation' (*M* 104–5). The death of the (m)other is experienced as what Freud calls *Ichverlust*,[12] a wound and an absence within the self. Later, Alexandre attempts to resurrect his mother within himself by forming a relationship with Daniel which is essentially *maternal* in nature. Daniel becomes identified with the boy Alexandre once was: 'je me demande si la pitié qui m'incline vers Daniel n'est pas un avatar de mon petit chagrin, en l'espèce la compassion que m'inspire le petit garçon orphelin que maman a laissé derrière elle. Narcisse se penche sur son image et pleure de pitié' (*M* 214). In one of the most horrific scenes of the novel (which precedes and prefigures the beginning of the Second World War), Daniel is killed by rats. Alexandre experiences this loss, like the loss of his mother, as a diminution of

---

[10] See Freud, 'On Narcissism: An Introduction', in *The Standard Edition*, xiv.

[11] See Jean Laplanche, *Vie et mort en psychanalyse*, p. 118; see also Laplanche and Pontalis, *Vocabulaire de la psychanalyse*, entry under 'Identification', where identification is described as 'l'opération par laquelle le sujet humain se constitue' (p. 188). Although Alexandre's discussions of his homosexuality seem to invite comparison with psychoanalytic theory, Tournier's infrequent references to psychoanalysis indicate hostility towards what he regards as its 'aspect réducteur' (*Vol* 31; see also *VP* 25, 202–3). The ambivalence of Tournier's attitude to psychoanalysis, and to modernity in general, is suggested in the short story 'Le Coq de bruyère', in which the Colonel explicitly rejects Freud's topology of the mind: 'Décidément on n'arrête pas le progrès! Eh bien moi, je dis non! Non au ça, non au surmoi, non au complot!' (*CB* 227). Nevertheless, the story seems to prove the analyst correct, and explicit rejection of Freudian theory coexists uneasily with a grudging assent inscribed within the very construction of the narrative. Tournier, it seems, is only half reconciled to the twentieth century.

[12] On *Ichverlust* (translated as ego-loss), see Freud, 'Mourning and Melancholia', in *The Standard Edition*, xiv. 249.

his own identity, and he discovers the interpenetration of self and other, life and death:

Suis-je encore vivant? Ce que j'ai identifié à Miramas comme le corps déchiqueté de Dani, n'était-ce pas en vérité mon propre cadavre rendu méconnaissable par les dents de la lune et les becs du soleil? Nous sommes d'invétérés égoïstes, et quand nous croyons pleurer sur un autre, c'est sur nous-mêmes que nous nous apitoyons. Après la mort de ma mère, c'est le deuil de son petit garçon Alexandre, devenu orphelin, que j'ai porté, et ce terrible matin mistralé de septembre, mon âme agenouillée a rendu un dernier et déchirant hommage à ma dépouille. (M 283–4)

Paul believes that the 'cellule gémellaire' and his own identity are immune from absence and the need for *autrui*. However, his brother Jean realizes that the twins' relationship is destined to break down for purely internal reasons. The 'cellule' is in fact a prison cell in which Jean, like Alexandre and like Edouard, is perpetually confronted with the precariousness of identity. The urgency of self-creation is made clear to Jean by what he calls the 'affaire du miroir triple'. In this episode, as in much of *Les Météores*, Tournier uses and adapts case histories derived from the work of the psychologist René Zazzo. In *Les Jumeaux: Le Couple et la personne* Zazzo describes the disorientation experienced by a twin who momentarily mistakes his own reflection in a mirror for that of his identical brother.[13] Tournier accentuates the significance of this incident by increasing its traumatic effect. The 'affaire du miroir triple' occurs when Jean, on a shopping expedition without his brother, enters a fitting room to see if a hat suits him:

Un miroir en triptyque dont les éléments latéraux tournaient sur des gonds permettait de se voir de face et sous ses deux profils. Je m'avançai sans méfiance dans le piège, et aussitôt ses mâchoires miroitantes se refermèrent sur moi et me broyèrent si cruellement que j'en porte les traces à tout jamais. J'eus un bref éblouissement. Quelqu'un était là, reflété par trois fois dans

[13] See René Zazzo, *Les Jumeaux: Le Couple et la personne* (henceforth referred to as *Les Jumeaux*), pp. 347, 470. Tournier makes numerous borrowings from Zazzo's work. Even the formula used by Jean-Paul, 'Bep, tu joues?', is a slight distortion of a phrase recorded by Zazzo: '*Béb tu joues?*' (p. 349). In *Le Vent Paraclet* Tournier quotes (slightly inaccurately) a phrase from Zazzo's work, but does not acknowledge its specific origin; compare *VP* 245 and *Les Jumeaux*, p. 482. In a radio conversation with Zazzo, of which a transcription is published in Zazzo's *Le Paradoxe des jumeaux*, Tournier admitted that the relationship of Jean and Paul was modelled on that of Jacques and Michel, twins whose case is discussed in *Les Jumeaux*, pp. 481–4, 592–6.

cet espace minuscule. Qui? La question à peine posée recevait une réponse qui faisait un bruit de tonnerre: *Paul!* Ce jeune garçon un peu pâle, vu de face, de droite et de gauche, figé par cette triple photographie, c'était mon frère-pareil, venu là je ne savais comment, mais indiscutablement présent. Et en même temps, un vide effroyable se creusait en moi, une angoisse de mort me glaçait, car si Paul était présent et vivant dans le triptyque, moi-même, Jean, je n'étais nulle part, je n'existais plus. (*M* 246)

The 'affaire du miroir triple' takes place around the time of Jean's puberty ('Je pouvais avoir treize ans', *M* 247) and corresponds to a psychological pattern which Zazzo describes in *Les Jumeaux*. He refers to the 'crise d'originalité' experienced by all children, but especially by identical twins, during adolescence.[14] At this time the twin often becomes aware of the disadvantages of twinship for the first time and feels the need to affirm a separate identity. Tournier uses the psychological evidence provided by Zazzo for his own purposes as he describes what can be regarded as a frightening reversal of the Lacanian 'stade du miroir'. According to Lacan, the synthetic construction of a unified identity is made possible when the young child begins to recognize and to identify with its own specular image.[15] In Tournier's reversal of the mirror phase, Jean *fails* to recognize his reflection. Rather than an original plenitude, he discovers only 'un vide effroyable'. After, and partly as a consequence of, this experience, Jean discovers the 'nomadisme qui a toujours été [son] destin secret' (*M* 246): like Alexandre (see *M* 281), he dreads *stasis*; and movement becomes the metaphor for a process of becoming which seeks to overcome, provisionally, the absence at the core of identity.[16]

After the account of the 'affaire du miroir triple', Jean and Paul describe their different attitudes to twinship in two juxtaposed fragments. Each of the fragments is constructed around the same basic opposition: the imperfect self-knowledge of the 'sans-pareil' and the perfect self-knowledge made available to the twin through the proximity of an identical and infallible copy. Paul insists that,

---

[14] Zazzo, *Les Jumeaux*, p. 678; see also p. 656: 'Les premières protestations des jumeaux contre les servitudes de la gémellité se manifestent aux approches de la puberté.'

[15] See Jacques Lacan, 'Le Stade du miroir comme formateur de la fonction du Je', in *Écrits*.

[16] For further discussion of the theme of travel in Tournier's writing, see 'Concluding Remarks: Between Synthesis and Scarcity'.

for the 'sans-pareil', there is no privileged perspective and hence no image which is not distorted:

L'homme sans-pareil à la recherche de lui-même ne trouve que des bribes de sa personnalité, des lambeaux de son moi, des fragments informes de cet être énigmatique, centre obscur et impénétrable du monde. Car les miroirs ne lui renvoient qu'une image figée et inversée, les photographies sont plus mensongères encore, les témoignages qu'il entend sont déformés par l'amour, la haine ou l'intérêt. (M 247)

Paul asserts that his own self-knowledge is immune from perspectival distortions because the presence of his brother provides 'une image vivante et absolument vérace de [lui]-même' (M 247). Jean's account of twinship relies upon the same distinction between the perfect and the imperfect image: 'Les sans-pareil ne connaissent de leurs voisins, amis, parents que des qualités particulières, des défauts, des travers, des traits personnels, pittoresques ou caricaturaux qui sont autant de différences avec eux. Ils se perdent sans ce détail accidentel et ne voient pas — ou voient mal — l'être humain, la personne qu'il recouvre' (M 247–8). Like Paul, Jean suggests that 'l'être humain' is normally masked by what he calls 'ce bric-à-brac pittoresque ou caricatural' (M 248). Twins cannot hide behind the caricatural detail; but, for Jean, the infallible copy gives rise to anxiety rather than reassurance: 'Le manteau bariolé de la personnalité qui arrête le regard sans-pareil est incolore et transparent au regard gémellaire, et lui laisse voir abstraite, nue, déconcertante, vertigineuse, squelettique, effrayante: l'Altérité' (M 248). 'L'être humain', the core of identity, when it is revealed, is an essential absence of selfhood. The 'détail accidentel' and the 'bric-à-brac pittoresque et caricatural' turn out to be necessary illusions when alterity is the only 'authentic self' behind the distorted perspectives through which we perceive others and ourselves.

For Paul, the disintegration of identity is something which happens from the outside, by accident or through contact with society. Being is static and cannot tolerate movement. Paul refers to the destruction of the twins' cell as a 'coup de hache' (M 64): a violent assault on a self-sufficient unit. But the experience of Edouard, Alexandre, and Jean suggests that identity is fragile and precarious, constructed rather than given. To avoid falling into the void of being, Tournier's characters choose perpetual movement and the flux of becoming. Even Paul will be forced to travel in the frustrated search for the lost equilibrium of childhood. Movement becomes the flight from a fundamental absence which can be overcome only provisionally: 'Je suis un condamné en sursis d'exécution,' says Alexandre (M 34); 'La menace reste imminente, la foudre peut fondre sur moi à chaque instant,' says Jean (M 245). Nevertheless, Les Météores continues to resist its own most radical insights into the absence at the foundation of identity. In the next section we shall see how the threat of alterity and the presence of death within life are simultaneously revealed and suppressed through the figure which comes to represent the novel's most frightening perceptions: woman.

(iv) Femininity and Sexual Identity

Alexandre has little time for women: 'Les femmes notamment existent si peu pour moi que je parviens difficilement à les distinguer les unes des autres, comme les nègres, commes les moutons d'un troupeau' (M 83). He dismisses female homosexuality as 'la conjonction de deux nullités' (M 205); and, although he is aware of the insufficiency of his views ('Je sais que j'ai de la femme une vision grossière, froide, désinvolte', M 218), he remains an unapologetic misogynist. Moreover, the misogyny of Les Météores is by no means restricted to one character. Throughout the novel the principal role accorded to woman is motherhood. On page nine of the text we learn that Maria-Barbara's 'vraie vie' began 'le jour où la femme savait qu'elle attendait un enfant' (M 9). Koussek refers to the 'indéracinable vocation maternelle' of women (M 126) and implies that even in procreation woman shows her natural inferiority: 'Le fardeau de la procréation écrase totalement les femmes, à moitié les hommes hétérosexuels' (M 125; see also M 25). Koussek goes on to describe women as parasites, whose husbands 'rampent sous le poids des femmes et des enfants dont ils ont vainement tenté de se délester pendant toute une vie de désordres, qui ne les lâchent pas et qui vivent de leur substance' (M 126).

The misogyny which is perceptible in Les Météores can be explained as a defensive reaction to the threat posed by woman. The potentially disturbing aspects of femininity are first adumbrated in the experience of Edouard. By marrying Maria-Barbara, Edouard makes himself the director of a factory in which over three hundred women are employed: 'Pour cet homme à femmes, devenir le patron d'une entreprise occupant trois cent vingt-sept ouvrières, c'était à la fois troublant et amer' (M 17). Initially Edouard proves 'incapable de restituer leur féminité aux silhouettes en blouses grises coiffées de fichus de couleur', and he has the impression of being 'le roi d'un peuple de larves' (M 17). The sexual identity of the women is hidden, and it requires long practice before Edouard is able to distinguish the female traits beneath their sexless clothing. Even so, the ability to recognize the signs of sexual identity does not neutralize the working woman's power to disrupt Edouard's views on the role of the sexes:

Et puis l'ouvrière restait pour lui un être inquiétant, infréquentable parce qu'elle déconcertait ses idées sur la femme. La femme pouvait bien travailler, mais à des choses domestiques, à la rigueur dans une ferme ou une boutique. Le travail industriel ne pouvait que la dénaturer. La femme pouvait bien recevoir de l'argent — pour la maison, pour l'ornement, pour le plaisir, pour rien. La paie hebdomadaire l'avilissait. (M 18)

The woman who works disconcerts Edouard's view of what Woman— 'la femme'—should be. Industrial labour 'ne pouvait que la dénaturer' since it threatens a view of female nature which has more to do with ideology than biology. Trapped between a 'peuple de larves' and a perpetually pregnant wife, Edouard is forced to confront his own futility: 'Mais il éprouvait parfois un grand accablement de solitude entre sa femme toujours enceinte et exclusivement préoccupée de ses petits, et la foule grise et laborieuse des Pierres Sonnantes. "Je suis le bourdon inutile entre la reine de la ruche et les abeilles ouvrières", disait-il avec une mélancolie enjouée' (M 18). In the midst of female activity, man feels painfully superfluous. Maria-Barbara discovers her 'vraie vie' in *pregnancy* rather than in marriage itself, and the father is irrelevant to that state once conception has taken place: 'Peu importait l'époux, le semeur, le donneur de cette pauvre chiquenaude qui déclenche le processus créateur' (M 9).

The narrator of Les Météores treats Edouard's notions of sexual stereotypes with an affectionate irony which betrays a degree of complicity: 'Telles étaient les idées de cet homme aimable et simple' (M 18). Woman occupies a relatively insignificant proportion of the text, and man makes himself the centre of his own discourse in order to preserve his precarious sense of necessity. Even so, Edouard will be subjected to a troubling confrontation with the slippage of sexual identity. He realizes that his Parisian friends consider him to be 'un Breton saisi par la débauche parisienne, une version mâle de

Bécassine, Bécassin en chapeau rond enrubanné et en sabots, avec un biniou sous le bras' (*M* 21). Edouard is regarded as a male version of a female model, whereas Florence, his Parisian mistress, has what Edouard considers to be a distinctly male characteristic: 'Florence l'avait étonné par sa lucidité drôle et amère, un trait qu'il aurait attendu davantage d'un homme que d'une femme' (*M* 21). Edouard is inevitably attracted and disconcerted by Florence (*M* 21); but he attempts to make their relationship conform to unambiguous sexual stereotypes by urging Florence to move into his Paris flat and to take the role of surrogate wife and housekeeper: ' — Une maison sans femme est une maison morte, argumentait-il' (*M* 23). At the end of the chapter, the narrator illustrates his complicity with Edouard's views by reasserting the authority of nature and affirming a clear distinction between the sexes:

Le malheur d'un homme comme lui — de beaucoup d'hommes — c'est d'avoir en leur vie assez de ressource pour faire au moins deux fois carrière de mari et de père de famille, alors qu'une femme est épuisée, rebutée bien avant d'avoir établi son dernier enfant. Le second mariage d'un homme avec une femme neuve, d'une génération plus jeune que l'ancienne, *est dans la nature des choses*. (*M* 24-5; my emphasis)

The text of *Les Météores* implies a hierarchy in which woman occupies the lowest position. The twin (forming half of the 'couple absolu'), the homosexual (copying the twin with imperfect means), and the heterosexual male (who attempts to imitate the homosexual; see *M* 126-7) all take precedence. At the same time the novel repeatedly extols maternity and underlines the relative insignificance of the father. Motherhood is the groundstone which makes all the other positions in the novel's hierarchical scheme possible; paternity is of relatively minor importance and at best only putative (see *M* 9 and 402). Moreover, the mother occupies a privileged position in the lives of her children. Maria-Barbara and Alexandre's mother command an intense affection never shared by their respective husbands. Even so, the familiar and for that reason ideologically loaded myth of the *alma genitrix* ('Majestueuse, l'alma genitrix dans toute sa sereine grandeur', *M* 33) contributes to the attempt to control femininity by assigning woman a clearly demarcated social and mythological role as mother.

This attempt to control femininity entails a denial of woman's complex sexual identity. In *Les Roi des aulnes* Tiffauges describes

female genitals as a 'ventre décapité' (*RA* 24) and thereby characterizes them by the absence of the phallus rather than in positive terms.
In *Les Météores* Alexandre gives a similar account. He regards
woman's 'ventre mutilé par la nature' as a 'navrante disgrâce' which
justifies his preference for the male body (*M* 202). However, this
summary dismissal of the female genitals is underlaid by fascination
and anxiety:[17]

> Mais notre curiosité s'animait et notre imagination travaillait quand on venait
> nous dire que ce sexe dont nous déplorions l'indigence était plus compliqué
> qu'il n'y paraissait, se composant de deux bouches verticales superposées
> dont les quatre lèvres — deux grandes, deux petites — pouvaient s'entrouvrir
> comme les pétales d'une fleur. Et puis il y avait une histoire de trompes —
> de deux trompes — bien propre à intriguer les adorateurs de Ganeça, mais
> enfouies, cachées, inaccessibles. Qu'importe. (*M* 202-3)

Alexandre begins by distinguishing between the poverty of the
female genitals and the plenitude of the phallus. He then concedes
that, far from being a simple absence, the female genitals share male
characteristics, and even go beyond the male since they have 'deux
trompes' rather than just one. The apparent poverty of the female
in comparison to the male is revealed as a greater complexity.
Knowledge of female anatomy diminishes the secure plenitude of
male sexuality, and Alexandre's abrupt 'Qu'importe' breaks off an
enquiry which is getting too close to the potentially traumatic mystery
of female sexuality.

Part of Tournier's text seems to corroborate Edouard's narrow
views on sexual stereotypes, but there is also a tendency in his writing
which is fascinated by the transgression of sexual identities. Woman,
in *Les Météores*, is the focus of the trans-sexual movement which
subverts sexual categories. She is either asexual or too ambiguously
sexual to be 'woman' in anything but the narrowly biological sense.
The workers in Edouard's factory are a 'peuple de larves' (*M* 17) or
'abeilles ouvrières' (*M* 18) whose sexuality is hidden; the silhouette
of Sabine Kraus is 'ronde, souple et asexuée' (*M* 510). Even Maria-
Barbara, the archetypal 'mère nourricière et adoptive, protectrice de

---

[17] On the fear of the female genitals, see, for example, Freud, 'Fetishism', in *The
Standard Edition*, xxi. 154; 'Probably no male human being is spared the fright of
castration at the sight of a female genital.' For discussion of Freud's analysis and of
the extent to which Freud himself shows the same fear, see Sarah Kofman, *L'Énigme
de la femme*, e.g. pp. 43-116, 213-28.

tous les habitants des Pierres Sonnantes' (M 278), is desexualized by her role as mother. She is the object of Edouard's 'soif de tendresse', but not his 'faim sexuelle' (M 24). Sexual relations seem irrelevant to her maternal vocation; like the Virgin Mary (see M 138), whose name 'Maria-Barbara' clearly recalls, she does not seem to require the preliminary of sexual contact in order to become pregnant. As Alexandre says, 'on aurait dit qu'elle se faisait féconder par l'air du temps' (M 33). The denial of female sexuality may be seen as a defence against its enigmatic or potentially disturbing nature. Indeed, when the sexuality of woman is recognized, it is too plural and ambiguous for male comfort. The transgression of sexual roles is most flagrant in the cases of Fabienne and her squire Eva. Alexandre uses masculine nouns and pronouns to refer to them on their first appearance, and only later realizes that 'le cavalier était une femme, le petit écuyer en était une autre' (M 198). Using a phrase which Tournier will repeat in Gilles et Jeanne to describe Joan of Arc, Alexandre calls Fabienne 'la fille-garçon' (M 224; see also GJ 9). Alexandre's homosexuality entails adherence to a narrow notion of virility, and he rejects the effeminacy of Fabienne's fiancé, Alexis de Bastie d'Urfé (though the similarity of their forenames perhaps indicates that they are more alike than Alexandre cares to admit). However, Fabienne teaches Alexandre the vital lesson of sexual mobility: 'il suffit parfois de changer de sexe pour que tout s'arrange!' (M 223). She is the femme phallique,[18] arrogating the rights of the male. Her tapeworm, which she loses in one of the most comic scenes of the novel, is a detachable phallus symbolizing the facility with which she passes from male to female, or to sexually indeterminate roles. After the untimely appearance of the tapeworm, Fabienne and Alexandre dance. All sexual identity, as well as all social propriety, are abandoned: 'L'amazone des ordures ménagères et le dandy des gadoues, ayant remisé chacun leur sexe au vestiaire, mènent le bal' (M 225).

The ambiguous sexuality of Florence and Fabienne exposes the fragility of conventional sexual identities. But this is not the most disconcerting aspect of what, in the course of Les Météores, becomes associated with femininity, as Edouard is once again the

---

[18] On the femme phallique, see Laplanche and Pontalis, Vocabulaire de la psychanalyse, entry under 'Phallique (femme ou mère —)', p. 310.

first to discover. He is ill and beginning to lose his appetite for life. Maria-Barbara suggests that he should see a doctor: 'Après une timide allusion à une éventuelle consultation, Maria-Barbara renonça et n'en parla plus, et ce fut Méline qui d'autorité le traîna chez le médecin de Matignon. Il accepta en riant, *pour faire plaisir aux femmes*, dit-il' (*M* 276; my emphasis). Edouard is diabetic; but he refuses to heed the doctor's diagnosis, along with the suggestion that sickness and death are already at work within his own organism. In his mind, it is women who have erected this *memento mori*: 'Il avait eu tort de *céder aux femmes* en faisant un premier pas dans la voie fatale' (*M* 277; my emphasis). Identified with maternity and the origin of life, women are also, at least for Edouard, reminders of the imminence and immanence of death. On leave for Christmas during the twilight war, Edouard first sees Maria-Barbara in Brittany as a symbol of life (*M* 278), and is then sensitive to the 'charme funèbre' of Florence's songs in Paris (*M* 279). This binary construction might suggest the mutual exclusion of opposites: Maria-Barbara/Florence, Brittany/Paris, life/death. Nevertheless, however much Edouard would like to maintain these oppositions (see *M* 306–10), *Les Météores* will insistently underline their dangerous interpenetration. Until his disappearance from the novel, Edouard will be haunted by the thought of his own demise. This is not in spite of his apparent love for life. On the contrary, it seems directly linked to it; as Paul observes, 'Ces hantises suicidaires sont moins rares qu'on ne pense chez des hommes profondément en accord avec la vie' (*M* 310). In the intense experience of life is the desire for a death which should be no less intense. One of the cruel ironies of *Les Météores* is that the heroic demise for which Edouard longs is usurped by Maria-Barbara. Edouard will die alone, sick, almost blind, and tragically unheroic.

The Pierres Sonnantes, presided over by Maria-Barbara, seem to symbolize life and vitality. But death already inhabits the Surin household, personified in the figure of Méline. The very name Méline may remind the reader of Mélanie, the girl fascinated by death in Tournier's story 'La Jeune Fille et la mort'. In *Les Météores* Méline acts as a portent of catastrophe: it is she who forces Edouard to see a doctor, and it is she who announces the arrival of the Germans who will arrest Maria-Barbara (see *M* 309). Sophie, Jean's fiancée, gives a description of Méline which underlines her function as an emblem of mourning and death:

Toujours vêtue de noir à l'exception d'un béguin gaufré blanc qui emprisonnait sa tête du front au chignon, elle ne portait pas le deuil, elle l'incarnait, ayant avec la mort des relations intimes, anciennes et comme familiales. J'ai cru comprendre que son mari, Justin Méline qui était ouvrier carrier était mort presque en même temps qu'Edouard Surin après avoir eu d'elle onze enfants dont pas un ne survivait. Ces morts enfantines avaient accompagné comme en contrepoint les naissances successives de la famille Surin, tellement qu'on aurait pu croire qu'il fallait qu'un Méline disparût pour qu'un Surin parût. Puis la mort des deux pères acheva de les souder l'un à l'autre comme si Justin Méline n'avait jamais été que l'ombre d'Edouard Surin. Seule Méline semblait indestructible — sans âge, éternelle, comme la mort elle-même. (M 352)

Méline is the inverted image of Maria-Barbara. One represents the life-giving force of maternity, whereas the other is the incarnation of mourning. But the dividing line between the poles of the opposition becomes blurred as the Surin and the Méline families become entangled with one another. Edouard Surin dies at the same time as Justin Méline. Maria-Barbara is deported by the Germans and never returns; and, in her absence, Méline becomes mistress of the Pierres Sonnantes and assumes the role of substitute mother to the twins. Maria-Barbara and Méline are *doubles*: like Jean and Paul, they are opposites who complement and complete one another. The story of one is entangled with the story of the other, and together they form a composite symbol of life and death.

The two sides of woman represented in *Les Météores* by Maria-Barbara and Méline are combined in *Le Roi des aulnes* in the figure of Frau Netta, the 'Heimmutter' of Kaltenborn. Through her innate knowledge of animals and plants, and through her instinct as nurse, she seems 'enracinée au plus concret de la vie' (*RA* 263). But she must also learn to accept the death of her wards and of her own children. When she is informed that one of her sons has probably been killed, she achieves a lucidity which would be improbable in the simple and instinctive woman she is supposed to be, but which perfectly expresses the dual vocation of woman in Tournier's texts. The repetition of 'porter' in the phrases 'porter l'enfant' and 'porter son deuil' suggests the inseparability of motherhood and mourning, life and death:

— La vie et la mort, c'est la même chose. Celui qui hait ou craint la mort, hait ou craint la vie. Parce qu'elle est fontaine inépuisable de vie, la nature n'est qu'un grand cimetière, un égorgeoir de tous les instants. Franzi est sans doute mort à cette heure. Ou bien il va mourir dans un camp de prisonniers. Il ne faut pas être triste. La femme qui porte l'enfant doit aussi porter son deuil. (*RA* 263)[19]

The enigma of femininity is associated in Tournier's fiction with the symbol of the labyrinth, which Tournier seems happy to use despite its association with the *Nouveau Roman*. In the story 'Tupik' a boy is told by his friend Dominique to meet him/her at the centre of the labyrinth in order to discover the secret of why s/he is allowed to use the women's toilets. The labyrinth in Tournier's story is described as a place of mystery and horror: 'Tupik était atterré. Le labyrinthe de buis [. . .] lui avait toujours inspiré de l'horreur' (*CB* 75–6). At the centre of the labyrinth is an absence: 'Là, sur un petit socle verdi par la moisissure, avait dû se tenir une statue. Elle avait disparu, et le socle attendait, souillé par les limaces' (*CB* 76). Tupik is 'plus mort que vif en se laissant absorber par le massif glauque' (*CB* 76). Standing on the base of the absent statue, Dominique, 'ce gros garçon paisible et maternel' (*CB* 75), waits for Tupik in order to reveal a second absence: 'Son ventre blanc et lisse se terminait par une fente laiteuse, un sourire vertical où jouait la trace d'un pâle duvet' (*CB* 76–7). The secret of Dominique's privilege is her ability to occupy both male and female roles simultaneously. Her absent penis signals the absence of unequivocal sexual identity, and Tupik believes that he can only escape his father's revolting virility by cutting off his own penis. Through the double absence at the centre of the labyrinth, Tupik discovers the enigma of female sexuality, which provokes his own suicidal self-immolation: 'il tira de sa poche un rasoir, un de ces anciens rasoirs à manche de nacre que l'on appelle parfois des coupe-chou. Il l'ouvrit et de sa main libre déboutonna sa braguette. Mamouse poussa un hurlement de bête en le voyant sortir son petit robinet d'enfant et en approcher le rasoir. Le sang jaillit' (*CB* 78).

In *Les Météores* Jean refers to the lives of the 'sans-pareil' as 'un dédale pittoresque dont personne ne sait où il mène, ni s'il mène quelque part' (*M* 240). Rejecting his brother's nostalgia for the closed cell of twinship, Jean affirms the tribulation and uncertainty of life: 'tout est bien ainsi' (*M* 240). However, Jean's affirmation is no less simplistic than Paul's crushing nostalgia, and Alexandre's

---

[19] Compare Prélat's comments in *GJ* 66–7. On the association of woman and death in Tournier's fiction, see also the figure of Lala Ramirez in *G* 101–8.

experience of the labyrinth, which parallels that of Tupik, does not corroborate his nephew's optimism. A pit has been filled with remains of barbed wire fences from local farms, and thereby transformed into a death trap for wild and domestic animals alike. Fabienne and Briffaut, a local rag-man, believe that the pit contains a pearl which is of limited value on its own, but priceless when matched with its twin, which Briffaut wears on his ear. The extreme economy of Tournier's best writing is shown by the way this episode is integrated within the thematic structure of the novel (through the themes of twins, doubles, duplication, *dépariage*) whilst also encouraging interpretation which goes beyond purely thematic analysis. In order to recover the lost pearl, Fabienne pays men to cut tunnels through the barbed wire. Walking near the pit one day, Alexandre hears a cry and Briffaut emerges from one of the tunnels, covered in blood and indicating that one of his ears has been cut off. The scene prefigures Paul's dismemberment in the tunnel under the Berlin Wall, but the text does not dwell on this thematic parallel. Alexandre enters the tunnel from which Briffaut has emerged in order to discover what has happened, and he finds himself lost in a labyrinth: 'Je me suis enfoncé dans la galerie d'où il était sorti. Ma surprise a été de me trouver dans un labyrinthe assez compliqué pour qu'on craignît de s'y perdre' (M 211). Eventually he comes across Fabienne, the *femme castratrice* who has cut off Briffaut's ear in order to retrieve the pearl attached to it. Fabienne stands aside to reveal the evidence of Briffaut's symbolic castration: 'Elle s'écarta pour me découvrir le sol. J'ai d'abord eu l'œil tiré par un lambeau de chair rouge et recroquevillée, et j'ai pensé à l'oreille de Briffaut' (M 212). But castration is not the final word of this scene. The *femme castratrice* is also the *femme initiatrice* who introduces Alexandre to death: 'Mais ce n'était rien encore. En regardant mieux, j'ai distingué une forme humaine à demi ensevelie dans la terre molle. Une tête de mort coiffée d'un lambeau de feutre riait de tout son râtelier au milieu des mottes de terre remuées' (M 212).

As an allegory of interpretation, the labyrinth suggests a meaning which can be obtained only with great difficulty: the recovery of buried knowledge is arduous and perilous, but nevertheless possible. 'Tupik' and Les Météores play upon this suggestion in order to subvert it. At the centre of the labyrinth, Tupik discovers an absent statue and an absent penis. The key to the enigma of Dominique's sexuality is promised but withheld: 'Tu comprendras ça plus tard,' says Dominique (*CB* 77). Far from knowledge, the discovery of a double absence at the centre of the labyrinth leads to further confusion, deferred understanding, and the false solution of Tupik's self-immolation, which leaves the mystery of femininity unresolved. In *Les Météores* the questions raised in the narrative (What happened to the second pearl? How did Briffaut lose his ear?) seem to be answered, if only hypothetically: 'On ne peut faire encore que des conjectures [. . .] mais les pièces du puzzle s'ajustent assez bien' (*M* 212). But the rapidity of Alexandre's exit from the labyrinth betrays an unexplained residue from which he, and the text, anxiously retreat: 'Je ne souhaitais pas en voir ni en entendre davantage. Sans un mot, j'ai tourné le dos à Fabienne et je suis sorti du labyrinthe' (*M* 212).

Rather than castration, the key to this enigma is the silent laughter of the skull: 'Une tête de mort [. . .] riait de tout son râtelier' (*M* 212). Tournier's account of what he calls 'le rire blanc' helps to explain, perhaps, why this laughter is so poignantly uncomic. Laughter, Tournier maintains, signals the approach of the absolute (*VP* 149); and 'le rire blanc', which is comparable to Baudelaire's 'comique absolu',[20] is described as 'l'absolu embusqué partout, minant tout ce qui se dit, tout ce qui se fait, frappant toute chose existante de dérision' (*VP* 193). It reveals 'la tragique condition humaine, cette brève émergence entre deux vides', and shows that 'rien n'a aucune importance' (*VP* 194). The laughter of the absolute represents an intolerable threat to the authority of reason, and in consequence 'Tout est fait pour que le rire blanc n'éclate pas' (*VP* 193). Tournier's own characters, with their mania for closed systems, coherent worlds, and totalizing interpretations, exemplify his version of Sartrean *esprit de sérieux*:

Nombreux sont ceux qui vivent et meurent sans avoir jamais éclaté de ce rire-là [. . .] Ils se veulent dupes de la cohérence, de la fermeté, de la consistance dont la société pare le réel [. . .] Lorsque les jattes disjointes de la passerelle où chemine l'humanité s'entrouvent sur le vide sans fond, la plupart des hommes ne voient rien, mais certains autres voient le rien. (*VP* 193–4)

Tournier's reference to the 'vide sans fond', which is the essential absence at the core of identity and meaning, recalls Alexandre's

---

[20] On the 'comique absolu', see Charles Baudelaire, 'De l'essence du rire', in *Œuvres complètes*, ii. 535–6.

insistence that 'la psychologie des femmes est un puits sans fond' (*M* 184). Perhaps what 'la plupart des hommes' are unwilling to see is femininity and the absence and transgression which it comes to represent in the course of *Les Météores*. The presence of death within life and the mobility of sexual and psychological identities gives rise to perceptions which simultaneously fascinate and repel. Tournier's text repeatedly enacts a gesture of recontainment by imposing sexual stereotypes and the role of motherhood on the vertiginous *sans-fond* of femininity. But woman perpetually refuses the positions ascribed to her. She embodies the deconstructive movement which unties and confounds the binary oppositions upon which the discourse of Tournier's novel relies: self/other, male/female, life/death. And woman is also at the centre of Alexandre's allegorical labyrinth, revealing a derisive silence which, far from solving the enigma of the text and elucidating its labyrinthine detours, discloses the absence of a final intelligible meaning and ensures that the labour of understanding is always incomplete. And, as we shall see in the next section, the frustrated promise of intelligibility plays a fundamental role in the poetics of Tournier's third novel.

(v) *The Mirror and the Abyss*

From his prominence in the final third of *Les Météores*, and from Tournier's comments in *Le Vent Paraclet*, Paul seems to occupy a position of particular importance in the novel. However, the text undermines the authority of its most dominant voice. Alexandre's experience of self-creation and Jean's discovery of alterity directly contradict Paul's rhetoric of immobile and immutable identity. Moreover, Alexandre's predilection for the copy and the copy of the copy, involving the possibility of imitation and infinite repetition, comes closer to Tournier's own aesthetics than Paul's uncompromising insistence upon the authority of the model. Alexandre's dictum 'l'imitation est plus que la chose imitée' (*M* 86) summarizes Tournier's own attitude to the use of literary sources. He aims to appropriate the legacy of literary tradition in order to 'Passer outre', to surpass the original usage of a given episode or theme (see *VP* 52–3). The Bloomian overtones of Tournier's relationship to his precursors are unmistakable; his 'anxiety of influence' is indicated, for example, by misreadings and simplifications of his source-texts.[21] On the credit side, his provocative stance also involves an attempt to rethink the relationship between the model and the copy, the real and the literary, from a perspective which goes beyond Alexandre's playful reversal of Paul's conventional hierarchies.

The notion of *mimesis*, most commonly understood as the imitation or representation of reality, has traditionally dominated aesthetic discussion since Plato and Aristotle, and it has maintained a powerful influence even over authors and painters who have attempted to give art a different function.[22] Tournier's admiration for the realist novelists of the nineteenth century, his rejection of surrealist and non-representational texts (see *VP* iii–13), and his own overtly referential practice of writing might suggest his adherence to the most conventional concept of art as the mirror of the real. However, his aphoristic pronouncements on the subject reveal a more slippery position which is neither fully inside nor fully outside the traditional concept of art as imitation. At moments Tournier clearly implies that art represents—or should represent—external reality, even if he combines this with a belief in the subversive potential of imitation: 'Plus platement on copiera le réel, plus intimement on le bouleversera' (*VP* 112). This notion is developed in Tournier's most recent and most self-referential novel, *La Goutte d'or*. The eccentric artist Milan photographs shop dummies arranged in natural settings:[23]

Et alors, vois-tu, il y a comme une contamination réciproque entre mes garçons-poupées et le paysage [. . .] mes mannequins jettent le doute sur le paysage. Grâce à eux, les arbres sont un peu — pas complètement, un

[21] On the 'anxiety of influence', see Harold Bloom, *The Anxiety of Influence* and *A Map of Misreading*. For Tournier's misreading of precursors, see particularly his comments on Defoe's *Robinson Crusoe* in *Le Vent Paraclet* (*VP* 220–3). Michael Worton discusses Tournier's writing in the light of Bloom's theory of misreading in 'Écrire et ré-écrire: Le projet de Tournier'; see particularly pp. 56–8, on Tournier's reading of *Robinson Crusoe*.

[22] On the history of the mimetic conception of art, see M. H. Abrams, *The Mirror and the Lamp*, pp. 30–46. For discussion of how attempts to break with the notion of *mimesis* are nevertheless influenced by it, see Jonathan Culler, 'The Mirror Stage', in *The Pursuit of Signs*, especially pp. 167–8. For a discussion of the meaning of *mimesis* in Aristotle's *Poetics* which takes issue with conventional interpretations, see Paul Ricœur, *Temps et récit*, e.g. pp. 59–60. On *mimesis* and representation in Tournier's fiction, see ch. 5, sec. (i) and sec. (iii).

[23] The character of Milan is based on the French photographer Bernard Faucon, whose photographs of shop dummies are collected in *Les Grandes Vacances*. I am grateful to Martin Roberts for drawing my attention to Faucon's work.

peu seulement — en papier, les rochers en carton, le ciel n'est en partie qu'une toile de fond. Quant aux mannequins, étant eux-mêmes déjà des images, leur photo est une image d'image, ce qui a pour effet de doubler leur pouvoir dissolvant. Il en résulte une impression de rêve éveillé, d'hallucination vraie. C'est absolument la réalité sapée à sa base par l'image. (*G* 210–11)

At other moments, however, Tournier deliberately and playfully reverses the conception of art, and especially of literature, as the representation of a pre-existent model. Art is described as a heterocosm, a world apart, which passes into a sort of Jungian collective unconscious and thereby plays an important role in the constitution of reality: 'Quand la caissière d'un café dit au serveur *je t'aime*, ils se comprennent, mais ils n'entendraient pas la même chose par ce mot si Platon n'avait pas écrit *Le Banquet* et Goethe *Werther*, bien qu'ils n'aient lu ni l'un ni l'autre.'[24] The power of the literary is such that it actually draws the real towards it and forces reality to become a copy of the fictional model. Tournier frequently reiterates this provocative idea, as, for example, in *Canada: Journal de voyage* when he takes issue with Simone de Beauvoir:

Et le génie littéraire consiste-t-il bien [. . .] à ressusciter et à capter les choses extérieures grâce à une certaine 'virtuosité' de plume? Ne serait-ce pas plutôt la faculté de *créer* d'un coup de force un monde différent du monde extérieur, ayant avec lui juste assez d'affinité pour l'attirer à lui, pour l'obliger à lui ressembler? Tel le monde balzacien qui s'impose souverainement comme l'archétype de la société de la Restauration, ou les salons du boulevard Saint-Germain de Proust doués d'une telle prégnance, d'une telle évidence que quiconque y a passé sa vie, lisant la *Recherche du temps perdu*, doit voir ses souvenirs s'évanouir comme des fumées et le théâtre proustien prendre irrésistiblement leur place? L'histoire imite le roman historique, l'amour s'efforce de ressembler au roman d'amour. Si les Américains vont dans la lune, c'est sous l'influence de la science-fiction; quant aux crimes que nous rapporte la presse, ils courent évidemment derrière les romans policiers. Le roman n'est rien d'autre que le modèle dont le réel s'inspire tant bien que mal pour prendre figure.[25]

---

[24] Tournier, *Vues de dos* (unpaginated), opposite the photograph of the 'Parc de Saint-Cloud'. For similar formulations of the same ideas, see *VP* 186–8 and *Vol* 390. On the novel as a heterocosm, see Tournier's 'Lettre-préface' to Manfred S. Fischer, *Probleme internationaler Literaturrezeption: Michel Tourniers „Le Roi des aulnes" im deutsch-französischen Kontext*, p. 8: 'Je vois le roman parfait comme un monde clos, sphérique, se suffisant à soi-même.'

[25] Tournier, *Canada: Journal de voyage*, pp. 31–2.

Tournier's lapidary theoretical pronouncements indicate his distrust of any simple opposition between the model and the copy. He maintains the conception of the relationship between art and reality as one of reflection, but on occasions he reverses the direction of the mirror and insists that life reflects art. It is clear, then, that neither of the two aphorisms 'Art copies life' and 'Life copies art' is adequate on its own, and it will be necessary to account for a more complex dialectic between the literary and the real. In *Les Météores* we find a clear thematic statement of this dialectical complicity when Jean explains his desire to travel:

— J'ai de chaque pays une connaissance livresque, expliquait-il. Je n'attends pas de notre voyage de noces qu'il détruise mes préjugés sur l'Italie, l'Angleterre, le Japon. Au contraire. Il ne fera que les confirmer, les enrichir, les approfondir. Mais ce que j'attends de ce voyage, c'est qu'il apporte à mes pays imaginaires la touche concrète inimaginable, le je-ne-sais-quoi qui est comme le cachet inimitable de réel. (*M* 346–7)

The 'connaissance livresque' precedes actual contact with the world, but does not preclude it. Ideally, at least, the real does not replace the literary, nor is it replaced by it: the two are mutually enriching.

This dialectical interdependence necessitates a reconsideration of the notions of 'model' and 'copy', 'real' and 'literary'. When Paul visits Venice in search of his lost brother, the proliferation of images subverts his belief in privileged perspectives. He observes that Venice and its image are always simultaneously present:

Spéculaire — du latin *speculum*, miroir — Venise l'est à plus d'un titre. Elle l'est parce qu'elle se reflète dans ses eaux et que ses maisons n'ont que leur propre reflet pour fondation. Elle l'est aussi par sa nature foncièrement *théâtrale* en vertu de laquelle Venise et l'image de Venise sont toujours données simultanément, inséparablement. En vérité, il y a là de quoi décourager les peintres. Comment peindre Venise qui est déjà une peinture? [. . .] En revanche il ne doit pas y avoir de lieu au monde où l'on fait une pareille consommation de pellicule photographique. C'est que le touriste n'est pas créateur, c'est un consommateur-né. Les images lui étant données ici à chaque pas, il fait des copies à tour de bras. (*M* 370–1)

As Paul distinguishes between creative and uncreative copying, he is tacitly adopting a criterion of creativity espoused by Alexandre and which he had rejected earlier in the novel (see *M* 336). Moreover, his conception of the model is undergoing an important change when he observes that 'Venise et l'image de Venise sont toujours données simultanément, inséparablement'. Venice is the source of a profusion of images—specular, literary, photographic, painted, imaginary. It becomes impossible to separate Venice 'as it is' from the over-familiar representations of it: 'Point n'est besoin d'être allé à Venise pour connaître cette ville, tant elle fait partie du paysage imaginaire de chaque Européen. Tout au plus y va-t-on pour la *reconnaître*' (M 367).

The 'real' Venice is indissociable from its specular and fictionalized images. Imagination contaminates perception, so that reality, as it is perceived, already bears traces of imaginary structuration: 'Comment peindre Venise qui est déjà une peinture?' (M 371). This insight inevitably has disruptive consequences for Paul's hierarchy of model and copy, as well as on any theory of art as representation. As M. H. Abrams points out in *The Mirror and the Lamp*, the theme of the mirror has traditionally been associated with the mimetic conception of art; and, given the self-consciousness of much recent French fiction, the contemporary reader is likely to be especially aware of the use of the mirror in *Les Météores* as a possible *mise en abyme* of Tournier's aesthetics. We have already seen the disruptive potential of the mirror in what Jean calls the 'affaire du miroir triple'. In Chapter Fifteen of *Les Météores*, entitled 'Les Miroirs vénitiens', Paul's discovery of the specular nature of Venice subverts his faith in the intelligibility and solidity of the real. This prepares his visit to a hall of mirrors, in which he is introduced to a world where there is no divine eye to guarantee against the madness of absolute perspectivism: 'Mais ces vastes pièces doivent plus encore leur prestige et leur mystère à la profusion des miroirs qui les démultiplient, brisent et recomposent toutes leurs lignes, sèment la folie dans leurs proportions, défoncent les plans et les creusent de perspectives infinies' (M 372). According to Giuseppe Colombo, the meteorologist who mistakes Paul for his brother, the particularity of the Venetian mirror is that it deflects the observer's attention away from self-contemplation:

Les miroirs de Venise ne sont jamais droits, ils ne renvoient jamais son image à qui les regarde. Ce sont des miroirs inclinés qui obligent à regarder ailleurs. Certes il y a de la sournoiserie, de l'espionnage en eux, mais ils vous sauvent des dangers d'une contemplation morose et stérile de soi-même. Avec un miroir vénitien, Narcisse était sauvé. (M 374)

Like the Venetian mirror, *Les Météores* has a centrifugal quality which throws the reader's attention outwards to a vast range of literary and philosophical texts. From the first sentence Tournier signs his own work as he describes himself as a precocious child (he would have been twelve in 1937 when the story begins) reading Aristotle's *Meteorologica* and also, of course, his own novel, seen in the hands of its author thirty-eight years before its publication: 'A 17 h 19 un souffle d'ouest-sud-ouest [. . .] tourna huit pages des *Météores* d'Aristote que lisait Michel Tournier sur la plage de Saint-Jacut' (*M* 7). Tournier's novel contains explicit references to works by Aristotle, Marivaux, Homer, Molière, Dumas, amongst many others, as well as a discussion of Jules Verne's *Le Tour du monde en quatre-vingt jours* and a long quotation from Casanova's *Memoirs*. The self-referential and intertextual quality of the text is most explicit in the chapter entitled 'L'Île des lotophages', which directly follows 'Les Miroirs vénitiens'. The very title alludes to the Island of the Lotus Eaters in Homer's *Odyssey*.[26] Within this literary frame, the text describes a night spent by Paul in Deborah's private library. The privileged referent here is literature itself:

Tout le monde est là. Livres anciens et classiques — Homère, Platon, Shakespeare — grands auteurs contemporains — Kipling, Shaw, Stein, Spengler, Keyserling — , mais la production française d'après-guerre — Camus, Sartre, Ionesco — témoigne que Deborah du fond de son désert n'ignorait rien, lisait tout, comprenait tout [. . .] C'est la nécropole de l'intelligence et du génie, les cendres de deux mille ans de pensée, de poésie et de théâtre après une apocalypse atomique. (*M* 418)

The pervasive and self-conscious literariness of *Les Météores* elicits differing reactions from Tournier's characters. On the one hand, Paul attempts to escape 'literature' into a non-literary, authentic relationship with the cosmos. At the end of the novel he will claim to have attained a state in which he is 'en contact immédiat, en prise directe avec le ciel et les intempéries' (*M* 529). Alexandre, on the other hand, has little time for such mystical aspirations. One day, when there is 'Rien à signaler sous le soleil', he discusses the word 'boustrophédon', which, it transpires, designates writing itself: 'Il

[26] On the Island of the Lotus Eaters, see Homer, *The Odyssey*, Book Nine, pp. 141–2, to which Paul refers in *M* 406. Tournier describes the couple on whom Ralph and Deborah are based in 'Cinq jours. . . cinquante ans. . . à Hammamet', in *Petites Proses*, pp. 38–52. Georges Perec describes a visit to the same couple at their home in Hammamet in *Les Choses*, pp. 110–11, to which Tournier refers in *VP* 260.

s'agit, je crois, d'un type d'écriture grecque archaïque serpentant en une seule ligne sur le parchemin, de gauche à droite puis de droite à gauche' (*M* 296). Unlike Paul, Alexandre seems reconciled to a practice of writing which takes itself as one of its most important themes.

This ambivalence towards self-representation is reproduced in Tournier's attitude to the *mise en abyme*, which he discusses briefly in the section of *Des clefs et des serrures* entitled 'L'Image abîmée'. Tournier begins his short essay in typically pedagogic fashion as he informs the reader of the etymology of 'abîme': '*Abîme*. Du grec *abussos*, dont on a tiré aussi *abysse*. Textuellement: qui n'a pas de fond. On commet donc un contresens en parlant du "fond de l'abîme" et un pléonasme en évoquant un "abîme sans fond".'[27] Like female psychology (see *M* 184), the abyss is, by definition, 'sans fond'. The aim of Tournier's subsequent discussion will nevertheless be to delineate and restrict this point of absence. As an example of the *mise en abyme*, Tournier refers to Benjamin Rabier's famous drawing of a cow, used on the label of a brand of processed cheese marketed as 'la Vache-qui-rit':

Cette vache porte en pendants d'oreilles deux boîtes de fromage de cette marque sur lesquelles est naturellement reproduite la même vache avec ses pendants d'oreilles, etc. Cette image de marque offre ainsi à l'œil une surface saine et solide, à l'exception de deux petites fondrières — les pendants d'oreilles — où le regard s'enfonce, perd pied, se trouve pris au piège d'un processus infini qui n'est freiné que par le rétrécissement que subit l'image à chaque étape. (p. 121)

The *abîme* is in principle bottomless; however, Tournier argues that in practice the 'processus infini' is arrested by the shrinking of the image *en abyme*. The threat which it poses to the spectator is thereby parried: 'Ce rétrécissement est d'une importance majeure, car lui seul met un terme à la fuite vertigineuse dans laquelle nous précipite l'image abîmée' (p. 123). The edges of the abyss are clearly demarcated and its influence is thereby restricted to a small portion of the otherwise unbroken surface of the text or image. Tournier's discussion in *Des clefs et des serrures* makes the concession of recognizing the potential threat posed by the *mise en abyme* in order

---

[27] Tournier, *Des clefs et des serrures*, p. 121. Further references will be given in the text.

to restrict it all the more effectively. The *abîme* marks a point of absence, but absence has its own clearly delineated place; and as such it is isolated, contained, controlled, and brought back under the hegemony of reason.

To illustrate how intelligibility is unimpaired by the *mise en abyme*, Tournier imagines a picture showing an old woman with a photograph of herself at the age of twenty. The hermeneut has no difficulty in explaining the 'abîme de temps' which this opens up: 'le demi-siècle qui sépare ces deux images saute aux yeux, lourdement aggravé par la sereine mélancolie de la vieillarde qui nous prend à témoin du ravage des ans' (p. 123). However, the promise of intelligible meaning is frustrated when Tournier takes the example of a *real* photograph by Arthur Tress, which is reproduced between the two pages of the short essay: 'Une jeune femme joue avec un chien. Au premier plan, une photo nous montre une petite fille embrassant une vieille femme. Entre ces deux couples — l'image et l'image de l'image — les fils et les pistes s'embrouillent. L'esprit se perd en troublantes hypothèses' (p. 123). Tournier suggests a possible interpretation of the photograph, but immediately dismisses it: 'Je connais Arthur Tress. Ses intentions sont rarement aussi limpides' (p. 123). The essay concludes inconclusively; and the attempt to control the *mise en abyme* ends by disclosing the author's inability to decipher the meaning of the image.[28]

Tournier's short account of the *mise en abyme* reveals a tension between the urge for intelligibility and the awareness that the moment of self-representation introduces an element into the image or text which frustrates interpretation. The same tension is reproduced in *Les Météores*. The Venetian mirrors confront Paul, as the novel confronts the reader, with a confusing array of fragmented perspectives. Paul, however, continues to insist upon the intelligibility of experience, as is illustrated by his treatment of Casanova's *Memoirs*. Unable to sleep after his visit to the Venetian mirrors, Paul reads and quotes Casanova's account of an episode from his time in prison. Casanova discovers what he believes to be the corpse of a dead friend, but then realizes that he is in fact holding his own

---

[28] For further discussion of Tournier's attempts to give a verbal interpretation of the visual image, see ch. 5, sec. (i). The passage from *Des clefs et des serrures* is reprinted in Tournier's *Petites Proses*, pp. 136–7, but interestingly the final paragraph, in which Tournier admits his failure to interpret a *real* photograph, is omitted.

left hand: 'je ne tenais dans ma main droite autre main que ma main gauche, qui, percluse et engourdie, avait perdu mouvement, sentiment et chaleur' (M 378). The use of quotation from Casanova's text illustrates the polyphonic construction of Les Météores: Casanova joins Alexandre, Paul, Jean, Sophie, and Hamida as one of the novel's first-person narrators. However, Paul's *use* of Casanova's text provides a significant example of the attempt to control the polyphony of Les Météores by reconciling the different voices within a single all-encompassing scheme. Paul appropriates Casanova's narrative by interpreting it in the light of his own situation and suggesting its relevance to his own concerns: 'Il y a là une allusion balbutiante à la gémellité, et singulièrement à la gémellité dépariée. Comme si ce sans-pareil invétéré [. . .] faisait un phantasme gémellaire' (M 378–9). Paul asserts the intelligibility of Casanova's experience when viewed from the privileged perspective of his 'intuition gémellaire'. In order to do this, he overlooks the final words of Casanova's text, which describe the inability of the solitary subject (Casanova, but evidently also Paul) to distinguish between truth and falsehood, reality and dream: 'Cette aventure, quoique comique, ne m'a pas égayé. Elle m'a au contraire donné sujet aux réflexions les plus noires. Je me suis aperçu que j'étais dans un endroit où, si le faux paraissait vrai, les réalités devaient paraître des songes, où l'entendement devait perdre la moitié de ses privilèges' (M 378). Paul describes the episode from Casanova's Memoirs as a 'phantasme gémellaire', but he refuses to see its more urgent relevance to the experience of the 'jumeau déparié'. Moreover, he interrupts Casanova's account in mid-sentence, and what he omits is perhaps more revealing than what he quotes. Casanova goes on to describe how 'la fantaisie altérée devait rendre la raison victime ou de l'espérance chimérique, ou de l'affreux désespoir'; and he turns to *philosophy* ('j'ai pour la première fois de la vie à l'âge de trente ans appelé à mon secours la philosophie') as a defence against the dangers of despair or fallacious hope.[29] Casanova's solution is also Paul's. After the departure of Jean, Paul becomes the self-blinded theorist of his own adventure and uses theory to protect himself against an inhospitable and unintelligible

---

[29] See Casanova, *Histoire de ma vie*, iv, ch. 12, p. 208. This is a modernized version of an older edition originally published between 1826 and 1838. Apart from minor alterations of punctuation, this modernized edition is identical to the text quoted by Tournier in Les Météores.

reality: 'Et moi, je cours derrière toi, mon bloc-notes à la main, et j'interprète ton itinéraire, je fais la théorie de ton tour du monde, je calcule l'équation de ta trajectoire' (M 492).

In this same episode the text both refuses (through Paul's attempt at understanding) and discloses (in Casanova's words) the frustration of the intellect and the subversion of the distinction between the real and the imaginary. This contradictory double gesture illustrates the conflicting imperatives at the core of Les Météores and of Tournier's fiction in general: on the one hand, the urge for the text to be translucent and rich in meaning, subordinate to the supreme value of intelligibility; on the other hand, the desire to liberate the literary text from the authority of unambiguous meaning. The Venetian mirrors disrupt all stable perspectives and confront Paul with an unwelcome insight into his own situation. And Venice itself, at least in Paul's account of it, reflects the tension inherent in Les Météores, a novel in which the promise of meaning is always renewed, but never finally honoured: 'Venise se présente constamment comme une ville chiffrée. Elle nous promet toujours une réponse imminente au prix d'un peu de sagacité, mais elle ne tient jamais cette promesse' (M 379).

(vi) 'Le Jumeau déparié'

Paul is described by his brother Jean as 'l'homme de toutes les plénitudes' (M 154). But Paul is forced to learn the lessons of absence and loss. After the departure of Jean he becomes aware of 'défaillances', 'trous', and 'taches d'obscurité' within his 'intuition gémellaire' (M 363). Plenitude is superseded by separation after what Paul calls the 'coup de hache' (M 363) has fallen: 'j'appelle Jean, je lui parle, je suscite l'apparition de son fantôme, et je bascule dans le vide quand je tente de m'appuyer sur lui' (M 364). From this point onwards, the principal theme of the novel will be loss in its various forms: le vide, amputation, dépariage.

For Paul, the departure of Jean entails the violent separation from his own specular image which guaranteed both identity and self-knowledge. In Venice, talking to Hamida, Paul concedes that the search for his errant twin is also the attempt to re-establish the foundations of his own identity: 'Aussi lorsque je vous dis: où est Jean? cela peut en effet signifier: où suis-je?' (M 395). The questions 'Où est Jean?' (M 394, 395, 425, 428, and 478) and

'Où suis-je?' (*M* 380 and 395) become subsumed in a more anxious self-interrogation: 'Qui suis-je?' (*M* 487 and 525). Paul discovers the fundamental insecurity of identity, and the search for Jean becomes the search for an impossible self-coincidence.

According to Tournier's discussion of *Les Météores* in *Le Vent Paraclet*, Alexandre's death is necessary to prevent him from arrogating too central a role in the novel: 'ce personnage bruyant et colore occupe indûment le devant de la scène' (*VP* 262). However, the spectre of Alexandre continues to haunt the text. With peculiar urgency, he is repeatedly resurrected within Paul's memory. After Alexandre's death Paul regrets the loss of his scandalous uncle: 'Et pourtant, j'aurais eu beaucoup à lui dire, beaucoup à apprendre de lui' (*M* 335). Later the memory of Alexandre returns more insistently:

Mais je songe surtout à [. . .] Alexandre, notre oncle scandaleux [. . .] Celui-là, je ne me consolerai jamais d'avoir manqué sa rencontre, son amitié [. . .] Son homosexualité — contrefaçon sans-pareil de la gémellité — aurait pu nous apporter des lumières précieuses, une méditation irremplaçable pour percer le mystère aussi bien gémellaire que sans-pareil. (*M* 360)

Here Paul accepts that the experience of the homosexual offers a different perspective, which might help him come to terms with his own experience of loss. On occasions Paul's text becomes the unacknowledged repetition of phrases and insights first used in the journal of the scandalous uncle.[30] The initial opposition between Paul and Alexandre has now been superseded by covert identification. This is made most clear whilst Paul is on the Canadian Pacific Railway:

Ici, le fantôme d'Alexandre hante mon esprit avec insistance [. . .] Quelle différence fondamentale y a-t-il entre Paul traversant la Prairie dans son train rouge et le dandy des gadoues installé dans le wagon immobile des collines blanches de Miramas? Jumeaux dépariés l'un et l'autre, Alexandre est affecté d'un dépariage de naissance, *congénital*, moi d'un dépariage *acquis*. (*M* 487–8)

Paul tries to suggest differences, but he accepts the fundamental similarity between his situation and that of his uncle. Earlier, Alexandre described the search for a companion as the eternal truth

[30] For Paul's unacknowledged use of parts of Alexandre's journal, compare their discussions of the size of the poor (*M* 96, 383) and the image of a fish swimming against the current (*M* 290, 472).

of those who live with absence: 'Au portier qui m'accueillait d'un air interrogateur, j'ai dit la vérité: "Je cherche quelqu'un." Vérité éternelle, la plus profonde de mes vérités, mon seul ressort depuis que j'existe' (M 327). Paul's search for his lost brother is anticipated in the life of his uncle; and, despite Paul's rhetoric of presence, Les Météores turns out to be a novel about separation, absence, and loss.

However, Paul's voyage initiatique prepares a reversal which it will be necessary to discuss at some length. In his rejection of adulthood (a trait which he shares with Tiffauges), Paul continues to believe that the happiness of childhood is both an origin and a destination: 'la préformation de l'aboutissement auquel je suis appelé' (M 488). In 'L'Âme déployée', the final chapter of the novel, Paul will claim to have regained, but also to have surpassed, the original plenitude of his childhood. In the course of his journey around the world he becomes aware that his aim is not simply to retrieve his errant twin. As he repeats and profits from his brother's experience, he begins to conceive of the possibility of assuming the total identity of Jean-Paul in one person: 'Jean n'a pas disparu, car je suis Jean. Et cela bien sûr sans cesser d'être Paul. En somme deux jumeaux en un seul homme, Janus Bifrons' (M 425). Paul states that he and Jean now share the same identity: 'je suis Jean.' But the phrase is, of course, ambiguous. In the context of Paul's pursuit of Jean, the possible derivation of 'je suis' from suivre is inevitably suggested. Paul simultaneously asserts that he has achieved full identity with his brother ('I am Jean'), but also indicates the distance which necessarily separates them ('I follow Jean'). As the Japanese servant Tanizaki reminds Paul three pages later ('seul il sait que je ne suis pas Jean', M 428), total identification has not yet been achieved. Even so, Paul begins to imagine the possibility of assuming his brother's identity whilst preserving his own; and, in consequence, Jean's death can be envisaged without trauma and even positively desired: 'Bref il faut oser l'écrire noir sur blanc: dès l'instant que je sens naître en moi la possibilité d'assumer en totalité la personnalité de Jean-Paul, la mort de Jean devient une éventualité acceptable, presque une solution' (M 426). Paul hopes to become Jean-Paul and to resurrect his possibly dead brother within himself: 'je m'engraisse de sa substance perdue, je m'incorpore mon frère fuyard' (M 467).

Paul's voyage initiatique culminates in the accident—or, as the text suggests, the ritual rebirth—in a tunnel under the Berlin Wall. This experience recalls the conversion of Saul (later St Paul) on the road to Damascus.[31] However, the finality of Paul's conversion is less assured than that of his biblical namesake. The stability of identity will be replaced by the uncertainty of metamorphosis: 'Nul doute que Paul vient de franchir un seuil décisif et va au-devant de métamorphoses radicales. Une vie nouvelle, une vie autre, la mort tout simplement peut-être' (M 522). The left half of Paul's body is crushed and later amputated. Earlier, Jean's experience of the triple mirror gave him a terrifying and unforgettable insight into the alterity at the core of his own identity. Verbal repetitions underline the parallels between Jean's experience and Paul's accident under the Berlin Wall:

Je m'avançai sans méfiance dans le piège, et aussitôt ses *mâchoires* miroitantes *se refermèrent* sur moi et me *broyèrent* si cruellement que j'en porte les traces à tout jamais. (M 246; my emphasis)

Il s'arc-boute [. . .] et lorsque la *mâchoire* molle et ruisselante *se referme* lentement sur son corps crucifié, il sent ces pièces dures le *broyer* comme des dents d'acier. (M 523; my emphasis)

Paul's body is now quite literally a 'corps morcelé'. Unlike Jean, he will not be able to escape from the memory of his experience through perpetual flight. However, in the final chapter of *Les Météores* the rhetoric of presence will reassert its ascendency over a text which up to that point has been dominated by themes of separation and loss. Unable to move independently, Paul will nevertheless claim to have rediscovered the primitive unity of self and world, thereby transforming failure into success, absence into presence, terror into affirmation, and physical infirmity into transcendence.

Whilst achieving these reversals, Paul begins to narrate his own, still-to-be-written text;[32] and this *aesthetic* activity is difficult to

---

[31] See Acts 9: 1–19. The period in *Les Météores* after the windows have been blacked out by the 'équipes d'aveuglement' (M 513) corresponds to Saul/Paul's blindness after his experience on the road to Damascus. For a further parallel between the conversions of the two Pauls, see the use of the number three in each account.

[32] On his first appearance in the text as a first-person narrator, Paul refers to 'le coup de hache qui nous a séparés, l'horrible amputation dont j'ai cherché la guérison de par le monde, enfin cette autre blessure m'arrachant une seconde fois à moi-même et me clouant sur cette chaise longue' (M 64). At this point he is clearly speaking after his accident under the Berlin Wall. At some points in his text, however, he seems much closer to the events which he describes; see, e.g., M 364. Paul uses at least two kinds of narrative (or three, if the final chapter of the novel is taken to be a form of interior monologue): a retrospective account which begins after the main action of the novel is complete, and a journal which is more or less contemporary with the events it describes. Failure to recognize this has led at least one critic into confusion;

reconcile with his claims to have reconquered full self-presence. Writing, throughout Tournier's texts, is essentially equated with absence and the deferment of fulfilment: Paul becomes an author only after the departure of Jean and the dislocation of the 'cellule gémellaire'. Tournier himself emphasizes the necessity of solitude, and even of failure, for artistic creation. The artist must never achieve more than a relative, restricted contentment if he is to continue his work: 'Les œuvres sont les fruits du désert et ne s'épanouissent que dans l'aridité' (*VP* 287). An author who needed nothing would not need to write. Alexandre and Paul (and perhaps also Tournier) use their texts to describe their attempts to establish or re-establish a form of happiness, and their narratives continue as long as their attempts fail. If Alexandre found his perfect partner, if Paul succeeded in bringing Jean back to the Pierres Sonnantes, and if Tournier found 'un frère idéal, une sœur idéale, tel ami, telle amie idéale' (*VP* 286-7), their literary works would be no longer necessary or viable. Tournier underlines this in *Le Vent Paraclet*: 'Seigneur, n'écoute pas mes supplications, et si d'aventure j'approche quelque jour l'oasis d'un cœur amical dans un corps accueillant, renvoie-moi à coups de pied au cul dans mes steppes familières où souffle le vent sec et glacé de l'idée pure! Car l'idéal éteint l'idée comme l'eau le feu' (*VP* 287). For Paul and Alexandre, as for Crusoé and Tiffauges, the written text is a partial substitute for an imaginary plenitude which, for the present at least, remains unrealized. As we shall see, Paul's conversion at the end of *Les Météores* is aesthetic rather than properly mystical; and human failure is the price of artistic success, though this in turn allows the possible reinscription of success within a life of solitude and loss, and within the text which describes them.

(vii) 'L'Âme déployée'

The stakes in 'L'Âme déployée' are high. By far the largest part of *Les Météores* portrays loss, separation, and quest; in less than twenty pages the final chapter attempts to reverse these terms and show reconciliation, presence, and discovery. In the accident under the Berlin Wall Paul repeats Jean's experience with the triple mirror and regresses to the state before the mirror stage. As he describes

see William Cloonan, *Michel Tournier*, p. 56. On Paul as an artist, see Jacques Chabot, 'Un frère jumeau du monde: Michel Tournier', p. 58.

his situation, Paul alludes to Lichtenberg's modification of the Cartesian Cogito (in which 'I think' is replaced by 'It thinks').[33] Simplified and reduced to an original, pre-individuated state, Paul rejects the grammatical subject 'je' in favour of the impersonal 'il':

Qui suis-je? Où suis-je? La petite fée Novocaïne en m'arrachant à la douleur m'a dépouillé de toute personnalité, de toute insertion dans l'espace et le temps. Je suis un moi absolu, intemporel et sans situation. *Je suis*, c'est tout [. . .] Je pense, je vois, j'entends. Il faudrait dire: il pense, il voit, il entend. Comme on dit il pleut ou il fait soleil. (*M* 525)

At this point Paul is still dependent upon anaesthetics to ease his pain; but, as he weans himself from pain killers, he continues to suggest that he has attained a state of existence which precedes and also surpasses individuation. Self and world, internal and external, are intimately fused:

Le ciel embrasé est devenu ma plaie. Je regardais fasciné ces vastes écroulements enflammés dont j'étais la conscience torturée. Mon corps souffrant encombrait le ciel, emplissait l'horizon [. . .] Mais mon cœur se gonfle d'espoir quand je constate que je suis en contact immédiat, en prise directe avec le ciel et les intempéries [. . .] Non plus le déchet organique pourrissant sur un grabat, mais le témoin vivant et nerveux des météores. (*M* 526, 529)

Paul seems to have resolved the conflict between movement and *stasis*, his brother's nomadism and his own sedentary nature, as he explores the world from the immobility of his bed or *chaise longue*. He is no longer alien to and alienated from his environment, and he has learned to take his place in the organic unity of the cosmos: 'Le ciel est un tout organique possédant sa vie propre, en relation directe avec la terre et les eaux [. . .] Il manque au physicien pour le savoir une dimension, celle précisément qui plonge en moi, articulant mon corps gauche déployé sur mon corps droit estropié' (*M* 541).

'L'Âme déployée' describes something akin to Crusoé's mystical experience at the end of *Vendredi ou les limbes du Pacifique*. If anything, however, Paul goes further than Crusoé in his identification

---

[33] The passage to which Paul alludes is Lichtenberg, *Gesammelte Werke*, i. 436: 'One should say "It thinks", just as one says "It is lightning" ' (all translations from German are my own unless reference is given to an English edition). Paul's claim to be a 'moi absolu' may also be an allusion to Fichte's Absolute Self, to which Tournier refers in *Vol* 92.

of self and cosmos. The keywords in 'L'Âme déployée' are 'ubiquité' and 'porosité': Paul claims to be everywhere and to participate in everything. He has achieved a state of absolute existence ('*Je suis*, c'est tout', *M* 525) and intense knowledge of the world ('hyperconnaissance', *M* 528). Observing his environment from an absolute, depersonalized perspective, Paul explicitly identifies his own vision with that of God: 'Grâce à la jumelle, je posais sur Méline un œil inquisiteur, perçant et hors d'atteinte, l'œil de Dieu en somme' (*M* 531; see also *M* 532).

It is striking that, in this most self-consciously literary and allusive of novels, the final chapter contains no *explicit* allusions to other texts. Paul's intense experience of reality would seem to exclude and be excluded by the mediation of literature. But here, more than anywhere else in the novel, Tournier is dependent upon literary models. The influence of literary Romanticism can be seen throughout the novel—in the cult of origins, the fantasy of fusion with the cosmos, as well as the themes of the double and the *voyage initiatique*.[34] In particular, *Les Météores* closely follows the structure of Novalis's unfinished novel, *Heinrich von Ofterdingen*.[35] Like Paul, Novalis's hero undergoes a long journey of initiation and anticipation until, as Tournier says in his essay on Novalis in *Le Vol du vampire*, 'Henri apprend à participer à un ordre cosmique supérieur' (*Vol* 69). The literary description of such a state clearly involves immense problems, which Novalis avoided by leaving his novel unfinished. In 'L'Âme déployée' Paul attempts to find a language adequate to his experience. He claims to have learned to understand a universal language, which resembles and surpasses the twins' cryptophasia. Paul's interlocutor is now the world itself: 'Doué d'ubiquité, le cryptophone déparié entend la voix des choses, comme la voix de ses propres humeurs' (*M* 540). This sentence clearly recalls Baudelaire's description of the poet as someone who 'comprend sans effort / Le langage des fleurs et des choses muettes'.[36] But 'la voix des choses' or 'le langage des fleurs' are not,

---

[34] On the Romantic theme of the journey of initiation, see Marcel Brion, *L'Allemagne romantique*, iii. *Le Voyage initiatique*, which Tournier discusses in 'Les Voyages initiatiques'.

[35] See Novalis, *Heinrich von Ofterdingen*, which Tournier discusses in *Vol* 68–9. On the projected conclusion of Novalis's unfinished work, see the account given by Ludwig Tieck, in *Heinrich von Ofterdingen*, pp. 207–19.

[36] See Charles Baudelaire, 'Élévation', in *Œuvres complètes*, i. 10. It is worth noting that the Pierres Sonnantes, as well as Le Guildo and the home for handicapped

and cannot be, the language adopted by the poet or the crippled twin in the text itself. The ineffable, by its very nature, does not lend itself to direct transcription, and so the author is obliged to search for an indirect means of approaching something which lies outside language.

'L'Âme déployée' resumes the experiment tentatively begun by Tournier in Chapter Ten of *Vendredi ou les limbes du Pacifique*. Paradoxically, the attempt to explore and to extend the limits of language involves an increased reliance upon language: allowed a degree of freedom, it may be capable of revealing something which the author could not deliberately constrain it to express. Nevertheless, Tournier remains unconvinced about the prospects of such an experiment, as can be seen from a brief examination of his ambivalence towards the notion of textual play. In the essay 'Novalis et Sophia' Tournier comments, in reference to the 'jeu de mots', that 'nous sommes déjà avec Novalis dans ce courant qui dure encore (Heidegger) et pour lequel le calembour a valeur d'intuition métaphysique' (*Vol* 68). It is not certain whether the phrase 'le calembour a valeur d'intuition métaphysique' should be taken as suggesting that the pun *gives rise to* metaphysical intuitions, and is therefore a legitimate tool for philosophical speculation, or that it *replaces* genuine thought. The latter reading would help to explain Tournier's lack of interest in recent French philosophy, which, following Heidegger's example, has often accorded a curious privilege to verbal play. But Tournier is aware that he belongs to 'ce courant qui dure encore', and his texts show that he takes great pleasure in the ambiguities and grey areas of language.[37] He evidently enjoys Novalis's pun 'Je suis philosophe parce que j'aime Sophie', because he quotes it in both *Le Vol du vampire* and *Le Vent Paraclet* (see *Vol* 68 and *VP* 275). He even reproduces it in the title of the final chapter of *Le Vent Paraclet*, 'Les Malheurs de Sophie', which also refers to a novel for children by the Comtesse de Ségur (also entitled *Les Malheurs de Sophie*). Nevertheless, Tournier is critical of the pun as he reproachfully associates it with the decline of *sophia*

children near Sainte-Brigitte, all exist. The Pierres Sonnantes are in fact a group of rocks in Brittany which emit a sound not unlike a cow bell when struck with a hard object. Perhaps this allows a less mystical explanation of what Paul means by the 'voix des choses'.

[37] See W. D. Redfern's discussion of Tournier's use of puns in 'Approximating Man: Michel Tournier and Play in Language'.

(wisdom) and the early death of Sophie von Kühn: 'Historiquement
ce touchant calembour sonnait le glas de la philosophie, de la sagesse
et de la fillette. Car c'est le romantisme qui fut le vrai fossoyeur de
la sagesse' (VP 275). In Le Vol du vampire, on the other hand,
Tournier takes a quite different view. Here he criticizes Novalis for
not going far enough in the surrender of intentional meaning to the
play of language. Novalis's poetry is described as 'trop menée sans
doute par les idées', whereas, Tournier continues, 'son contemporain
Hölderlin savait, lui, laisser les mots jouer leur jeu divin' (Vol 70).

Tournier's dilemma, and perhaps the dilemma of contemporary
French theory and fiction in general, is that he is attracted to, but
knows that he cannot fully embrace, the possibility of creative textual
freedom unlimited by all semantic and referential constraints. He
will not confine his texts to the prison house of self-referentiality,
although this would perhaps be the easiest solution to the problem of
writing in an age which has lost faith in the referential capability
of language. In 'L'Âme déployée' Paul adopts a fragmentary mode of
narration which foregrounds language but which nevertheless aims
to establish a playful and productive exchange between word and
meaning. This is illustrated by Paul's meditation on the word 'travail'
which begins when he overhears his doctor who observes that '*Il
faudrait* [. . .] *qu'il fasse un peu travailler sa carcasse*' (M 528). This
reminds him of the etymology of 'travail':

Travail. Je me souviens, oui. Du bas latin *tripalium*, chevalet formé de trois
pieux servant à mater les chevaux rétifs et à accoucher les femmes. Je suis
un cheval rétif, écumant et piaffant sous la douleur du *travail*. Je suis une
femme en *travail*, hurlante et cabrée. Je suis l'enfant qui vient de naître: le
monde pèse sur lui avec le poids d'une grande souffrance, mais il doit assimiler
cette souffrance, en devenir l'architecte, le démiurge. (M 528)

Paul's meditation resembles free association and produces an open-
ended textual chain which could be indefinitely extended but which
is constantly drawn back to its source in the suffering of the speaker:
'piaffant sous la douleur', 'hurlante et cabrée', 'le poids d'une grande
souffrance'. A later passage again illustrates the same principle. Paul's
description of the changing consistency of the clouds depends as much
on verbal resonance as on the form of external reality. The clouds
provoke a series of images and sensations which lead from a '*fil*
d'épée' to '*fil*aments délicats', and then to a whole series of words
for cloth, which suggest the presence of animal and finally human

figures. What is interesting here is not the objective accuracy of the description, but the interplay of external form, subjective sensation, and textual production:

Ce matin le ciel était limpide et clair comme un diamant. Pourtant des frôlements de lame de rasoir, des coupures fines et profondes, la douloureuse vibration d'un fil d'épée dans l'épaisseur de ma cuisse annonçaient un changement. En effet, le ciel s'est strié de filaments délicats, de griffes à reflets soyeux, de cristaux de glace suspendus comme des lustres à des altitudes prodigieuses. Puis la soie cristalline a épaissi, elle est devenue hermine, angora, mérinos, et mon ventre s'est enfoncé dans cette toison douce et bienveillante. Enfin le corps nuageux est apparu, cortège solonnel, massif et arrondi, grandiose et nuptial, — nuptial, oui, car j'ai reconnu deux silhouettes unies, rayonnantes de bonheur et de bonté. (M 537)

The silhouettes which Paul has recognized are those of his dead parents, Edouard and Maria-Barbara. The passage begins with the description of physical pain: 'la douloureuse vibration d'un fil d'épée dans l'épaisseur de ma cuisse'. The chance association of words, objects, and ideas leads away from, but also back to, the suffering which is its point of departure. As Paul recalls his dead parents, '[son] corps droit recroquevillé sur sa couche pleurait de nostalgie et de douceur' (M 538).

It will be clear by now that Paul's belief that he can attain a state of communion with his environment does not entail an end to his sense of loss. This discrepancy between his aspirations to plenitude and the continuing disclosure of suffering illustrates the principal problem of interpretation posed by 'L'Âme déployée': should we accept Paul's claims to have achieved, or to be approaching, apotheosis, or is he merely deluding himself and the reader as to his actual situation? As in Le Roi des aulnes, the ending of Les Météores is subject to mutually exclusive interpretations, which unsettle the reader's anticipation, frequently encouraged within Paul's narrative, that the conclusion of the text will retrospectively explain what precedes. This is emphasized by the ambiguity of the final word of the novel. Having described the way in which the heat of the sun makes the snow evaporate without first becoming water, Paul brings the text to a close with a single-sentence paragraph: 'Cela s'appelle: sublimation' (M 542). This observation is open to a number of possible readings. Firstly, there is the literal interpretation: in chemistry, the word 'sublimation' does indeed· describe the direct passage of a substance from solid to gaseous form. However, as the final word of the novel, 'sublimation' bears a great deal of emphasis, and other implications vie for the reader's attention. In essays on Novalis and Kant, Tournier himself explores the polysemy of the word and suggests a number of possible meanings (see *Vol* 60–1 and 67–8). The most important of these in the present context is the Romantic sense, as used for example by Novalis, which refers to the possibility of human transcendence into the realm of the gods.[38] This would seem to support Paul's account of his situation at the end of *Les Météores*. However, the meaning of sublimation in psycho-analytical theory, which uses the term to describe the redirection of libidinal energy into intellectual and especially artistic activity,[39] authorizes a more sceptical attitude towards Paul's text. Rather than a *roman d'initiation*, in which the protagonist finally accedes to a higher order of knowledge, the profound drama of *Les Météores* would be that of a *Künstlerroman* which recounts how Paul becomes the author of his own novel. Indeed, *Les Météores* leaves us at the point when its principal narrator is beginning to narrate (parts of) the novel we have just read. Paul may have achieved a form of magical transcendence, in spite of or because of his accident, or he may be channelling his unused sexual energy into the art object which his text becomes; he may have finally achieved understanding of his destiny or he may have succumbed to an aesthetic urge which will make him the self-blinded author of his own text. Earlier, Sophie had indicated that Méline's speech was not made incomprehensible by the absence of meaning in her mutterings: 'Mais le peu que j'en ai saisi m'a toujours paru non dénué de sens, au contraire, et j'ai le sentiment que c'était plutôt l'excès de signification, d'implication qui le rendait inintelligible' (*M* 351). The superabundance of meaning frustrates attempts at understanding. Similarly, the word 'sublimation', and the chapter which precedes it, allow a variety of possible but irreconcilable interpretations. Polysemy may not be dissemination, but its effect on the ideal of intelligibility is potentially no less disruptive.[40]

---

[38] Tournier quotes Novalis's aphorism: 'Si l'univers est un précipité de la nature humaine, le monde des dieux en est la sublimation. Les deux se font *uno actu*' (*Vol* 67).

[39] On sublimation, see Laplanche and Pontalis, *Vocabulaire de la psychanalyse*, entry under 'Sublimation', pp. 465–7.

[40] On the distinction between polysemy and dissemination, see Jacques Derrida, *La Dissémination*, e.g., p. 32. See also Sarah Kofman, *Quatre romans analytiques*, p. 23: 'la polysémie, par l'excès de sens qu'elle détient, équivaut à l'absence de sens.'

The departure of Jean makes Paul aware of the insufficiency of his own powers of understanding (see M 362); and so, through the separation of the twins, Les Météores dramatizes the frustration of the intellect, which plays an essential role in Tournier's poetics and which is given a final illustration in the ambiguity of Paul's ultimate 'sublimation'. In 'L'Âme déployée' amputation becomes a figure of irreparable physical and semantic loss, inscribed on the body and in the text:

Ce bras et cette jambe qui me manquent, je m'aperçois que dans la nuit noire de ma souffrance je les identifiais confusément à mon frère-pareil disparu. Et il est bien vrai que tout être cher qui nous quitte nous ampute de quelque chose. C'est un morceau de nous-même qui s'en va, que nous portons en terre. La vie peut bien continuer, nous sommes désormais des invalides, plus rien ne sera jamais comme avant. (M 535)

Nevertheless, the absence of Jean, the dismemberment of the body, and the frustration of the search for unambiguous meanings are not unmitigated. Through Alexandre's experience of bereavement, we saw how the death of the loved one introduces absence within the self. But, by identification and incorporation, the lost figure is resurrected within the grieving subject. Paul realizes that Jean is not entirely lost: 'Mais il y a un mystère et un miracle gémellaires, et le frère-pareil disparu revit toujours de quelque façon dans le jumeau déparié survivant' (M 535). The dead live on, in a certain manner, even if the life of the living is also diminished. Jean is absent, but also present in the memories and fantasies of his crippled brother. The redeeming power of memory and the magical transformations effected by the imagination help to compensate for the reality of absence; and they also form the substance of Paul's *text*. In 'L'Âme déployée' there is no explicit indication that Paul's narrative is written. His illness at the beginning of the chapter even makes such a hypothesis highly improbable. Nevertheless, Paul has become the narrator of his own story. He has learned to value metamorphosis, creation, and openness to the outside world, even though these qualities were initially associated with Alexandre and presented as incompatible with the plenitude of the 'cellule gémellaire'. In Chapter Eighteen of Les Météores ('Les Jardins japonais'), Shonïn describes the artist Paul will become: 'Ainsi le lettré dans sa modeste demeure, le poète devant son écritoire, l'ermite dans sa caverne disposent à volonté de tout l'univers' (M 468). Drawing on Shonïn's belief in the creative power of vision (see *M* 445), Paul learns to equate creation and contemplation and explicitly relates his experience in 'L'Âme déployée' to the lessons of the Zen gardens. The musical and scriptural metaphors reveal how Paul conceives his newly acquired relationship with the world in aesthetic terms:

Le travail de création qui s'accomplit dans mes deux plaies trouve sa leçon dans les jardins miniatures japonais. JUMO vient d'élever les prairies de la Cassine de la dignité de jardin de thé — où l'on se promène en devisant — à celle de jardin Zen où seuls les yeux peuvent se poser. Mais à Nara mes yeux de profane ne voyaient dans les jardins Zen qu'une page blanche — cette nappe de sable ratissé, ces deux rochers, cet arbre squelettique, ce n'était évidemment qu'une portée vierge attendant les notes de la mélodie. Après les mutilations rituelles de Berlin, je ne suis plus ce profane, et le vide a fait place à une magnifique surabondance. (*M* 532-3)

Paul uses the analogy of art to describe his perception of the world: 'le vide' is also 'une page blanche' or 'une portée attendant les notes de la mélodie'. The creative potential of which Paul now becomes aware makes his amputation tolerable and his text possible. Moreover, his discovery of the power of language also entails an exultant recognition of the *natural* richness which linguistic differences allow us to perceive. Paul learns the names of the plants in his garden from an old book; the 'joie intense' which he describes is simultaneously and indistinguishably a joy in the music of names and the joy of discovering nature:

Je me suis fait apporter par Méline le grand herbier aux gravures en couleur qui a appartenu au père de Maria-Barbara — mon grand-père maternel — et j'ai démêlé avec une joie intense dans la masse confuse du regain frais toutes sortes d'espèces répertoriées, les trèfles blancs et violets, le lotier corniculé, la flouve odorante, la crételle et le pâturin des prés, l'avoine jaunâtre et la pimprenelle sanguisorba, ailleurs l'houlque laineuse, la fétuque, le brome, le fromental, la fléole, le raygrass, le dactyle et le vulpin, plus loin, dans le coin marécageux, les renoncules, les scirpes et les carex. (*M* 532)

The linguistic richness of 'L'Âme déployée' does not negate the loss at the source of the text and to which the text constantly returns. But it does suggest the possibility of reconciliation with loss, and perhaps even a paradoxical satisfaction in the withholding of presence. If Jean had not fled from the stifling atmosphere of the 'cellule gémellaire', the twins would literally have no story to tell and would have remained enclosed in a sterile environment immune from the corrosive atmosphere of narrative fiction. *Dépariage* has compensations which are not negligible, such as the discovery of an aesthetic vocation and the celebration of nature. Another such compensation is desire. The 'cellule gémellaire' represents a state of permanent satisfaction from which desire is excluded. But desire need not necessarily be understood as the adjunct of a fallen state. Like so much else in *Les Météores*, it can be interpreted in a variety of different ways. After the death of Daniel, Alexandre equates it with a form of exile: 'Je me demande même si le désir n'est pas une certaine folie, la folie particulière provoquée par cet exil, la folie errante d'un visage dépossédé de son corps' (*M* 264). However, Alexandre's account of his first homosexual experience illustrates how desire is also, on the positive side, a creative mode of being in the world and an enriching relationship with the other: 'C'était ma première rencontre avec le désir, vécu non plus solitairement et comme un honteux secret, mais dans la complicité, j'allais dire — mais ce serait bientôt vrai — dans la communauté' (*M* 36). The magical encounter with desire makes it possible to affirm the state of exile and dispossession which are at its source: 'Pas encore revenu. . . Comme j'aime cette expression juste et touchante qui suggère un pays inconnu, une forêt mystérieuse au charme si puissant que le voyageur qui s'y est aventuré *n'en revient jamais*. Saisi d'émerveillement, cet émerveillement ne le lâche plus et lui interdit de revenir vers la terre grise et ingrate où il est né' (*M* 36-7).

L'Âme déployée' invokes the paradoxes of *qui perd gagne*: pain inaugurates and is mitigated by artistic creation, and, whilst continuing to disclose its origin in suffering, art also becomes part of a necessary veiling process which assumes and surmounts suffering.[41] The inevitability of human failure is transformed—precariously—into Paul's, and Tournier's, aesthetic success: 'je ne suis plus ce profane, et le vide a fait place à une magnifique surabondance' (*M* 533).

---

[41] For further discussion, see ch. 6, sec. (iii) and sec. (iv).

4

Meaning and Intention

(i) *Reading*

Although Tournier's autobiographical, critical, and theoretical writings sometimes elucidate his literary texts indirectly, they are often unsatisfactory or frustrating when they deal explicitly with the genesis or meaning of his fiction. In *Le Vent Paraclet* Tournier offers an explanation for the discrepancy between his novels and his explanations of them through his acceptance that the author is never entirely in control of his work. The reflection on literary meaning which this insight provokes culminates in the theory of reading elaborated in *Le Vol du vampire*. In that text, superficially at least, Tournier allows the literary work complete freedom from the constraints of authorial intention, and he transfers the onus of meaning from author to reader. However, the liberation of the reader which this entails is less straightforward, and less generous, than it initially seems; and the principal concern of this chapter is Tournier's struggle for control over his own texts as suggested in his theory of reading and in practice in *Gilles et Jeanne*.

In *Le Vent Paraclet* Tournier seems resigned to what he calls 'l'auto-genèse de l'œuvre' (*VP* 203). He describes how the novel becomes independent of its creator: 'Il échappe à ma maîtrise, et se prend à vivre d'une vie propre. J'en deviens alors le jardinier, le serviteur, pire encore, le sous-produit, ce que l'œuvre fait sous elle en se faisant' (*VP* 179; see also *VP* 153–4 and 203). Tournier echoes Heidegger in the suggestion that the work makes the author as much as the author makes the work.[1] The very notion of an author is described as an 'aberration causaliste' (*VP* 154). Tournier continues

---

[1] See Martin Heidegger, 'Der Ursprung des Kunstwerkes', in *Holzwege*, p. 7: 'On the usual view, the work arises out of and by means of the activity of the artist. But by what and whence is the artist what he is? By the work; for to say that the work does credit to the master means that it is the work that first lets the artist emerge as a master of his art. The artist is the origin of the work. The work is the origin of the artist.'

to use traditional aesthetic terminology, but subjects it to his own redefinition. Invoking the authority of Stendhal and Cocteau, he advocates a 'dédramatisation du génie' (*VP* 290) according to which genius should no longer be the sole prerogative of the artist: 'Le génie est là dès lors que quelqu'un existe, agit, marche, sourit, parle d'une façon inimitable, unique, évoquant l'infini que contient tout acte créateur' (*VP* 288). Genius and creativity are democratized, and Tournier seems opposed to the Romantic myth of the artist as a privileged being.

Tournier insists that the receiver should participate in the creative act. Indeed, the degree of participation may be used to establish a hierarchy of the arts. Films require only passive acceptance from their spectators, whereas poetry, 'le plus éminent des arts', demands a large degree of active involvement from the reader (*VP* 169). Criticism, as a form of reading, must be creative, and the critic of a literary text may 'recognize' qualities of which the author was unaware: 'Car la vraie critique doit être créatrice et "voir" dans l'œuvre des richesses qui y sont indiscutablement, mais que l'auteur n'y avait pas mises' (*VP* 203; see also *Vol* 54).

In theory, then, Tournier relinquishes mastery over his own texts and allows the reader a significant degree of creative freedom. However, all too often Tournier's comments on his own fiction do not accord with his theoretical positions. He is clearly still attempting to control the meaning and reception of his texts, when, for example, he repudiates any reading of *Le Roi des aulnes* which concentrates on its historical setting rather than the formal prominence of *phorie*. He refers to 'cette "phorie" qui constitue le seul sujet du roman' (*VP* 53), and later, using almost exactly the same phrase, 'cette notion de phorie qui constitue le seul véritable sujet du roman' (*VP* 120).[2] Referring to *Les Météores*, Tournier warns against 'un risque de contresens' if readers take Alexandre as anything other than a secondary character (*VP* 250). This desire to defend his fiction

---

[2] See also Tournier's 'Lettre-préface' to Manfred S. Fischer, *Probleme internationaler Literaturrezeption: Michel Tourniers ,,Le Roi des aulnes" im deutsch-französischen Kontext*, p. 9. In this case Tournier's comments can be explained by the fact that they are directed specifically at the German-speaking readers of Fischer's study. As Fischer reports, some critics, notably Jean Améry, had accused *Le Roi des aulnes* of coming dangerously close to espousing Nazi ideology. Tournier attempts to disarm such a reading and defend his own text by highlighting the formal aspects of the work.

against what he regards as deviant readings is accompanied by an aggressive gesture of mastery over other critics. Tournier lambasts those readers of *Le Roi des aulnes* who draw 'false' conclusions from Tiffauges's interest in pre-adolescent boys: 'Car il est clair que l'interprétation pédérastique que des critiques paresseux, expéditifs ou laborieusement malveillants ont parfois donné d'Abel Tiffauges va à l'encontre de toute la ligne du roman' (*VP* 117). Tournier claims a privileged and indisputable insight into the meaning of his own texts, and anyone who disagrees is dismissed as 'paresseux', 'expéditif', or 'laborieusement malveillant'. The reader of Tournier's texts is free to see 'des richesses [. . .] que l'auteur n'y avait pas mises' (*VP* 203); but the freedom of the critic may be withdrawn if he sees defects in the work, or proposes an interpretation contrary to Tournier's own reading. Tournier's reader may apparently praise, but not blame.

Tournier contests the Romantic myth of the artist by his 'dédramatisation du génie' and the democratization of creativity. But he has not entirely discarded the Romantic heritage. His provocative defence of the executed collaborator Robert Brasillach, on the grounds that he wrote better than his judges, entails the full-blooded reinstatement of the myth of the artist. The humble Reader must listen in awe to the polemic of the Author:

Moi, écrivain français, j'ai le privilège de par ma francité supérieure de pouvoir si bon me semble accabler la France des pires critiques, des injures les plus sales, vous qui me lisez, si vous n'êtes pas vous-même écrivain français, je vous accorde tout juste le droit de m'écouter debout et découvert, comme si vous entendiez *La Marseillaise*. (*VP* 86)

The title essay in *Le Vol du vampire* (1981) represents an attempt to develop the disparate comments on reading in *Le Vent Paraclet*. Published four years after Tournier's autobiographical essay, it gives evidence that the author has read a certain amount of literary theory, especially Sartre's 'Qu'est-ce que la littérature?', and that he is at least aware of some more recent thought on the problems of literary meaning. After the provocative stance adopted in *Le Vent Paraclet*, Tournier now makes a show of respect for his reader. The 'liberté créatrice du lecteur' must not be compromised, he claims (*Vol* 14; see also *Vol* 11). True creation is contagious and appeals to 'la créativité des lecteurs' (*Vol* 11).[3] The reader contributes to the creation of

---

[3] See also *GMB* 77; 'Car le spectacle de la création doit être contagieux, et les chefs-d'œuvre ne sont pleinement eux-mêmes que lorsqu'ils suscitent la naissance

meaning, becoming the 'indispensable collaborateur de l'écrivain' (*Vol* 10). Readers are the 'co-auteurs' of the text (*Vol* 16), so that no work is the product of a single author–creator: 'Un livre n'a pas un auteur, mais un nombre indéfini d'auteurs. Car à celui qui l'a écrit, s'ajoutent de plein droit dans l'acte créateur l'ensemble de ceux qui l'ont lu, le lisent ou le liront' (*Vol* 10). The author accords equality to his reader, since it is only through the act of reading that the book acquires full existence: 'Un livre écrit, mais non lu, n'existe pas pleinement' (*Vol* 10). Unread, the book is pure virtuality (*Vol* 10), awaiting the 'actualisation effectuée par le lecteur' (*Vol* 24) to realize its latent potential.

Ever since *Les Météores* Tournier has insisted upon the virtual coexistence of contradictory states within the work of art. Shonïn, the Japanese sage, asserts that 'le jardin Zen contient en puissance toutes les saisons de l'année, tous les paysages du monde, toutes les nuances de l'âme' (*M* 455). This perception of infinite possibilities informs a more general theory of art. In Urs Kraus's portraits, his girlfriend Kumiko appears simultaneously as child, adolescent, and old woman; these 'expressions aussi contradictoires' are possible because the artist captures 'l'élan vital à sa source même, au point où toutes les implications sont encore réunies à l'état virtuel' (*M* 463).[4] All possibilities are simultaneously present; contradictory perceptions arise when the observer focuses upon particular qualities contained within the virtual plenitude of the artwork (see *M* 455 and 463).

Tournier conceives the literary text, like the painting, as being full of contradictory meanings, eliciting radically opposed—but nevertheless equally appropriate—responses from different readers. Despite his frequent references to the importance of content and the philosophical foundation of his fiction (see, for example, *VP* 174 and 190), in 'Le Vol du vampire' Tournier accepts that literature, as opposed to non-fictional texts, should have no pre-inscribed, intentional meaning: 'Mais, s'il s'agit d'un poème, d'un roman ou d'une pièce de théâtre, la présence d'une thèse, exposée explicitement et s'imposant sans ambiguïté, nuit gravement à la valeur de l'œuvre

---

d'autres chefs-d'œuvre.' For further discussion of Tournier's theory of reading, see Michael J. Worton, 'Use and Abuse of Metaphor in Tournier's "Le Vol du vampire" '.

[4] For discussion of Paul's reference to Bergson's *élan vital*, see ch. 5, sec. (iii) and n. 36. On the virtualities of the work of art, see also *Canada: Journal de voyage*, p. 128.

[. . .] Un roman peut certes contenir une thèse, mais il importe que ce soit le lecteur, non l'écrivain, qui l'y ait mise' (*Vol* 14; see also *Vol* 375). Meaning is produced through the interaction of reader and text rather than originating in conscious authorial intention. In *Le Vent Paraclet*, Tournier refers to the pluri-dimensionality of myth (see *VP* 183–4); but it is clear there that the naïve reading of the child and the sophisticated reading of the metaphysician (Tournier refers to Deleuze's essay on *Vendredi ou les limbes du Pacifique*) complete and enrich, rather than positively contradict, one another. In 'Le Vol du vampire', the radical absence of determinate meaning has replaced the different *levels* of meaning in the mythological novel. No single reading, not even one which accounts for the pluri-dimensionality of myth, exhausts the virtualities of the text. In consequence, different interpretations may be contradictory without being mutually exclusive.

As in *Le Vent Paraclet*, Tournier uses conventional terms such as 'inspiration' and 'création', but, following Paul Valéry,[5] he situates them in the experience of reading rather than the act of writing; and, despite his traditional terminology, his views bear comparison with the thought of contemporary theorists. His discussion recalls, for example, the dissolution of the privilege of the author in structuralist criticism; and the rejection of any single pre-inscribed meaning in the literary text and the emphasis on the creative role of reading recall Barthes's description of the 'texte scriptible' in *S/Z*. As opposed to the 'texte lisible', in which the reader passively receives the author's message, Barthes's 'texte scriptible' or 'texte pluriel' transforms its reader into a 'producteur de texte'.[6] Tournier interprets structuralist and post-structuralist theory in the light of his own interests. He takes the plurality of possible readings as evidence of the infinite virtualities of the literary text and the creativity of the reading public:

Car l'interprétation — tendancieuse ou non — relève de la seule compétence du lecteur, et la pluralité des interprétations — à la limite aussi nombreuses que les lecteurs eux-mêmes — mesure la valeur et la richesse de l'invention poétique, romanesque ou théâtrale du public [. . .] De ce point de vue le critère du chef-d'œuvre est facile à définir: c'est la participation à la joie créatrice qu'il offre à son lecteur. (*Vol* 14, 19)

---

[5] Tournier refers to Valéry's insistence that inspiration should be a state induced in the reader rather than the condition of the poet; see *Vol* 24, *VP* 169, and *M* 455. Valéry discusses the idea to which Tournier refers on several occasions; see, e.g., Paul Valéry, 'Propos sur la poésie', in *Œuvres*, i. 1378.

[6] See Roland Barthes, *S/Z*, pp. 9–10.

The most important single influence on 'Le Vol du vampire' is Sartre's 'Qu'est-ce que la littérature?'. In his early discussion of literature Sartre affirms that 'la lecture est création',[7] and argues that the novel exists only through an exchange with its reader: 'Mais l'opération d'écrire implique celle de lire comme son corrélatif dialectique et ces deux actes connexes nécessitent deux agents distincts [. . .] Il n'y a d'art que pour et par autrui.'[8] The key terms in the relationship between author and reader are creation and freedom: 'Ainsi l'auteur écrit pour s'adresser à la liberté des lecteurs et il la requiert de faire exister son œuvre. Mais il ne se borne pas là et il exige en outre qu'ils lui retournent cette confiance, qu'ils reconnaissent sa liberté créatrice et qu'ils la sollicitent à leur tour par un appel symétrique et inverse.'[9] Clear references to 'Qu'est-ce que la littérature?' indicate Tournier's knowledge of and debt to Sartre's account of reading;[10] and Tournier also reproduces one of the central paradoxes of Sartre's early essay. In 'Qu'est-ce que la littérature?' Sartre affirms that 'la lecture est création', but also that 'la lecture est création *dirigée*'.[11] The reader creates, but is nevertheless dependent upon the generosity of the text. What he creates is already *given* in the work of art: 'En un mot, le lecteur a conscience de dévoiler et de créer à la fois, de dévoiler en créant, de créer par dévoilement.'[12] As Sartre explains two pages later, the reader's creativity is required to give existence to what is in fact already present in the text: 'Ainsi, pour le lecteur, tout est à faire et tout est déjà fait.'[13] On the one hand, Sartre affirms that reading is a free creative act; on the other hand, it is also 'un genre de fascination':[14] the reader is possessed and compromised by the work of art. Tournier rediscovers this paradox in the ambiguity of the word 'inventer', which means 'to invent' but also, in its legal and etymological sense, 'to find' (Tournier quotes the phrase 'l'inventeur d'un trésor').[15] The

---

[7] Jean-Paul Sartre, 'Qu'est-ce que la littérature?', in *Situations*, ii. 107.

[8] Ibid. 93.   [9] Ibid. 101.

[10] Tournier explicitly refers to *Situations*, ii, in *Vol* 15; he also borrows a chapter heading from Sartre's early work when he asks the question 'Pour qui écrit-on?' (*Vol* 20), and his subsequent analysis of literary patronage shows a clear debt to Sartre's discussion.

[11] Sartre, *Situations*, ii. 107 and 95 respectively; my emphasis on 'dirigée'.

[12] Ibid. 94.   [13] Ibid. 96.

[14] See Sartre, *L'Imaginaire: Psychologie phénoménologique de l'imagination*, p. 217.

[15] See *Vol* 54: 'Nous retrouvons ici l'admirable ambiguïté de mot *inventer* qui veut dire couramment créer de toutes pièces, et, juridiquement, découvrir ce qui existait auparavant à l'état dissimulé (le code civil parle de "l'inventeur d'un trésor").' 'I find'

reader both creates and finds what is already present in the text: 'C'est cela la dimension fictive: cette co-création par le receveur des images et des impressions qu'il reçoit de l'auteur' (*Vol* 19). Reading is creative, Tournier's rhetoric suggests, in as far as the text allows it to be so. Whereas Sartre's reader is *fascinated* by the text, Tournier's is *infected* as if by a contagious disease: 'Ainsi toute création se veut-elle *fondamentalement contagieuse* [. . .] Tous les sentiments incarnés dans tous les personnages [. . .] doivent être *doués de contagiosité* et se retrouver dans le cœur du lecteur' (*Vol* 11, 17; my emphasis).

For Tournier, as for Sartre, the reader is less free in respect of the text than the rhetoric of 'Le Vol du vampire' or 'Qu'est-ce que la littérature?' would have us believe. At moments it becomes clear that Tournier is not fully committed to his stated intention of respecting the liberty and creativity of his reader. He describes the text as a trap ensnaring an unsuspecting victim: 'Que signifie donc *majestueux*? Le dictionnaire nous l'apprend: empreint d'une gravité imposante. Rien d'incompatible avec la drôlerie: les deux mots se renforcent pour marquer seulement une mainmise irrésistible sur le spectateur ou le lecteur. Il est "pris". Il ne peut échapper à ce qu'on lui présente' (*Vol* 18). The reader or spectator is seized ('une mainmise irrésistible') and cannot escape. Even so, Tournier is not advocating a mode of writing which adopts the shock tactics of Sade or Genet. On the contrary, he insists that the reader should retain 'assez de liberté pour qu'il ne puisse se plaindre d'être "victime" d'une violence, même sous la forme d'un envoûtement' (*Vol* 18). The pleasure of reading may be used to ensnare more effectively than overt hostility. Tournier still insists that the reader retains a degree of freedom; but his own discussion indicates that respect for this 'freedom' may be a strategy of writing rather than the author's profound conviction. This possibility is suggested at the end of 'Le Vol du vampire', where Tournier shows a marked scorn for what he calls the 'écrivain de talent': 'il met en forme les idées, les sentiments et les rêves que la société lui a livrés à l'état brut' (*Vol* 22); he is 'le jouet doré d'une certaine société, son esclave favori, mais pas son maître' (*Vol* 23). The scorn for the merely talented author suggests Tournier's desire to be recognized as genius and the master of his audience. He disguises

is, of course, a common meaning of the Latin *invenio* and 'invent' is still used in the sense of 'find' in English archeological terminology.

his *hubris* by according his reader the freedom to participate in the act of creation. This theoretical liberation is nevertheless accompanied by a renewed gesture of mastery. Towards the end of the essay Tournier indicates the price he expects his reader to pay for his or her freedom: 'Je te donne mon livre, dit l'écrivain au lecteur, qu'il fasse de toi un inspiré, fais de moi un auteur de génie' (*Vol* 24). The reader is put in the paradoxical situation of a freed slave who still owes obedience to his former master.

Tournier's discussion of reading in 'Le Vol du vampire' begins with a series of analogies which are intended to illustrate the productive exchange between author, text, and reader. Without a reader, the book is 'une virtualité, un être exsangue': 'L'écrivain le sait, et lorsqu'il publie un livre, il lâche dans la foule anonyme des hommes et des femmes une nuée d'oiseaux de papier, des vampires secs, assoiffés de sang, qui se répandent au hasard en quête de lecteurs. A peine un livre s'est-il abattu sur un lecteur qu'il se gonfle de sa chaleur et de ses rêves' (*Vol* 10). Here, in the image from which 'Le Vol du vampire' draws its title, the virtual plenitude of the book appears as a radical *absence* of substance. The text is a vampire awaiting living prey, taking sustenance from the blood of its victims. In the following sentence, Tournier compares the author and the reader to the father and mother of the child–text. This suggests a sexual analogy: 'Ensuite, la lecture terminée, le livre [. . .] attendra un autre vivant afin de féconder à son tour son imagination' (*Vol* 11). The sexual analogy is extended as Tournier compares the book to 'un coq qui tamponne successivement un nombre indéfini de poules' (*Vol* 11). The word 'tamponne' suggests a sexual act which is impersonal, loveless, and perhaps even painful. The text seduces the reader; but this seduction is more like a rape, carried out whilst the victim is distracted by the book he is reading.

Tournier's concession to contemporary theory is less generous than it initially seems, and the liberation of the reader does not curtail his struggle for control over his own texts. The reader is confronted with an impossible double bind, being exhorted to create freely on the one hand, but to obey and lionize the author on the other; and the notion of reading-as-creation serves to ensure the reader's collaboration in his own demoralization: 'Mais comment plaire — ou faire plaisir — en communiquant à l'âme des sentiments qui au premier degré seraient déplaisants? La réponse est simple: en faisant en sorte que ce soit l'âme elle-même qui invente — ou co-invente avec l'écrivain ou l'auteur dramatique — ces sentiments' (*Vol* 19). Tournier accepts that reader and text should not be subordinate to the constraints of authorial intention or to any single tendentious interpretation. But the pleasure of reading can be used by the author as a means of exposing the reader to 'des sentiments qui au premier degré seraient déplaisants'. In his critical writing Tournier only unwillingly relinquishes control over the meaning of his fiction; and in *Gilles et Jeanne* he will attempt to use the semantic indeterminacy of the literary text as an instrument of his hostility towards the reader.

However, *Le Vol du vampire* reveals a final twist to Tournier's perception of the author–text–reader relationship in the essay on Perrault's story 'La Barbe bleue'. 'Barbe-Bleue ou le secret du conte' begins as an exercise in literary classification, as Tournier distinguishes between the *nouvelle*, the *fable*, and the *conte*. The *nouvelle* is characterized by 'un strict et gris réalisme'; it is 'dépourvue de toute signification, moralité ou autre message' (*Vol* 36). The *fable*, on the other hand, draws a moral lesson from what it describes: 'On ne peut fabuler sans enseigner' (*Vol* 37). As in the discussion of philosophy and poetry in *Le Vent Paraclet* (see *VP* 199–201), Tournier opposes two extremes in order to introduce an intermediary position which corresponds fully to neither pole of his own opposition and which is in consequence of particular interest to him. In *Le Vent Paraclet* it is the novel which has neither the transparency of philosophy nor the opacity of poetry; in *Le Vol du vampire* the *conte* occupies the intermediary position: 'A mi-chemin de l'opacité brutale de la nouvelle et de la transparence cristalline de la fable, le conte [. . .] se présente comme un milieu translucide, mais non transparent, comme une épaisseur glauque dans laquelle le lecteur voit se dessiner des figures qu'il ne parvient jamais à saisir tout à fait' (*Vol* 37). The *conte* is a *nouvelle* masquerading as a *fable*. It hints at the presence of a disguised message but ultimately proves to be 'indéchiffrable' (*Vol* 37). At the end of 'La Barbe bleue' Perrault makes a mockery of his reader's anticipation of meaning by drawing an ironic lesson from his story which Tournier summarizes as: 'la curiosité est un vilain défaut!' (*Vol* 40).[16] At the end of Tournier's *Gilles et Jeanne* the testimony of François Prélat at Gilles de Rais's trial plays a similar role: Prélat's explanation explains nothing.

---

[16] Tournier is referring to 'La Barbe bleue', in *Contes de Perrault*, p. 128: 'La curiosité malgré tous ses attraits / Coûte souvent bien des regrets.'

Most significantly, however, it is not only the reader who is compromised by the text. Tournier imagines Perrault when he has almost completed 'La Barbe bleue', 'la plume en l'air, pris au piège du conte qui nous fait sans cesse soupçonner une signification, mais se refuse toujours à passer aux aveux' (*Vol* 40). The author is caught in the trap of his own text, since he too awaits the meaning which the *conte* never delivers. Perrault appends a false moral to his story: 'Évidemment il se moque de nous, il se moque de lui-même' (*Vol* 40). As we shall see, in this account of Perrault's self-mockery Tournier describes a benign version of his own sense of estrangement from his work.

(ii) *Paradox:* Gaspard, Melchior et Balthazar *and* Gilles et Jeanne

'There can be no intermediate between contradictories; any given predicate must be either affirmed or denied of the same subject.'[17] With this definition of the Law of Excluded Middle, Aristotle insists upon a binary logic of truth and falsehood. In similar vein, the Law of Contradiction, described as 'the most certain of all principles' and 'this ultimate law on which all others rest',[18] states that, 'The same attribute cannot at the same time belong and not belong to the same subject in the same respect.'[19] Since Aristotle, philosophers have tended to dismiss paradox as nonsense, confusion, or error. Literary authors, on the other hand, have often allowed paradox to become an essential element of their style and of their perception of reality in spite of, or because of, the offence to logic which it entails. Tournier enjoys paradox; however, an important tendency in his writing, most evident in *Gaspard, Melchior et Balthazar*, suggests that opposing attributes are only apparently or provisionally in conflict, and that they may be ultimately resolved in the light of a higher truth. *Gilles et Jeanne*, on the other hand, allows no such resolution, and

[17] Aristotle, *Metaphysics*, 'The Law of Excluded Middle', p. 142.
[18] Aristotle, *Metaphysics*, 'The Axioms Included in the Object of Metaphysics', pp. 123 and 124. In recent years this view has been challenged by thinkers working outside the Anglo-American analytic tradition; see, for example, Deleuze, *Logique du sens*, p. 9: 'Le bon sens est l'affirmation que, en toutes choses, il y a un sens déterminable; mais le paradoxe est l'affirmation des deux sens à la fois.'
[19] Aristotle, *Metaphysics*, 'The Axioms Included in the Object of Metaphysics', p. 123.

in that text Tournier uses paradox in an attempt to unsettle the reader's expectations of intelligibility.

In *Gaspard, Melchior et Balthazar* the resolution of paradox and conflict is made possible by the miracle of Bethlehem, which unites God and man in the person of Christ. Tournier's fourth novel adopts a recapitulatory mode of narration, which shows the repetition of psychological, political, and metaphysical conflicts in the lives of Gaspard, Melchior, Balthazar, and Herod. The birth of Christ interrupts the narrative and heralds a break within the conflictual cycle of history. Herod's search for reconciliation with his family and his subjects will never be successful because he will not recognize the significance of Christ's birth, but Gaspard, Melchior, and Balthazar return from Bethlehem with a message of hope. Christ represents the union of 'attributs incompatibles, la grandeur et la petitesse, la puissance et l'innocence, la plénitude et la pauvreté' (*GMB* 73).[20] Both human and divine, flesh and spirit, He embodies the 'impossible mariage de contraires inconciliables' (*GMB* 207). For Balthazar, this entails 'la réconciliation de l'image et de la ressemblance' (*GMB* 207);[21] Melchior, concerned with political power, learns 'la force de la faiblesse, la douceur irrésistible des non-violents' (*GMB* 211);[22] Gaspard, recovering from an ill-fated love affair, discovers 'la rencontre totale de l'amant et de l'aimé' (*GMB* 213). Like Gaspard in *Les Rois Mages*, Tournier's own rewriting of *Gaspard, Melchior et Balthazar*, each of the kings is 'guéri pour toujours, réconcilié avec lui-même et avec son peuple par le miracle de Bethléem'.[23]

Taor, the effete prince who appears in the final section of Tournier's novel, is given a trivial introduction to paradox when his envoys

---

[20] These apparently contradictory attributes do not in fact 'belong to the same subject in the same respect' (Aristotle, *Metaphysics*, p. 123): 'grandeur', 'puissance', and 'plénitude' are the *spiritual* attributes of Christ, whereas 'petitesse' and 'pauvreté' refer *literally* to the size and material conditions of the infant. The resolution of paradox is made possible when it is recognized that different levels of reference must be distinguished from one another. One of the important ways in which *Gilles et Jeanne* differs from *Gaspard, Melchior et Balthazar* is that the *récit* allows no such appeal to a spiritual dimension, in which paradoxes are resolved.

[21] On the distinction between 'image' and 'ressemblance', see *GMB* 45–6. The distinction is taken from the medieval theologian Saint Bernard of Clairvaux; see Étienne Gilson, *La Théologie mystique de Saint Bernard*, pp. 64–72. Tournier may have learned, or have been reminded of, the distinction from his reading of Zazzo; see Zazzo, *Les Jumeaux*, p. 513.

[22] On the strength of the weak, see also *M* 15.

[23] Tournier, *Les Rois Mages*, p. 41.

return from Judaea with a jar of locusts preserved in honey. Salt and sugar combine to surprising effect: ' — Moi qui déteste le sel, la sincérité m'oblige à proférer cette vérité stupéfiante: le sucré salé est plus sucré que le sucré sucré. Quel paradoxe!' (GMB 179). Having left his 'paradis puéril' (GMB 192) in search of the recipe for 'rahat loukoum' (Turkish delight), he discovers the conflict of adulthood as he gradually becomes estranged from his servant Siri and his pet elephant Yasmina. After his encounter with Gaspard, Melchior, and Balthazar on their return from Bethlehem, Taor is made increasingly aware of paradox. The children of Bethlehem enjoy a regal feast prepared by his cooks, culminating in a 'pièce montée' which evidently recalls the wedding cake in Flaubert's Madame Bovary;[24] at the same time, the infant brothers of the children are being slaughtered by Herod's troops. In Taor's mind, these scenes form 'deux images apparues en même temps, et pourtant violemment opposées' (GMB 227). However, the images of joy and massacre are united by 'une affinité secrète', so that, despite their contrast, they are 'd'une certaine façon complémentaires' (GMB 227). Now, Taor begins to anticipate the future resolution of paradox and conflict: 'Il y avait là un paradoxe intolérable, mais aussi une clef pleine de promesses' (GMB 227).

In the rest of the novel Taor is initiated to the paradoxes of Christianity exemplified in Christ's Sermon on the Mount (see GMB 261–2). Earlier, when Melchior was forced to beg for alms in his own kingdom, he referred to his experience as an 'Admirable et bénigne inversion!' (GMB 86). Undergoing a similar (properly Christian) reversal of fortunes, Prince Taor learns poverty and humility. At the same time, his life acquires meaning and finality: 'Il assistait subjugué à la métamorphose de sa vie en destin' (GMB 232). He learns the value of selflessness, accepting a thirty-three-year sentence in the saltmines of Sodom in place of another man. A fellow prisoner reports the words of Christ which retrospectively confirm the coherence of his own destiny (GMB 260); and his prolonged self-sacrifice prepares the most dramatic of all Christian inversions. The final words of the novel are 'le premier', as Taor is carried to Heaven after being the first to receive the Eucharist: 'Les deux anges, qui veillaient sur lui depuis sa libération, le cueillirent dans leurs

---

[24] Compare GMB 222–3 (where the phrase 'pièce montée' is used twice) with the 'pièce montée' at Emma Bovary's wedding in Gustave Flaubert, Madame Bovary, p. 33.

grandes ailes, et, le ciel nocturne s'étant ouvert sur d'immenses clartés, ils emportèrent celui qui, après avoir été le dernier, le perpétuel retardataire, venait de recevoir l'eucharistie le premier' (*GMB* 265). The last is the first, as Tournier's novel fulfils the pattern of benign inversion described by Christ Himself: 'For everyone who exalts himself shall be humbled; and whoever humbles himself will be exalted.'[25]

Gaspard, Melchior et Balthazar has the most unambiguous conclusion of any of Tournier's novels. Even so, Melchior expresses a telling reservation about this conclusion when he suggests that the reconciliation promised by the birth of Christ is effective in the spiritual dimension only. It does not entail any interruption in the cycle of historical conflict, since 'la violence et la peur sont les ingrédients inexorables du royaume terrestre' (*GMB* 210). What Melchior calls 'la concorde parfaite' will never be achieved on earth: 'Le royaume de Dieu ne sera jamais donné une fois pour toutes ici ou là' (*GMB* 212). Melchior will withdraw from society and found a community of like-minded believers, all living 'dans l'attente de l'Avènement' (*GMB* 212), in a state of permanent expectation of a revolution which they know will never occur in *this* world. Like Tiffauges, Taor must pay for his final transcendence with his life, since only death gives access to the other-worldly domain in which conflict is resolved.

The Sodomites, to whom Tournier devotes a short section of *Gaspard, Melchior et Balthazar* have 'une vision en ombres noires, anguleuses, coupantes, plongeant dans des abîmes vertigineux': 'Chez le Sodomite, toute hauteur de vue se résolvait en analyse fondamentale, toute ascendance en pénétration, toute théologie en ontologie, et la joie d'accéder à la lumière de l'intelligence était glacée par l'effroi du chercheur nocturne qui fouille les soubassements de l'être' (*GMB* 253–4). Here, philosophical vocabulary acquires scatological and sexual connotations ('*analyse* fondamentale', 'pénétration', 'soubassements de l'être').[26] But Tournier (regrettably, perhaps) does not dwell on the Sodomite perspective. In his novel of resolved

---

[25] Luke 14: 11; see *GMB* 259, which refers to the parable from which this is taken.

[26] On the relationship between philosophy and scatology, see Tournier's much-quoted remark in *Le Vent Paraclet*, which clearly should not be taken too seriously: 'Eh bien, c'est un fait, on dirait que jetée dans le creuset romanesque, l'ontologie se métamorphose partiellement en scatologie!' (*VP* 257).

conflict, he substitutes theological hope for the 'abîmes vertigineux' opened up by existential analysis. *Gaspard, Melchior et Balthazar* is, for Tournier, an unusually benign text. Like Taor, the reader undertakes a journey into conflict and paradox, but finally sees the possibility of transcendent resolution. In *Gilles et Jeanne* Tournier's treatment of paradox allows the reader no such recourse to a higher level of truth in which incompatibles coexist without friction.

Perhaps the most important immediate source of *Gilles et Jeanne* is Tournier's own *Le Roi des aulnes*, from which images and episodes, as well as the discussion of malign and benign inversions, are taken.[27] But the *récit* also uses and alludes to a wide range of other texts in a manner which, one critic has suggested, has more to do with plagiarism than intertextuality.[28] Huysmans's *Là-bas*, which includes a short biography of Gilles de Rais, Perrault's 'Le Petit Poucet' (see *GJ* 53–5) and 'La Barbe bleue' (the legendary Bluebeard is often confused with the historical Gilles de Rais), and *Gilles und Jeanne* by the German Expressionist dramatist Georg Kaiser, are evident precursors.[29] Another important source, which will also provide a useful point of comparison, is *Le Procès de Gilles de Rais*, an account of Gilles de Rais's life and crimes by George Bataille, published together with documents translated by Pierre Klossowski. Bataille and Tournier share a common attraction to the gruesome story of Gilles de Rais and they use many of the same details in their accounts; both authors, for example, recount Gilles de Rais's habit of choosing, and then kissing the severed head of his most attractive victim.[30] Details such as this are historically attested, and, as in previous texts, Tournier attempts to integrate historical research into a literary narrative. However, Bataille and Tournier seem to

---

[27] Compare, e.g., *RA* 22–3 (the incident with Pelsenaire's knee) with *GJ* 28 and *RA* 316–18 (the capture of Lothar) with *GJ* 52–3. For further discussion of the relationship between *Le Roi des aulnes* and *Gilles et Jeanne*, see Susan Petit, '*Gilles et Jeanne*: Tournier's *Le Roi des aulnes* Revisited'.

[28] See Colin Nettelbeck, 'The Return of the Ogre: Michel Tournier's *Gilles et Jeanne*', p. 43: 'it is difficult even to approach [Tournier's] work without being confronted by questions of plagiarism.'

[29] The article by Colin Nettelbeck drew my attention to the play by Georg Kaiser and its importance for Tournier's *récit*. Tournier acknowledges his debt to Huysmans in *Des clefs et des serrures*, p. 194. For discussion of the distinction between Gilles de Rais and the 'Barbe bleue' of legend and of Perrault's short story, see Georges Bataille, *Le Procès de Gilles de Rais*, pp. 11–16.

[30] Compare Bataille, *Le Procès de Gilles de Rais*, p. 49, and *GJ* 132.

make quite different use of the same material.[31] In *Le Procès de Gilles de Rais* Bataille describes the frustration of one of the judges, Pierre de l'Hôpital, when confronted with the lack of motivation for Gilles de Rais's crimes:

Ce que demande le président de l'Hôpital est simple. C'est ce que veut savoir un homme que la raison commande. Pourquoi Gilles a tué? à la suite de quelles instigations, de quels exemples, il procéda de cette manière, non d'une autre? L'explication du crime importe au juge. . . A l'opposé, Gilles n'aperçoit qu'une vérité tragique, monstrueuse, dont il fut l'expression aveugle. Ce fatal besoin de tuer, de tuer sans raison, qu'aucune phrase ne pouvait éclairer, qui l'avait tenu comme le galop tient la bête emballée. . . Il n'importait pas au coupable d'apprendre ou de révéler l'origine de ses crimes. En lui, ces crimes avaient été ce qu'il était lui-même, ce qu'il était profondément, tragiquement, si bien qu'il n'imagina rien d'autre. Aucune explication.[32]

The key terms in Bataille's account are *frénésie*, *ivresse*, *démesure*, *déraison*. Refusing any explanation which relies upon notions of purpose and utility, Bataille accepts the lacunae in his own account. For him, Gilles de Rais's experience transgresses the limits of reason and so remains intractable to rational explanation.

Tournier's extensive use of quotation from historical documents, as well as the references to exact dates and locations, serve to give *Gilles et Jeanne* a firm grounding in historical reality. At the same time, *Gaspard, Melchior et Balthazar* and *Gilles et Jeanne* are written 'dans les blancs laissés par les textes sacrés et historiques'.[33] In his attempt to explain Gilles de Rais's crimes, Tournier uses his *récit* to *complete* the story told in the historical texts which he has consulted. Moreover, he feels free to modify historical detail when it suits his purpose. The final lines of the *récit* are a case in point. At the end of his trial Gilles de Rais was condemned to be burned at the stake. Bataille demonstrates with historical documents that Gilles, unlike Jeanne d'Arc, was already dead when he was tied to the stake and that his body was removed from the pyre before being

---

[31] In detail also Tournier seems to take issue with Bataille. The account of Gilles de Rais's assault on the castle of Saint-Étienne-de-Mermorte given in *Gilles et Jeanne* appears to be a direct refutation of Bataille's interpretation of the incident; compare *GJ* 106 and Bataille, *Le Procès de Gilles de Rais*, pp. 83–4.

[32] Bataille, *Le Procès de Gilles de Rais*, pp. 20–1.

[33] Quoted from the 'Prière d'insérer' to the 'Folio' edition of *Gilles et Jeanne* (Folio 1707, published 1985), p. 5.

consumed by flame.[34] With total disregard for historical evidence, Tournier accentuates the parallels between the deaths of Jeanne and Gilles by having Gilles burned alive at the stake, so that he can call out for Jeanne as she had called for Jesus.

Tournier's modifications of historical facts serve to reinforce the coherence of his narrative. Whereas Bataille confronts his reader with an experience which defies rational explanation, Tournier reassures his public by implying that reason, sanity, and intelligibility retain their privilege over their most disturbing contraries. The ruse of Tournier's text is in the suggestion that, initially at least, there is nothing extraordinary in the experience of Gilles de Rais. He is described as 'un brave garçon de son temps, ni pire ni meilleur qu'un autre, d'une intelligence médiocre, mais profondément croyant' (*GJ* 14). Neither better nor worse than his contemporaries, he appears to be a noble Christian, aware of the dark side of his nature, but sincerely seeking salvation through Jeanne d'Arc (see *GJ* 22). As in *Le Roi des aulnes*, the initial ordinariness of Tournier's protagonist makes the revelation of his latent sadistic qualities and the escalation of his crimes all the more striking. In *Le Vent Paraclet* and *Le Vol du vampire* Tournier insists that the reader should identify with and then be exalted and ennobled by the heroes of fiction through a process which he calls 'auto-hagiographie' (*VP* 220; see also *Vol* 17). But his practice hardly concurs with his theory. The ordinariness of Gilles de Rais develops into an extraordinary experience of Evil, and Tournier's aim is to mislead rather than to ennoble his reader.

François Prélat proposes a provocative moral defence of his employer's conversion to Evil. He echoes the Gnostic belief that 'le mal s'explique par l'ignorance'[35] when he assures Père Blanchet that 'Toute science est bonne! L'ignorance c'est le mal, purement et simplement' (*GJ* 83). The search for knowledge is represented as the perilous endeavour to save light from darkness: 'Il faut plonger, père Blanchet, il faut avoir le courage de plonger dans les ténèbres pour en rapporter la lumière' (*GJ* 68). If knowledge is accepted as a supreme value, then Evil practised in the pursuit of knowledge must ultimately be recognized as Good. Gilles de Rais, under the guidance of Prélat, combats Evil through Evil and seeks redemption through

---

[34] See Bataille, *Le Procès de Gilles de Rais*, pp. 92–3, 335.

[35] Serge Hutin, *Les Gnostiques*, p. 18; see also p. 125 for a list of Gnostic themes in modern literature which correspond to elements of Tournier's fiction.

crime.[36] Prélat argues that his master may one day, like Jeanne d'Arc, be accepted as a saint (see *GJ* 137).

In some Gnostic cosmogonies, the God of Light is carefully distinguished from the Evil Demiurge, sometimes identified as the Old Testament Jehovah, who is responsible for the creation of the material world. Jehovah is considered to have imprisoned man in a world of ignorance and misery; Lucifer, identified with the serpent in Eden, initiates Adam and Eve to knowledge of Good and Evil and so helps them advance towards Good.[37] In *Le Roi des aulnes* Tiffauges asserts that the Fall of man should not be situated 'dans l'épisode de la pomme — qui marque une promotion au contraire, l'accession à la connaissance du bien et du mal' (*RA* 26; see also *CB* 56–7). In consequence, as *Gilles et Jeanne* makes explicit, Lucifer may be seen as an agent of redemption rather than damnation. Prélat seems unconcerned by Blanchet's warning that his quest for knowledge may be motivated by 'quelque chose de diabolique': ' — Diabolique? Pourquoi pas? Le Diable pourrait bien avoir lui aussi sa raison d'être' (*GJ* 68). Like the Guardian Angel in Claudel's *Le Soulier de satin*, Prélat believes that, in the quest for salvation, 'Le péché aussi sert.'[38] Of course, Prélat goes much further than Claudel in his revaluation of sin and the designation of contingent Evil as ultimate Good. Far from being a force of darkness, Lucifer is literally the 'Bearer of Light', a necessary intermediary between man and God:

N'oubliez pas que Lucifer — le Porte-Lumière — était originellement le plus beau des anges. On en fait le Prince des ténèbres, le Mal absolu. C'est une erreur! L'homme, pétri de fange et animé par le souffle de Dieu, a besoin d'un intercesseur entre Dieu et lui. Comment voulez-vous qu'il entre directement en rapport avec Dieu? Il a besoin d'un intercesseur, oui, et qui soit son complice dans tout le mal qu'il pense et qu'il fait, mais qui possède aussi ses entrées dans le ciel. (*GJ* 82–3)

Gilles et Jeanne is Tournier's most provocative treatment of the ambiguity which frustrates man's search for semantic, moral, and metaphysical certainty. One of the principal themes of the *récit* is the failure to make an adequate distinction between irreconcilable opposites:[39]

---

[36] On the search for redemption through crime, see ibid. 70–2.
[37] See ibid. 74.
[38] See Paul Claudel, *Le Soulier de satin*, in *Théâtre*, ii. 819.
[39] Jean Anouilh also raises the problem of distinguishing between God and the Devil in *L'Alouette*, his version of the story of Joan of Arc; see, for example,

— Il y a un feu en toi. Je le crois de Dieu, mais il est peut-être d'enfer. Le
bien et le mal sont toujours proches l'un de l'autre. De toutes les créatures,
Lucifer était le plus semblable à Dieu. (*GJ* 27)

— Ce qui me trouble, oui, dans la pitié, c'est l'immense volupté que j'y trouve
[. . .] Mon père, cette pitié-là est-elle de Dieu ou du Diable? (*GJ* 48)

Qu'est-ce que c'est que cette odeur? [. . .] Mais dites-moi, est-ce une odeur
de fagot ou une odeur de sainteté? (*GJ* 56–7)

Il y a d'immenses clartés en vous, mais j'ignore s'il s'agit de la lumière du
ciel ou des flammes de l'enfer.

C'était relancer Prélat sur l'un de ses thèmes favoris.

— Lumière du ciel et flammes de l'enfer sont plus proches qu'on ne pense.
(*GJ* 82)

As Prélat explains, God and Satan share the same attributes; and
this similarity between what should be most radically opposed
invalidates all simple distinctions between Good and Evil:

— Seulement voyez-vous, seigneur Gilles, ajoutait-il [Prélat], si Yahvé aime
la chair fraîche et tendre des enfants, le Diable, qui est l'image de Dieu,
partage ces goûts. Comment en serait-il autrement? (*GJ* 101)

— Satan est l'image de Dieu, poursuivit Prelati avec une douceur affectée.
Une image inversée et difforme, certes, mais une image cependant. Il n'est
rien de Satan qui ne se retrouve en Dieu. (*GJ* 136)

Prélat resumes Tiffauges's meditation on the problem of inversions;
and, as we found in *Le Roi des aulnes*, he discovers that the *inversion
maligne* is made possible and uncontrollable because of the interdependence of malign and benign:

Le Florentin semblait fonder ses expériences sur l'ambiguïté fondamentale
du feu, lequel est vie et mort, pureté et passion, sainteté et damnation. Il
professait que le pèlerin du ciel — ainsi se nomme l'alchimiste en quête —
n'atteint l'un de ces pôles que pour se trouver aussitôt rejeté vers l'autre
pôle par un phénomène d'inversion, comme l'excès de froid provoque une
brûlure, ou comme le paroxysme de l'amour se confond avec la haine. Et
cette inversion pouvait être bénigne ou maligne. (*GJ* 98)

The alchemist's attempt to control the passage from negative to
positive poles will be frustrated because malign and benign already

---

pp. 48, 83. Ultimately, in Anouilh's play, Joan of Arc solves the problem by affirming
her faith in herself and hence by embracing a form of humanism which has no
equivalent in Tournier's *récit*.

coincide in the same states and the same actions: 'La Sainte Inquisition ne torturait et ne brûlait que dans un esprit de sollicitude maternelle' (*GJ* 98). In *Gilles et Jeanne*, as in the final section of *Le Roi des aulnes*, the interpenetration and mutual contamination of apparent incompatibles do not permit the reconciliation of opposites which seems to be promised in *Gaspard, Melchior et Balthazar*. In Tournier's *récit* the transcendent dimension is never presented as a realm of harmony and absolute justice in which earthly conflicts are resolved, since sacrifice is more essential than self-sacrifice (in the non-literal Christian sense) to man's striving for union with God. This is suggested most vividly by Prélat's (somewhat unorthodox) inter-pretation of the Crucifixion. Jehovah's lust for blood, illustrated in the stories of Cain and Abel and Abraham and Isaac (see *GJ* 100; see also *GMB* 166), culminates in the torture and sacrifice of his own son: 'Jésus, ah, cet enfant-là, Yahvé ne l'a pas manqué! Flagellation, croix, coup de lance. Le père céleste riait aux anges' (*GJ* 100).

At the end of *Gilles et Jeanne* François Prélat attempts to make Gilles's crimes intelligible to his accusers, as he had earlier justified them to his employer. However, Prélat knows less than he says; he is an agent of disinformation, who spreads confusion and invites distrust where he promises enlightenment. On the final page of the *récit* Gilles himself still believes in the possibility of his salvation: 'Suivez-moi dans mon salut, comme vous m'avez suivi dans mes crimes' (*GJ* 140). As yet, however, no rehabilitation has taken place, and the crimes of Gilles de Rais are neither explained nor justified by Prélat's most bold hypotheses concerning the convertibility of Evil into Good. In the light of this failure to give an adequate account for the experience of Evil, it becomes clear that Tournier's interest in the story of Gilles de Rais has a greater affinity with Georges Bataille's study than at first appears. Bataille simply confronts his reader with Gilles de Rais's pre-reflexive *déraison*, which frustrates all rational explanation. Tournier seems to tell a more coherent story, in which the most obscure paradoxes are explained by Prélat. But Prélat never succeeds in explaining the significance of Gilles's crimes. Nor is the ultimate 'meaning' of *Gilles et Jeanne* the rich plurality of possible interpretations which offers the reader what Tournier calls 'la participation à la joie créatrice' (*Vol* 19). At the core of *Gilles et Jeanne* lies the unsolved but urgent enigma of ethical limits and the limits of ethics:

En vérité je suis l'homme le plus exécrable qui fut jamais. L'énormité de ma faute est insurpassable.

Il y avait tant d'orgueil dans ces aveux que les juges se sentirent humiliés plus encore que sous les injures dont Gilles les avait accablés l'avant-veille. (*GJ* 121)

In *Gaspard, Melchior et Balthazar* Taor's experience parallels that of the reader, as both are confronted with paradoxes but shown the possibility of ultimate resolution through the union of man and God in Christ. The paradoxes encountered in *Gilles et Jeanne* are less benign, and this may be explained by Tournier's very different relationship with his putative reader, which is presented *en abyme* through the character of Eustache Blanchet, Gilles de Rais's confessor. Blanchet is blithely unaware of paradox when he makes his first appearance in the *récit*: 'Blanchet avait une âme sans détour et croyait sincèrement qu'à toutes les questions de foi et de morale, il existe une réponse simple et évidente' (*GJ* 47). The historical Blanchet was less innocent than he appears in *Gilles et Jeanne*.[40] Tournier portrays Blanchet as naïve in order to make him all the more susceptible to the disruptive encounter with paradox. Gilles de Rais confesses to the combination of 'pitié' and 'volupté' which he discovers in the suffering of others:

— Ce qui me trouble, oui, dans la pitié, c'est l'immense volupté que j'y trouve.

Du coup Blanchet sentit qu'il commençait à perdre pied. (*GJ* 48)

Confronted with the problem of distinguishing between God and the Devil (*GJ* 48) or 'une odeur de fagot' and 'une odeur de sainteté' (*GJ* 57), Blanchet can offer no solution. The process of discomfiture to which he is subjected culminates in his visit to the Florence of the early Renaissance and his encounter with François Prélat. Blanchet is 'ébloui et scandalisé' (*GJ* 58) by the spectacle of Renaissance Tuscany. He is equally dazzled and shocked by the vertiginous facility of Prélat's rhetoric. Prélat confronts Blanchet, as the text confronts the reader, with the 'incroyable paradoxe' (*GJ* 63) according to which wealth engenders selflessness, generosity, and charity;

---

[40] An indication of the fact that Blanchet was less innocent and naïve than he appears in *Gilles et Jeanne* is given by Bataille when he shows that Prelati was by no means the first necromancer whom he had procured for Gilles de Rais; see Bataille, *Le Procès de Gilles de Rais*, pp. 74–5.

life and death are described as inseparable (see *GJ* 66–7), and Heaven and Hell as indistinguishable (see *GJ* 82). Blanchet is fascinated and horrified by the web of contradictions in which he becomes entangled:

En vérité le pauvre Blanchet se débattait dans un réseau de contradictions qui le mettaient au supplice. A tout instant le spectacle de cette civilisation novatrice mais suspecte l'enchantait et l'effrayait, comme les propos de Prélat imposaient à son esprit des évidences inacceptables, découlant de raisonnements spécieux mais inattaquables. (*GJ* 75)

The discussion of art, which occurs in the middle of the episode in Florence and almost at the exact centre of the text, reinforces the impression that Blanchet's encounter with Prélat serves as a *mise en abyme* of Tournier's relationship with his reader. Tournier is disclosing the intended effect of his own narrative when he describes the disorientating effect of perspective on Blanchet:

Il lui semblait que l'image plate, édifiante, sage de sa pieuse enfance se gonflait soudain d'une force magique, se creusait, se tordait, se précipitait hors de ses limites, comme possédée par un esprit malin. Debout devant des fresques ou penché sur des gravures, il croyait voir se creuser sous ses yeux une profondeur vertigineuse qui l'aspirait, un abîme imaginaire où il avait l'affreuse tentation de plonger, la tête la première. Prélat au contraire nageait comme un poisson dans l'élément nouveau sécrété par l'art, la science et la philosophie modernes.

— Crever la surface des choses pour y voir des fantômes s'agiter, disait-il. Devenir soi-même l'un de ces fantômes. . . Par la perspective, le dessin fuit vers l'horizon lointain, mais il s'avance aussi et emprisonne le spectateur [. . .] La porte s'ouvre sur l'infini, mais vous vous trouvez définitivement compromis. C'est ça la perspective! (*GJ* 75–6)

Blanchet represents Tournier's fantasy of an innocent reader, lured into a world of paradox and definitively compromised. Prélat's verbal dexterity makes him an apt self-portrait of the novelist himself, taking pleasure in the demoralization of his victims: '— Prélat, vous me faites peur! On dirait que vous éprouvez un malin plaisir à m'épouvanter' (*GJ* 76). And Prélat knows that Blanchet will not be able to forget his experiences in Florence when he returns to France; the fruit of knowledge causes an irreversible fall from the paradise of ignorance: 'Vous savez bien que désormais plus rien ne sera pour vous comme avant votre voyage. Vous en avez trop vu, trop entendu

[. . .] Que vous le vouliez ou non, vous avez mangé du fruit de la connaissance, et vous n'êtes pas près d'en oublier le goût' (*GJ* 81–2).

Gide describes the tendency of the literary text to exceed the author's intentions and control as 'la part de Dieu'.[41] Sartre borrows the notion but refers instead to 'la part du diable'; and he also envisages the possibility that the novelist might use the uncontrollable aspects of language and the literary text as part of his intentional project. Genet, for example, is an author who explores the indeterminate grey areas of language, so that 'C'est le sens intentionnel qui, lui, sera non-sens'.[42] Given Tournier's admiration for both Gide and Sartre,[43] it seems probable that he is familiar with the ideas behind 'la part du diable'. Moreover, the actual phrase occurs twice in *Gilles et Jeanne*; and on both occasions it refers to the attempt to control and utilize what in principle cannot be controlled. On the first occasion, Blanchet reprimands Prélat for calling on Evil in the quest for knowledge: 'C'est la part du diable qu'on réserve, comme on fait la part du feu' (*GJ* 83). Prélat wants to cut his losses ('faire la part du feu'), giving the devil his due in order to minimize and utilize his power. Later, at Gilles de Rais's trial, Prélat reveals his formula for the invocation of the evil spirit Barron: 'Viens à ma volonté, et je te donnerai ce que tu voudras, excepté mon âme et l'abréviation de ma vie' (*GJ* 135).[44] The prosecutor seems sceptical about the possibility of making any such bargain with the Devil:

— Croyez-vous qu'on fait ainsi la part du Diable!
— Certainement. Il n'est que de savoir lui parler. (*GJ* 135)

These references to 'la part du diable' illustrates how *Gilles et Jeanne* is, amongst other things, a parable of writing. Tournier attempts to harness the text's self-liberation from the author's intended meaning by making ambiguity the ultimate signified of his

[41] For Gide's reference to 'la part de Dieu', see the 'Prière d'insérer' to *Paludes*, in *Romans, récits et soties, oeuvres lyriques*, p. 89.

[42] Jean-Paul Sartre, *Saint Genet, comédien et martyr*, p. 362. Although Sartre attributes the phrase 'la part du diable' to Gide, I have been unable to find an occasion on which Gide uses it with the meaning given to it by Sartre.

[43] As an indication of Tournier's admiration for Gide and Sartre, see 'Cinq clefs pour André Gide' and 'Jean-Paul Sartre, romancier cryptométaphysicien', both in *Le Vol du vampire*.

[44] This formula is authenticated by the documents of Gilles de Rais's trial; see *Le Procès de Gilles de Rais*, p. 253.

récit. However, inevitably, the author must at the same time renounce any privilege of adjudication over his own text. In *Le Vent Paraclet* Tournier describes his ambition to write philosophical novels informed by his studies of Descartes, Spinoza, Leibniz, Kant, and Husserl 'pour ne citer que quelques modèles majeurs' (*VP* 174–5). In *Le Vol du vampire*, on the other hand, the novel is described in terms of radical emptiness rather than latent plenitude: 'C'est une virtualité, un être exsangue, vide, malheureux qui s'épuise dans un appel à l'aide pour exister' (*Vol* 10). Devoid of substance, the text only comes into existence when it feeds off the blood of its reader–victims. And the author of the text fares no better than his reader. In *Le Vent Paraclet* Tournier describes how he becomes estranged from his own creation. Here, it is the author who is made victim of the vampire–text: 'Je vis dans la servitude d'un monstre naissant, croissant, multipliant, aux exigences péremptoires [. . .] à l'appétit dévorant, l'œuvre pie, la pieuvre. . . Et quand elle me lâche, quand gorgée de ma substance elle commence à rouler de par le monde, je gis exsangue, vidé, écœuré, épuisé, hanté par des idées de mort' (*VP* 179). In *La Part du feu* Blanchot describes, in strikingly similar terms, the state between life and death to which the author is condemned by his own work:

L'écrivain se sent la proie d'une puissance impersonnelle qui ne le laisse ni vivre ni mourir: l'irresponsabilité qu'il ne peut surmonter devient la traduction de cette mort sans mort qui l'attend au bord du néant; l'immortalité littéraire est le mouvement même par lequel, jusque dans le monde, un monde miné par l'existence brute, s'insinue la nausée d'une survie qui n'en est pas une, d'une mort qui ne met fin à rien.[45]

The author is subject to contradictory imperatives which he can never reconcile: 'Efface le lecteur' | 'Efface-toi devant le lecteur', 'Écris pour ne rien dire' | 'Écris pour dire quelque chose.'[46] Tournier insists that he writes in order to be read (see *Vol* 10), but paternal benevolence towards the reader is revealed, in *Le Vol du vampire*, as disguised hostility. Author and reader are compromised by the vampiric text; and reading completes the cycle of aggression and estrangement which begins when the author first raises his pen.

Despite his indications to the contrary, Tournier is clearly not ready to abandon his text to the self-engendering play of writing and

---

[45] Maurice Blanchot, *La Part du feu*, p. 327.   [46] See ibid. 303–4.

the freely creative act of reading. In *Gilles et Jeanne* ambiguity and paradox are privileged themes which serve the author's provocative intentions rather than signs of the independence of the text from intentional meaning. Tournier sets out too deliberately to locate, delineate, and utilize 'la part du diable', and for that reason he necessarily fails: the uncontrollable always resides somewhere *other* than where the author attempts to isolate it. *Gilles et Jeanne* compares unfavourably with Tournier's earlier, more substantial fiction; and perhaps the 'part du diable' makes its presence felt in the *récit* through Tournier's failure to reproduce the disruptive power of his immediate source, *Le Roi des aulnes*.

5

Art and Truth

(i) *Theoretical Positions*

Visual art occupies a privileged but ambiguous position in Tournier's writing. The image is an object of respect and fear, and the conflict between the iconoclasts and the art-lovers in *Gaspard, Melchior et Balthazar* indicates an ambivalence which is reflected throughout Tournier's fiction. On the one hand, art seems capable of depicting the very essence of its subject; on the other hand, especially in *La Goutte d'or*, the image is endowed with a malicious force which seems to justify its suppression. Tournier's practice is no less ambivalent in his two books of commentaries on photographs, *Vues de dos* and *Des clefs et des serrures*. The commentary aims to elucidate the image, but also distracts from the image by foregrounding language. Only once is Tournier interrupted by the realization that the photograph contains something which resists his commentary: 'L'image est belle, chargée de secrets et de symboles indéchiffrés. Consentons pour une fois à n'être qu'un œil.'[1] Even if, for once, Tournier acknowledges his inability to decipher the secret of the photograph, he does not abandon the assumption that it contains a disguised message which only the hermeneut can raise to the dignity of language.

This conception of visual art as a form of language underlies Tournier's opposition to much contemporary thinking on the subject. Lyotard, for example, writes that, 'on ne peint pas pour parler, mais pour se taire'; if paintings are 'absolument muettes' and 'vraiment impénétrables', it is, he says, 'parce qu'elles ne cachent rien'.[2]

---

[1] Tournier, *Vues de dos* (unpaginated), opposite picture of 'Jardin du Luxembourg, Paris'. On art as meaningful, see 'Le Peintre et son modèle', episode from *La Goutte d'or* not included in the final version of the novel and published in *Petites Proses*, pp. 155–67; see especially *Petites Proses*, p. 167, for reference to 'un portrait-signification'.

[2] Jean-François Lyotard, *Des dispositifs pulsionnels*, p. 88. For the refusal to subordinate art to language, see also Jacques Derrida, *La Vérité en peinture*, pp. 28, 133, 178, and Sarah Kofman, *Mélancolie de l'art*, pp. 22–5.

Lyotard is opposing an aesthetic tradition, exemplified in the thought
of Kant and Hegel, which unquestioningly privileges the verbal over
the non-verbal. In the *Critique of Judgement* Kant affirms the
supremacy of the verbal arts, and evaluates other art-forms through
an analogy with language which is never justified.[3] Despite his
opposition to the subjectivism of Kant's aesthetics, Hegel repeats
his predecessor's faith in the ascendency of language by placing
poetry at the summit of his hierarchy of the arts and imposing a law
of intelligibility (*Verständlichkeit*) on painting. The silence of the
painting is regarded as an absence which must be filled by the
supplement of language.[4]

In *Le Vent Paraclet* Tournier readily accepts the influence of Kant
and Hegel (see VP 27 and 174-5); and, when he addresses himself
to the problem of art in his critical writings, he places his faith in
the power of language as he attempts to define the nature and role
of the visual image.[5] The discursive activity of the theorist tends to
contain and confine art within the limits of language. Tournier
does not question the legitimacy of this form of discourse or the
assumptions which underlie it. However, his theoretical positions
never entirely dominate his literary texts; and Tournier's fictional
uses of the theme and theory of art exceed the limits of what might
otherwise be a restrictively conventional enquiry.

Since the final hundred pages of *Les Météores*, the visual arts have
occupied a central role in Tournier's fiction. Urs Kraus (in *Les
Météores*), Véronique (in 'Les Suaires de Véronique', published in
Le Coq de bruyère), Assour (in *Gaspard, Melchior et Balthazar*) and
Ahmed ben Salem (in 'Barberousse ou le portrait du roi', published
as part of *La Goutte d'or*) are all engaged in the production of visual
images. The privileged status of visual art in Tournier's fiction can
be illustrated by the treatment of the three artists who appear in
Gaspard, Melchior et Balthazar. One is 'un poète, un littéraire, un
bavard' (*GMB* 155) and also, as it happens, a donkey. The poet is

---

[3] See Kant, *Kritik der Urteilskraft*, pp. 175-82.
[4] For Hegel's hierarchy of the arts, see Hegel, *Vorlesungen über die Aesthetik*,
in *Werke in zwanzig Bänden*, xiii-xv; on *Verständlichkeit* as the first law of painting,
see xv. 94-5.
[5] See, for example, Tournier, *Canada: Journal de voyage*, pp. 123-9; this
passage is reprinted almost exactly under the revealing title 'Qu'est-ce que la peinture
abstraite?' in *Le Point*, Sept. 1972.

(literally) a garrulous ass who must 'surveiller [son] goût excessif pour les mots' (*GMB* 159) to avoid cluttering up his narrative with superfluous babble. The *conteur* Sangali is 'naïf et fragile' (*GMB* 104), exaggeratedly deferential, and, when we last see him, a vast smile covers his 'face poupine' (*GMB* 121). In contrast, Assour, the painter and sculptor, is spared the irony to which Sangali and the donkey are subjected. His search for a viable art-form is 'ardente' and 'angoissée' (*GMB* 77); he has 'des mains véritablement magiques' (*GMB* 93); he is 'transfiguré' by the birth of Christ, and Balthazar sees in his face 'l'aurore d'un art nouveau' (*GMB* 207). The painter is in the vanguard of an aesthetic revolution in which the verbal arts participate only indirectly.

The discussion of surrealism in *Le Vent Paraclet* helps to explain the privileged status of visual art in Tournier's writing. Tournier makes a sharp distinction between the art and the literature of surrealism. The latter is characterized by its imprecision: 'le flou, le rêve, l'inconscient, l'à-peu-près, l'écriture automatique, les mots en liberté' (*VP* 112). Surrealist painting, on the other hand, is a subversive blend of humour, fantasy, and *absolute precision of detail*: 'ils font confiance plus à la sûreté infaillible du trait qu'au tremblé atmosphérique du rêve. Plus platement on copiera le réel, plus intimement on le bouleversera' (*VP* 112). Tournier insists that rigorous attention to detail is more effective in the subversion of reality than the simple abandonment of representation. Modern literature has taken a false path by following the example of Mallarmé, Verlaine, and Rimbaud instead of that of Gautier, Flaubert, and Maupassant. Tournier identifies with Dali and Magritte rather than Breton and Éluard: 'C'est du côté des peintres que je me sens chez moi' (*VP* 112). This account of surrealism enables Tournier to justify his own aesthetic options in opposition to literary modernism. Rather than 'les mots en liberté', he advocates 'un objectivisme poussé jusqu'à l'hallucination' (*VP* 112).

What this entails is a rearguard defence of *mimesis*. All the artists who appear in Tournier's fictional texts are primarily figurative (even if some of Urs Kraus's paintings in *Les Météores* combine incongruous elements in a surrealist manner). Tournier's preference for mimetic art does not, however, mean that for him art is simply or essentially the imitation of visible forms. When asked about his paintings, Ahmed ben Salem, the court artist in 'Barberousse ou le portrait du roi', says, 'Je peins la vérité' (*G* 43); his portrait of the king is *also* 'le portrait même de la royauté' (G 43). Figurative art copies the visible world; but the most essential function of painting is the revelation of essences and truths which are normally hidden from the human eye. This is made possible by the implication of a continuity between visible form and invisible truth. As Ahmed insists, 'la profondeur d'un être transparaît sur son visage' (G 45). In *Les Météores* Kraus's portraits show the 'élan initial qui est à la source même de chaque être' (M 466); Ahmed paints the 'voix de l'âme' of his model and the 'chant profond' of humanity (G 47). Christian art in *Gaspard, Melchior et Balthazar* is deemed to depict the reconciliation of divine and human made possible by the Incarnation: Christ is described as 'Dieu incarné dans un petit enfant' and 'devenu visible' (GMB 207). God, the invisible and unrepresentable, is made flesh, given a visible form, and so He becomes susceptible to visual representation.

Tournier's discussions of art suggest a remarkably eclectic range of influences. An obvious precursor is Hegel, for whom art makes possible what he calls 'the sensible representation of the Absolute'[6] by acting as a point of mediation between Spirit and the material world. Plato's *Timaeus* is possibly a more distant source, with its description of how the Demiurge creates the cosmos by making a sensible copy of an eternal pattern.[7] Heidegger's discussion of the Greek designation of truth as *aletheia* (unveiling) is recalled by the metaphors of veils and masks which abound in Tournier's discussion: the 'autre chose' which the artist depicts is 'masquée par un rideau d'images'[8] and the artist tears the 'voile gris que notre fatigue jette sur le monde' (VP 289). Tournier associates the vocabulary of unveiling with the Kantian notions of noumenon, phenomenon, and thing-in-itself: the eye is not normally allowed the 'vision directe des noumènes' (*Canada*, p. 125); but the 'univers nouménal' is 'dévoilé par l'art abstrait' (p. 129) and it pierces the 'masque figuratif' in mimetic art (p. 125); the artist 'peint des choses en soi' (p. 125) and the thing-in-itself is the 'seul véritable sujet du peintre' (p. 129).

A short paragraph from *Le Vagabond immobile* is even more rich in possible resonances. Commenting on a sketch by Jean-Max Toubeau of ordinary household objects, Tournier writes:

---

[6] The German phrase is: 'die sinnliche Darstellung des Absoluten' (Hegel, *Werke in zwanzig Bänden*, xiii. 100).   [7] See Plato's *Timaeus*, 28–9.
[8] Tournier, *Canada: Journal de voyage*, p. 125; in the rest of this paragraph references to *Canada: Journal de voyage* are given in the text.

Le véritable sens de la nature morte, c'est plutôt, semble-t-il, de considérer les objets d'usage — normalement oblitérés à nos yeux par leur utilité — hors de tout usage non seulement actuel, mais possible. Leur présence, habituellement très effacée dans notre vie, devient tout à coup exorbitante. Le dessin les fait passer du relatif à l'absolu. La cafetière et le pot à tabac se refusent désormais à contenir du café ou du tabac. Ce sont des archétypes, des idées platoniciennes.[9]

Tournier's use of the word 'utilité' recalls Heidegger's discussion in 'The Origin of the Work of Art' of the 'Dienlichkeit des Zeuges' (utility of the utensil) and how it is affected in the work of art. In the painting, the utensil is at rest, removed from its practical usage, and so its being ('das Zeugsein des Zeuges') is revealed. Heidegger's example is a pair of shoes, and, he writes, 'The work of art revealed what the pair of shoes is in truth.'[10] Heidegger's discussion of the depiction of the banal object in the work of art itself echoes a passage from Hegel's *Lectures on Aesthetics*. In ordinary life, Hegel says, we only consider the external purpose ('äussere Zweckmässigkeit') of everyday objects; they are considered as means rather than as ends in themselves. By representing the ordinary, painting 'tears [. . .] all the bonds of need, attraction, inclination and disinclination [. . .] and brings us closer to the objects in their authentic life as ends in themselves'.[11] Hegel, like Tournier, believes that our relationship to the everyday is radically altered by the work of art. In the painting we are given a new perception of the banal object because it is removed from its normal system of relationships.

At the end of his discussion of the still life Tournier asserts with characteristic assurance: 'Ce sont des archétypes, des idées platoniciennes.' In the famous discussion of art in Plato's *Republic* Socrates condemns the artist because he copies the material world rather than the perfect ideal Forms.[12] The neo-Platonic interpretation of Plato's philosophy brought a radical reassessment of the artist's role. Plotinus suggests that the artist bypasses material forms and may even have an intuition of the suprasensible principles from which nature itself

[9] Tournier, *Le Vagabond immobile*, p. 69.
[10] Martin Heidegger, 'Der Ursprung des Kunstwerkes', in *Holzwege*, p. 24.
[11] Hegel, *Werke in zwanzig Bänden*, xv. 65. For a similar view, see Schopenhauer, *Die Welt als Wille und Vorstellung*, in *Sämmtliche Werke*, i. 257.
[12] See Plato, *The Republic*, Book Ten, 597–8.

is derived.[13] This aesthetic exerted a powerful influence on the theorists of the Renaissance as well as the Romantics and German idealists. Schelling writes that the portrait should be 'more like the person, that is the idea of the person, than he is himself in isolated moments'.[14] Similarly, Hegel says that, if a portrait succeeds in depicting the spirit of a person, 'then it can be said that the portrait is, as it were, more accurate, more like the individual, than the real individual himself'.[15] The work of art is deemed to be more than a copy of the material world; in fact, it may come closer to the essence of its subject than its material manifestation, since it escapes the vicissitudes of time and captures what is permanent within temporal flux. Tournier places his own texts under the authority of this idealist tradition. In the first instance, the artist, or at least the figurative artist, copies the sensible world; but the most fundamental and important part of his art is the unveiling of the ideal form, noumenon, essence, or soul of the model. The representation of the world gives rise to and is subsumed under the self-presentation of truth in the work of art.

Tournier seems to be proposing a philosophical discourse on art derived from sources as diverse as Plato, Plotinus, Kant, Hegel, and Heidegger. However, it is important to emphasize that Tournier's reading of the history of aesthetics involves an appropriative infidelity to the texts from which he derives his own positions. For example, he uses Kantian terminology to suggest that the 'univers nouménal' is 'dévoilé par l'art abstrait'[16] and that the value of figurative art depends upon its ability to show the noumenon underneath the phenomenon: 'Si rien ne perce, la peinture ne vaut rien.'[17] However, the aesthetics of the *Critique of Judgement* bear no relation to these assertions, and Kant never suggests that the artist paints the thing-in-itself. Tournier uses Kantian terminology to support a position which has nothing to do with Kantian aesthetics and which in fact seems closer to Hegel. And, even though Tournier seems to echo Hegel in his account of how the banal object is transformed by its

---

[13] See Plotinus, 'On the Intellectual Beauty', Eighth Tractate, Fifth Ennead, in *The Enneads*, pp. 422–3. On art as the imitation of Platonic Ideas, see Schopenhauer, *Die Welt als Wille und Vorstellung*, Third Book.

[14] Schelling, *Sämmtliche Werke*, v. 547.

[15] Hegel, *Werke in zwanzig Bänden*, xv. 104.

[16] Tournier, *Canada: Journal de voyage*, p. 129.

[17] Ibid. 125.

depiction of art, he makes a giant leap between two systems of thought by associating this with the idea that the artist copies the 'idées platoniciennes'. The vocabulary of unveiling and the suggestion that the being of the utensil is revealed in the work of art may seem to bear witness to a dependence upon Heidegger. But in 'The Origin of the Work of Art' truth is an event which takes place in the painting rather than a state independent of it. What is revealed in the work of art has little in common with the Platonic concept of immobile eternal Forms, and the 'happening of truth' (*Geschehnis der Wahrheit*) cannot be understood as the simple unveiling of a static essence.

Without marking the transitions, Tournier's rhetoric slips smoothly from Kant to Hegel, from Hegel to Plotinus. The elisions and simplifications which this involves are passed over in silence and Tournier exhibits a wilful blindness towards the differences between the texts from which he derives his own aesthetics. However, this appropriation of the thought and terminology of his philosophical percursors is one means by which Tournier clears space for his own writing to begin. Moreover, his theoretical positions never command the composition of his fiction to the extent which he sometimes suggests. In the next section of this chapter we shall see how the powerful *erotic* force of the image disrupts the identification of art with truth which Tournier's texts attempt to impose.

(ii) *Vision, Knowledge, and Desire*

In philosophical discourse on the senses, vision is traditionally accorded a privileged status. For Descartes, it is 'le plus universel et le plus noble' of the senses; for Kant also it is the most noble of the senses, and for Hegel the most spiritual because the least dependent upon material stimuli; and Schopenhauer describes how only the eye is capable of direct contemplation of the Platonic Forms.[18] In accordance with the philosophical tradition in which he was trained, Tournier gives vision a privileged role in his theory of art. But for Tournier vision also has an important erotic function; and an examination of the role of the eye in the arousal of desire

---

[18] See Descartes, *Œuvres et lettres*, p. 180; on the place of vision in Kant's philosophy, see Derrida, 'Economimesis', in S. Agacinski *et al.*, *Mimesis des articulations*, p. 85; for Hegel, see *Werke in zwanzig Bänden*, xiii. 61; and for Schopenhauer, see *Die Welt als Wille und Vorstellung*, in *Sämmtliche Werke*, i. 284–5, 340.

necessitates a reconsideration of the place of visual art in his fiction.

In *Les Météores* the theme of vision acquires particular significance when Paul visits Japan and discovers Urs Kraus's paintings of Jean.[19] Chapter Eighteen ('Les Jardins japonais') alternates between Paul's account of his experiences in Japan and the meditations of Shonïn, the sage and theorist of Japanese gardens whose presence in the novel is confined to this chapter. Shonïn makes the initial connection between art and vision in his first appearance in the text, scarcely a page into the chapter: 'Pourquoi sculpter avec un marteau, un ciseau ou une scie? Pourquoi faire souffrir la pierre et mettre son âme au désespoir? L'artiste est un contemplateur. L'artiste sculpte avec son regard. . . ' (*M* 445). In the following meditation on the beauty of stones, the references to the importance of vision continue. 'Pour créer cette beauté, il n'est que de savoir regarder,' Shonïn insists; the instrument vital for the collection of pebbles is 'l'oeil du ramasseur'; and gardens created through the judicious collection of stones are 'l'oeuvre d'un oeil' (all *M* 446). Shonïn's esoteric discussions of Japanese gardens seem to have little to do with Paul's search for his lost brother, and he seems a cryptic, foreign voice in a text that would hardly suffer from his absence. But in fact his presence in *Les Météores* is far from superfluous. He heralds and theorizes an important reorientation in the novel and in the corpus of Tournier's fiction through the elaboration of an aesthetic which is founded upon the privileged status of visual perception.

On his arrival in Japan, Paul is worried that his 'oeil d'Occidental' will not be able to distinguish the Japanese one from another (*M* 446). His initiation to the power of vision is prepared by his visits to the statue of Buddha (*M* 454) and then to the statues of the 'déesse miséricordieuse Kannon' (*M* 456-7). At first, he thinks that the statues of this goddess are identical, but Shonïn corrects his mistake: 'Cependant mon maître Shonïn a bien vite détrompé mon illusion' (*M* 456). The statues are only identical 'pour le regard grossier du profane occidental' who is deceived by the 'attributs accidentels' and does not perceive spatial difference and its 'relation intime avec l'essence des choses' (*M* 456-7).

---

[19] For the theme of the eye in Tournier's earlier fiction, see, e.g., *V* 21, 149, and *RA* 276-7, where Blättchen points out that the German word *Auge* (eye) is contained in Tiffauges's name.

This initiation to the ability of the eye to distinguish the essential from the accidental precedes and prepares Paul's discovery of Kraus's paintings: 'Cette rencontre [. . .] était bien faite pour en préparer une autre' (M 457). Paul becomes an art critic, and the alternation between his commentaries on Kraus's paintings and Shonïn's theoretical discussions suggests an affinity between the sage and the artist, who are joined through their sacred vision of depths. In Shonïn's words, only the 'regard du sage' is normally capable of seeing the 'vie profonde' that lies underneath the surface (M 459). Metaphors of depth are also used by Paul to characterize the peculiar power of the artist's vision. Kraus achieves 'une vision particulièrement pénétrante des êtres et des choses' (M 460); in his landscapes he paints a 'relation directe au cosmos' which is 'plus profonde' than what the eye normally perceives (M 463); and his portraits attain a 'pénétration en quelque sorte métaphysique' (M 462). Kraus is able to show what normally cannot be seen. His landscapes reveal the 'formule cosmique du Japon', which is 'devenue sensible' so that it can be recognized 'au premier coup d'oeil' (M 462). Through the agency of art and in the intimacy of the eye, the passage from outer form to inner truth is effected.

In the final chapter of Les Météores Paul realizes the full power of vision. He refers to '[ses] yeux devenus hypersensibles' (M 529) and asserts that his eye has become 'un oeil inquisiteur, perçant et hors d'atteinte, l'oeil de Dieu en somme' (M 531). Earlier, his 'yeux de profane' were incapable of realizing the power of vision; but now, he affirms, 'je ne suis plus ce profane' (M 533). With the aid of his binoculars, which he describes as his 'instrument d'hyperconnaissance', he is able to see with an 'oeil divin' (M 532) and has achieved 'une connaissance plus intime, plus possessive par [son] seul regard d'infirme' (M 533).

We saw in the previous section that Hegel is an important influence on Tournier's aesthetics. In Hegel's Lectures on Aesthetics the 'sensible representation of the Absolute' achieved by art depends upon a continuity between visible and invisible which makes it possible for the former to represent the latter. In painting, the internal is revealed through its external form and the representation of reality is the condition for the self-presentation of truth. In order to maintain this position, both Hegel and Tournier must deny that there is any radical difference or discontinuity between visible and invisible. At one point in the Lectures on Aesthetics Hegel envisages a possibility which threatens the premises of his own aesthetic theory. Internal excellence, he says, may be contained in a body which, from the point of view of simple external form and considered in itself, may be ugly.[20] The *locus classicus* to which Hegal refers is the notorious ugliness of Socrates.[21] Art, however, must overcome this all-too-disturbing exception. To express spiritual or intellectual beauty, art must, according to Hegel, avoid (*vermeiden*), tame (*bändigen*) or transfigure (*verklären*—the word used for the Transfiguration of Christ, *die Verklärung*) the ugliness of external forms. With this, Hegel gives a rather incomplete and unsatisfactory solution to a problem which threatens his theory of art; and in the same sentence he moves on to say that the artist may depict physical ugliness, but that this is only permissible as a representation of moral and spiritual deformity.

Tournier also indicates that ugliness must be overcome if the painting is to represent the nobility of its model. In 'Barberousse ou le portrait du roi' Barberousse asks the painter if his portraits would show any 'disgrâce physique, verrue, nez cassé, œil torve ou crevé' that his subject might have (G 43). Ahmed says that he would, but that the 'visage rendu laid et ridicule par une difformité' would also be transformed by the hand of the artist (G 44). If the king had a wart on his nose, the painting would make it seem 'si royale qu'il n'est personne qui ne serait fier d'en porter une pareille sur le nez' (G 43). Art is capable of *exalting* the ugly and making it an expression of internal excellence. The painter depicts, but also overcomes, the physical blemishes of his model, so that physical ugliness is after all reconcilable with spiritual beauty.

In the theory of art which Tournier's texts seem to espouse, vision is the faculty which allows the observer to pass from contemplation of the sensible to knowledge of the suprasensible. Art seems to have a privileged relationship to truth; but further consideration of the role of vision in Tournier's fiction indicates that the eye, and hence also the image, are neither primarily nor necessarily concerned with objective truthfulness.

The short story 'Le Coq de bruyère' seems to demonstrate most clearly the equivalence of 'seeing' and 'seeing the truth' in Tournier's

---

[20] See Hegel, *Werke in zwanzig Bänden*, xv. 101.
[21] On the ugliness of Socrates, see Plato, *Symposium*, 215 A–B. On the problem posed by Socrates' ugliness to the aesthetics of Hegel and his contemporaries, see Stephen Bungay, *Beauty and Truth: A Study of Hegel's Aesthetics*, pp. 116, 206 n. 32.

fiction. The vocabulary of vision, and its uncontrolled slippage between literal, metaphoric, and moral meanings, play a central role in the story. The abbé's advice that the baronne should 'turn a blind eye' ('fermer les yeux', *CB* 213) to her husband's infidelity causes her psychosomatic blindness. Her refusal to 'see' a moral blemish coincides with a quite literal loss of vision. When the colonel gives up his adulterous affair to look after his wife, she recovers her sight. With the collusion of the abbé, she decides not to inform her husband straightaway. She believes that it would be more prudent to allow 'un dévoilement progressif de la vérité' (*CB* 220). The truth, however, will not submit to the discretion of a slow unveiling: 'Elle éclata un beau dimanche après-midi [. . .] avec une brutale indiscretion' (*CB* 220). The *éclatement* of truth involves a series of visual perceptions. Out walking with his wife, the colonel sees Mariette, his former mistress, with another man. He looks towards his wife ('Il leva vers elle un regard inquiet', *CB* 221) and sees ('Et ce qu'il vit. . . ', *CB* 221) that she smiles and then laughs. He sees that Mariette has a new lover and that his wife has recovered her sight: 'elle avait vu la même chose que lui [. . .] elle voyait en vérité aussi bien que lui' (*CB* 222).

The truth is *seen*; however, the eye may also *refuse* to see a truth which offends it. The analyst consulted by the colonel suggests that the baronne goes blind because of 'quelque chose qu'elle ne veut pas voir' (*CB* 227), which he then describes as 'Quelque chose de laid, d'immoral, de bas, de dégradant, d'abject, une ignominie si proche d'elle-même en même temps qu'il n'y a qu'un moyen pour ne pas la voir: devenir aveugle' (*CB* 227). The analyst's diagnosis has clear sexual overtones; and in 'Le Coq de bruyère' the refusal to see, literal, moral, or metaphoric, is consistently the refusal to face the evidence that others have been involved in the sexual act. The abbé says that he has decided 'de ne [s]'apercevoir de rien' (*CB* 191) when the baronne alludes to the pregnancy of one of his unmarried parishioners. The phrase 'fermer les yeux' has sexual connotations throughout the story. A local architect 'aurait un peu fermé les yeux' to his wife's affair with a man in a position to help his business (*CB* 196); the abbé advises the baronne to 'fermer les yeux' to her husband's affair (*CB* 213); and later, reunited with Mariette, the colonel in turn decides to 'fermer les yeux' to *her* infidelity (*CB* 230).

The 'truth' which offends the eye is a sexual truth. On his wedding night, the protagonist of the one-act play 'Le Fétichiste' is traumatized by the sight of his wife's naked body: 'J'ai fini par détourner les yeux, tellement j'étais malheureux' (CB 286). The baronne in 'Le Coq de bruyère' is subject to the same anxiety when confronted with the evidence of sexuality. She is, according to her husband, not interested in sexual relations: 'ces choses dont vous parlez, admettez donc que pour vous elles n'ont *jamais* été de saison' (CB 197). However, this apparent lack of interest may be the sign of a powerful but inadmissible fascination with sexual matters. What the eye refuses to see most vehemently is what it most desires to see. This is suggested when the baronne and her maid Eugénie accidently discover erotic pictures and magazines belonging to the colonel. This discovery prompts an unambiguous moral condemnation: 'Encore ces saletés!', the baronne exclaims (CB 203). The naked bodies are described as being 'd'une laideur', and only men with their 'sale désir de mâles' could be interested in them (CB 203); only women who are 'vicieuses' could expose their bodies to male desire (CB 204). However, the text indicates an interest which is not openly acknowledged. When the baronne has recognized the 'flot d'images et de publications érotiques' for what they are, she picks them up: 'Elle les ramassa, les rassembla, et y jeta un coup d'œil écœuré' (CB 203). The baronne knows what she has in front of her, and she has no need to examine the pictures more closely. Her 'coup d'œil écœuré' perhaps indicates that her moral outrage does not negate a deeper desire to see the objects of male desire. The attitude of Eugénie is equally ambivalent. She obediently concurs with the baronne's disgust: ' — Pour ça oui, approuva Eugénie penchée sur son épaule' (CB 203). Eugénie leans over the shoulder of her mistress, since she too is anxious to see the pictures of which she so unambiguously disapproves. Desire and disgust, it seems, go hand in hand.

The baronne contrasts the 'sale désir des mâles' with an ideal relationship suggested to her when she was a girl. By the bath at the convent school which she attended was 'une sorte de cape en grosse toile écrue': 'C'était pour se déshabiller, se laver et se rhabiller sans voir son propre corps' (CB 204). The first time she took a bath, she did not use this cape. The 'surveillante' reproached her for having been 'nue en pleine lumière', saying: 'Vous ne savez donc pas que votre ange gardien est un jeune homme?' (CB 204). The baronne concludes: 'Oui, je n'ai jamais cessé de penser à ce jeune homme, très doux, très pur, très chaste, qui est à tout instant près de moi, comme un compagnon fidèle, un ami idéal. . . ' (CB 204). This 'ami idéal' anticipates the analyst's reference to the super-ego later in the story.[22] At the same time, the baronne's recollections have an evident sexual significance. The cape is described as 'cette sorte d'éteignoir' (CB 204): by covering the body and making it inaccessible to the eye, it extinguishes or represses the desire associated with nudity, the 'sale désir des mâles'. The baronne covers her body so that she cannot see herself or be seen. Yet she fantasizes about a permanent companion who is always present to observe the scrupulously hidden body. The baronne is torn between the desire to see the naked body and the moral condemnation of nudity and sexuality as dirty and base; between the desire to see herself and the nuns who prohibit self-observation; between the fantasy of being observed and the urgent need to cover the body. Forms of voyeurism, narcissism, and exhibitionism all conflict with a puritanical repression of sexuality; and in each case the eye is the locus of desire and the transgression of moral prohibitions. In a paper entitled 'The Psycho-Analytic View of Psychogenic Disturbance of Vision' Freud describes how the sexual function of the eye can come into conflict with the moral demands of the ego (or, in his later terminology, the super-ego).[23] By a version of the Law of Talion ('An eye for an eye, a tooth for a tooth'), the offending organ is the organ which must be punished. The eye is responsible for the baronne's desire, and so the appropriate punishment must be blindness.

The equation of vision and desire has disruptive consequences for Tournier's idealist aesthetics. In Gaspard, Melchior et Balthazar Balthazar believes that the birth of Christ will save art from the Judaic prohibition of the image, but this does not explain the intensity of his love for art. A reading of Tournier's text will suggest that, despite Balthazar's theoretical and religious convictions, desire is an essential element in the aesthete's relationship to the visual image.

Balthazar concedes that his 'éducation érotique et sentimentale' is 'incomplète et comme dérisoire' (GM 68). This is not because of his lack of sexual experience but because of the 'excès de facilité' with which the crown prince can obtain any woman he wants. A

---

[22] The baronne's reference to her 'ami idéal' also recalls the term 'Ichideal', which Freud used before coining the term 'Über-Ich' (super-ego). On the relationship and possible differences between the Ichideal and the Über-Ich, see Laplanche and Pontalis, Vocabulaire de la psychanalyse, entry under 'Idéal du moi', pp. 184–6.

[23] See Freud, 'The Psycho-Analytic View of Psychogenic Disturbance of Vision', in The Standard Edition, xi.

less privileged young man 'fortifie et nourrit son désir' in the struggle to obtain sexual satisfaction, whereas the prince needs make only 'un geste de la main ou même des paupières' (*GMB* 68). The facility of Balthazar's sexual relations spoils the pleasure of conquest: 'Facilité affadissante et débilitante qui le frustre de l'âpre joie de la chasse, ou du subtil plaisir de la séduction' (*GMB* 68). However, this dissatisfaction with physical relationships can be traced further back than his first erotic experiences. From his early childhood Balthazar pursues *visual* beauty. For the young prince, the butterfly is the incarnation of 'la beauté pure, à la fois insaisissable et sans aucune valeur marchande' (*GMB* 57). Beauty in its pure form is 'insaisissable'. Balthazar can chase after it, he can observe it, but he can never fully possess it. The essence of beauty is its unattainability, and its unattainability makes it all the more desirable. This will prove to be an important factor in Balthazar's experience of art. As a young man, he falls in love with a portrait; and when he is asked to choose a wife, he asks for the girl shown in the picture. But it is the portrait he loves, not its human model: 'Mais pour moi, c'était le portrait qui se trouvait à l'origine de tout [. . .] L'image me suffisait. C'était elle que j'aimais, et la jeune fille réelle ne pouvait m'émouvoir que secondairement, dans la mesure où je trouvais sur ses traits un reflet de l'œuvre adulée' (*GMB* 71). When he makes love to his wife, the real object of his desire is the portrait (see *GMB* 71); and, as his wife grows older and ceases to resemble her image, Balthazar curtails his sexual relations with her (see *GMB* 72–3).

For Balthazar, the work of art replaces woman as the object of desire. He leaves his kingdom to hunt for art treasures as other men chase women, and as earlier he had chased after the unattainable pure beauty of the butterfly. His vocabulary suggests the sexual aspects of his relationship to the work of art: 'Seule la passion de la pure et simple beauté enflammait ma jeunesse', he writes (*GMB* 54); and he describes himself as 'passionné de dessin, peinture et sculpture' (*GMB* 206). When his art collection is destroyed in a wave of religious fanaticism, the destruction of the objects of his desire has a direct effect on his body and particularly on his sexual organ: 'En quelques heures, mes cheveux ont blanchi et ma taille s'est courbée, mon regard s'est voilé et mon ouïe s'est durcie, mes jambes se sont alourdies et mon sexe s'est rabougri' (*GMB* 77).

A powerful tradition in aesthetics refuses to acknowledge the bond of desire at the origin of Balthazar's intimate involvement with the destiny of his art collection. Kant insists that aesthetic pleasure should be dispassionate and disinterested, and Hegel describes the contemplation of works of art as calm and without desire ('ruhig' and 'begierdelos').[24] Freud, however, rejects this tradition in an important note added to the *Three Essays on Sexuality* in 1915: 'There is to my mind no doubt that the concept of "beautiful" has its origins in sexual excitation and that its original meaning was "sexually stimulating".'[25] Aesthetic beauty excites the eye in the same way as an erotic stimulus, and it engages the beholder in a process similar to that which leads to the sexual act. Freud argues that 'Visual impressions remain the most frequent pathway along which libidinal excitation is aroused'.[26] In the sexual act, seeing causes sexual excitement, which leads to physical contact and to copulation. Perversion, for Freud, is the refusal to complete the sexual act; and seeing becomes a perversion when, instead of acting as a preliminary to coition, it *replaces* it. The voyeur does not progress beyond the initial stage of looking at the object of desire.[27]

The art-lover shares the voyeur's perversion. If Balthazar and his wife have children, it is possible only because he uses her as a substitute for her portrait, to which he makes love 'par personne interposée' (*GMB* 71). Balthazar coins the word *iconophile* to describe someone afflicted by 'l'étrange perversion dont [il était] possédé' (*GMB* 71). His 'iconophilia' is a form of aesthetic voyeurism. The eye becomes an erogenous zone which is excited by the sight of beauty, but there is no orgasm because the true object of desire is not touched and possessed. Balthazar's desire thrives on the unbridgeable distance which separates the work of art from its beholder. He maximizes his pleasure by deferring or refusing its final fulfilment. In orgasm, desire is temporarily satisfied; the distance essential to the contemplation of art is necessary to desire, and at the same time prevents its total satisfaction. The chase after a sexual partner may come to

---

[24] See Kant, *Kritik der Urteilskraft*, pp. 46–8; Hegel, *Werke in zwanzig Bänden*, xv. 134.

[25] Freud, *Three Essays on Sexuality*, in *The Standard Edition*, vii. 156 n. The note is added to the sentence in which Freud makes his first published use of the term 'sublimation'.

[26] Ibid. 156.

[27] On voyeurism, see Freud, ibid. 156–7. Freud discusses seeing and touching in the same passage and writes of the latter that 'lingering over the stage of touching can scarcely be counted a perversion, provided that in the long run the sexual act is carried further' (p. 156).

an end, but with art the chase never ends. Even when the object is owned, it is never possessed and so desire is never finally satiated.

As we saw in Chapter 3, Alexandre from *Les Météores* often has a lucid insight into areas which Tournier himself seems able to confront only through the oblique perspective of (what he regards as) his secondary characters. Balthazar attempts to mask the erotic function of vision by making art subordinate to religious faith. But Alexandre recognizes that vision is unreliable as an organ of truth, since it serves desire rather than knowledge:

Mettez un chat dans un jardin. Croyez-vous qu'il appréciera le tracé des allées, la perspective des frondaisons, l'équilibre des pelouses et des bassins? Il n'en aura cure, il ne verra rien de tout cela. Ce qu'il verra d'un coup d'œil infaillible, c'est la vibration insolite d'un brin d'herbe qui trahit le passage d'un mulot.

Je suis ce chat. Ma vision n'est que la petite servante de mon désir. *Ancilla libidinis*. Tout est flou autour de moi hormis l'objet de mon désir qui brille d'un éclat surhumain. (*M* 83)

Tournier's turn from the Judaic origins of Christianity in *Gaspard, Melchior et Balthazar* to the Islamic context of *Le Goutte d'or* is less abrupt than it might seem, since Tournier finds in Judaism and Islam the same prohibition of the visual image. This prohibition reflects an anxiety which appears throughout Tournier's fiction, and which can be explained partly at least as fear of the power of frustrated desire. Balthazar thrives on frustration, but his aesthetic voyeurism is relegated to the level of minor theme in a text which attempts to neutralize the force of the image by showing the reconciliation of the love for art with religious faith. In *La Goutte d'or* Idriss travels to Paris and finds himself in 'le pays des images' (*G* 131). The dangerous sexual force of the disembodied image is made explicit when he visits a peep-show in the rue Saint-Denis and he is separated from the object of his desire by a glass screen. Achour warns him that 'Elle existait pour tes yeux, mais pas pour tes mains' (*G* 191). Idriss can see but not touch, and he leaves the peep-show 'tremblant de désir frustré' (*G* 191).

The story 'La Reine blonde', incorporated within *La Goutte d'or* in counterpoint to 'Barberousse ou le portrait du roi', deals explicitly with the erotic fascination of the image.[28] The portrait of the

---

[28] For further discussion of the erotic force of the work of art in 'La Reine blonde', see Françoise Merllié, 'La Reine blonde: De Méduse à la Muse, ou comment les mots délivrent de l'image'.

blonde Queen gives her beauty a timeless, intense quality which causes 'une passion absolue et sans espoir' in all those who see it (G 239). The Queen herself grows old, but the portrait continues to excite and frustrate those who see the image but cannot touch the body. 'La Reine blonde' gives an undisguised description of the relationship between visual art and sexual excitement; and the poet and calligrapher Ibn Al Houdaïda explains how the author may respond to the dangerous erotic force of the image and overcome the fascination of art:

L'image est douée d'un rayonnement paralysant, telle la tête de Méduse qui changeait en pierre tous ceux qui croisaient son regard. Pourtant cette fascination n'est irrésistible qu'aux yeux des analphabètes. En effet l'image n'est qu'un enchevêtrement de signes, et sa force maléfique vient de l'addition confuse et discordante de leurs significations [. . .] Pour le lettré, l'image n'est pas muette [. . .] Il n'est que de savoir lire. . . (G 243)

The visual image must be translated into rhetorical figure (see G 243–4). The beholders of the portrait protect themselves against the power of art with language, which becomes the new focus of sublimated desire. In 'La Reine blonde', then, Tournier achieves a heightened insight into his use of the theme of art and his own practice as novelist by representing the transmutation of unfulfilled desire into written text.

(iii) *The Refusal of Mourning*

As we have seen, the question of *mimesis* is fundamental to Tournier's aesthetics. Figurative art depicts the suprasensible by imitation of the sensible. But some forms of imitation are better than others. In *Gaspard, Melchior et Balthazar* the artist Assour and the art-lover Balthazar are in complete agreement with the Judaic prohibition of the image if all art represents is 'nos pauvres carcasses fiévreuses et faméliques' (GMB 95); no artist, 'à moins de perversion' (GMB 95), would want to celebrate the human form for its own sake. Balthazar believes that the union of God and man through Christ makes art permissible: 'L'image est sauvée, le visage et le corps de l'homme peuvent être célébrés sans idolâtrie' (GMB 208). Nevertheless, the birth of Christ does not justify all forms of art, and Balthazar knows that 'l'image peut être menteuse et l'art imposteur' (GMB 206–7; see also GMB 95). The image must show the possibility of man's reconciliation with the divine: 'le reflet, la grâce, l'éternité noyée dans la chair, intimement mêlée à la chair, et transverbérant la chair' (GMB 95). Despite the optimism of Balthazar's final appearance in Gaspard, Melchior et Balthazar, art is not liberated from the controls of religious dogma.[29] It can only be justified under the condition that it accepts its subordination to the miracle of the Incarnation and so depicts the presence of God in man, and the reconciliation of eternal and temporal, sacred and profane, made possible by the birth of Christ.

In line with a tradition which goes back as far as Plato,[30] Tournier implicitly distinguishes between a good and a bad mimesis. This is illustrated by the discussion of art in the short story 'Barberousse ou le portrait du roi'. The aesthetics of Ahmed, the court painter, depend upon a series of conventional dualisms: body/soul, accident/essence, surface/depth, temporal/eternal. In each case, a bad mimesis attains only the former pole, copying the surface but not penetrating to the essence. Of course, a bad mimesis is always possible; and 'Barberousse ou le portrait du roi' suggests that it may even be more essential to the pleasure derived from art than rigorous fidelity to the truth. The king ousted by Barberousse is described as 'chétif et de piètre apparence' and 'voué à la défaite et à l'humiliation' (G 39). He is oppressed and depressed by the pressures of governing and the measures made necessary by the exercise of power. He cannot bear 'l'image de lui-même qu'il voyait se refléter dans l'œil du bourreau, du supplicié ou du simple soldat' (G 46). When the king goes to see his portraits, he is 'pâle, découragé, écoeuré par les basses œuvres de son métier' (G 46). In contrast to this sorry figure, Ahmed's paintings show the king in all his regal splendour, 'triomphant, dominateur, épanoui dans toute sa gloire' (G 39). By

[29] Balthazar's optimism on his final appearance is, to say the least, premature. His defence of Christian art, on the grounds that it shows the visible manifestation of divinity rather than just the human form, is essentially that adopted by the opponents of the Iconoclasts. However, the use of icons was still considered by many to be a form of idolatry. The Iconoclast Controversy was not resolved until AD 747, when icons were accepted under the condition that they portrayed a strictly limited number of traditional themes; and, despite this temporary resolution, the issue of icon-worship continued to be a cause of violent confrontation in the later history of the Christian Church. For discussion, see E. H. Gombrich, The Story of Art, pp. 97–8.

[30] For the implicit distinction between good and bad mimesis, see Plato, The Republic, Book Ten, 596 B–597 E, where Socrates distinguishes between the imitation of Forms practised by the carpenter and the imitation of copies practised by the artist.

the art and artifice of the painter, the portraits show a king freed from the contamination of power: 'A leur lumière, il se lavait de toutes les souillures du pouvoir. Il se regonflait à vue d'oeil de sa fierté de roi. Il reprenait confiance en lui-même. Je n'avais pas un mot de réconfort à prononcer. Il me souriait et partait rasséréné' (G 46-7). The artist stakes the authority of his paintings on their ability to represent an essential truth. But, despite his claims to the contrary, Ahmed is a flatterer. His art is a bad *mimesis*, concerned with preserving one image of kinghood amongst others, when nothing justifies the artist's arbitrary distinction between essential and accidental attributes. The king goes to see Ahmed's paintings in order to exchange an image which is true but intolerable, the image of a king who governs reflected in the eye of the executioner, for an image which is partial or even mendacious, that of a serene and glorious ruler unsullied by time and power.

In Tournier's fiction the theme of art is associated with the rejection of contingency and mortality. Art proclaims the fixity of identity and essences, and the existence of the eternal and the absolute beneath the mask of the temporal and the relative. This is made clear during Tiffauges's visit to the Louvre in Le Roi des aulnes when he attempts to explain his reaction to a statue of Apollo:

Rien n'illustre mieux que cette statue la fonction essentielle de l'art: à nos coeurs rendus malades par le temps — par l'érosion du temps, par la mort partout à l'oeuvre, par la promesse inéluctable de l'anéantissement de tout ce que nous aimons — l'oeuvre d'art apporte un peu d'éternité. C'est le remède souverain, le havre de paix vers lequel nous soupirons, une goutte d'eau fraîche sur nos lèvres fiévreuses. (RA 95)

Art is the promise of 'un peu d'éternité', whereas life is subject to time, decay, and death. The metaphors of illness are revealing. Our hearts are 'rendus malades par le temps', our lips are 'fiévreuses'; art is the 'remède souverain'. Time is the sickness for which art is the cure; art restores the eternity from which we come and to which we shall return. But, as 'Barberousse ou le portrait du roi' shows, it restores by falsification rather than imitation. Responding to the voice of desire rather than the dictates of truth, it creates the illusion of a stable essence by abstracting its subject from time. The 'fonction essentielle de l'art' is not the unveiling of truth, but the veiling of temporality.

In a short paper entitled 'On Transience' ('Die Vergänglichkeit'), Freud describes the reaction of a poet to the realization that even natural beauty is ephemeral. He writes: 'All that he would otherwise have loved and admired seemed to him to be shorn of its worth by the transience which was its doom.'[31] Mourning, for Freud, is the reaction which occurs when the subject's libido is still directed towards an object that has died or gone away: and the intolerable knowledge that beauty is not immune from the ravages of time gives what Freud calls a foretaste of mourning ('Vorgeshmack der Trauer').[32] In *Mélancolie de l'art*, Sarah Kofman draws on Freud's essay and interprets the attempt to save art from the temporal and the contingent, which Tournier's *Gaspard, Melchior et Balthazar* shows to be an essential feature of the Christian tradition, in psycho-analytical terms.[33] Kofman describes how art imposes stability on the flux of identity by introducing duration and fixity into the transitoriness of life. Art camouflages the ephemeral nature of the flesh by spiritualizing it; painting thereby masks the truth at the very moment when it proclaims its own truthfulness. It is precisely this infidelity to the decay of the living which recommends art to the tribunal of posterity. In Kofman's phrase, art is the 'refus du deuil de la beauté':[34] it gives expression to the demand for eternity and helps to overcome the intolerable insight that everything, even beauty, is ephemeral.

Art's lie against time is in the assertion that all is well: the noumenon is intact underneath the phenomenon, the essence is untarnished by the accident, time is underlaid by eternal truths, and identity is safe from difference. The function of art in Tournier's fiction, and to a certain extent the function of the fiction itself, is not to reveal the truth, but to mask the evidence of transitoriness and contingency. As Tournier himself insists, 'Le portrait a pour source première l'ambition de vaincre la mort.'[35]

However, the theme of art in Tournier's fiction is not exhausted by the nostalgia for fixed identity and the permanence of beauty. Tournier also describes the possibility of a quite different aesthetic,

[31] Freud, 'On Transience', in *The Standard Edition*, xiv. 305.

[32] On mourning, see Freud, 'Mourning and Melancholia', in *The Standard Edition*, xiv; on the 'foretaste of mourning', see Freud, 'On Transience', in *The Standard Edition*, xv. 306.

[33] See Sarah Kofman, *Mélancolie de l'art*, especially pp. 60–70, on which the following discussion is based.

[34] Ibid. 68. See also Derrida on the 'travail de deuil dans le discours de la beauté', *La Vérité en peinture*, pp. 104–5.

[35] Tournier, *Petites Proses*, p. 168.

in spite of and sometimes contrary to explicit statements made about art in the course of his texts.

In *Les Météores* Paul alludes to Bergson when he describes how Kraus's portraits of his girlfriend Kumiko capture her 'élan vital à sa source même' (*M* 463). Bergson's *élan vital* is a process of differentiation which leads away from the original coexistence of virtualities.[36] Unable to accept the fluctuation of identity, Paul insists that the function of art is to depict the *élan vital* at its source, before temporal and spatial differentiation have begun to affect the virtual plenitude of the self. The artist is deemed to reattain the original moment when, in Paul's words, 'toutes les implications sont encore réunies à l'état virtuel' (*M* 463). In accordance with this aesthetic, Kraus's landscapes are able to reveal 'une essence, un chiffre' which constitute the 'formule cosmique du Japon' (*M* 462). However, Paul *also* suggests that the 'formule cosmique' is strangely absent from the painting: 'Dans chaque tableau, on percevait confusément la présence occulte de cette formule. Elle émouvait sans éclairer. Elle débordait de promesses dont aucune n'était vraiment tenue. Un mot se présente sous ma plume: l'esprit des lieux. Mais l'image qu'il évoque n'est-elle pas celle d'un peu de soleil filtrant à travers beaucoup de brume?' (*M* 462). The essence is, after all, not fully revealed in Kraus's paintings, and its presence in the painting is no more than a 'présence occulte'; its revelation is promised but not yet achieved.

Paul's discussion of Kraus's paintings culminates in his account of the eleven portraits of Jean. As in the description of the landscapes, he begins by suggesting that the paintings capture and reveal an original moment before the fluctuation of identity in time and space. This original moment is described as 'l'élan initial qui est à la source même de chaque être' (*M* 466). In the course of the discussion it nevertheless becomes clear that the 'élan initial' is not an atemporal essence, but the fundamental urge for movement which constitutes Jean's only identity:

Dans ce masque je ne vois qu'une fièvre de vagabondage qui tourne à la panique dès qu'un séjour quelconque menace de se prolonger. C'est une étrave

---

[36] For this interpretation of the *élan vital*, see Deleuze, *Le Bergsonisme*, pp. 92–119. As Tournier indicates in *Le Vent Paraclet* (*VP* 267–8), the discussion of space in *Les Météores* is derived from Bergson's notion of duration. Compare Deleuze's account of the latter (*Le Bergsonisme*, pp. 23–4) with Paul's discovery that location alters identity, or, in Kraus's words, that '*il n'y a pas de translation sans altération*' (*M* 475).

usée par le sillage, une figure de proue creusée par les embruns, un profil de perpétuel migrant affûté par les souffles aériens. Il y a là de la flèche et du lévrier, et le seul reflet d'une rage de départs, d'une fringale de vitesse, d'une folie de fuite vers des ailleurs indéterminés. Du vent, du vent et encore du vent, c'est tout ce qui reste dans ce front, ces yeux, cette bouche. Ce n'est plus un visage, c'est une rose des vents. (M 466)

The portraits show a mask behind which there is no face. Jean is only present in the form of an essential non-presence. There is no reunification of an original identity in the work of art, and the 'élan initial' leads to the disappearance of the subject rather than to its ultimate reconstruction: 'On dirait qu'il est en train de se désagréger pour se dissiper totalement à la fin' (M 466–7).

When Paul first sees one of Kraus's eleven portraits of Jean, he describes it as a 'portrait parfaitement ressemblant de Jean' (M 457). However, he also acknowledges that there are differences between the paintings when he describes them as stages ('étapes', M 466) on the way to knowledge of his brother. Paul interprets the differences between the paintings as the consequence of the increasing accuracy with which Kraus is able to portray Jean's 'élan initial'. But this suggestion is contradicted by Kraus's explanation of his art. According to Kraus, each of the portraits is different from the others and different from its model because it occupies a distinct and unique position in time and space (see M 475–6). Moreover, as we have seen, Jean has no stable or unified identity for the artist to represent. Rather than a model, of which Kraus's portraits are mere copies, Jean can be regarded as a paradigm in the sense given to that term by Derrida:[37] he is the source of a series of non-identical portraits which cannot be judged in terms of how accurately they portray his features. The artist's aim is not simply to reproduce a faithful image of his original subject. Resemblance to the paradigm is only one criterion, and not necessarily the most important, in an aesthetic practice which *also* values the play of difference.

In Tournier's fiction the proliferation of images reveals and exacerbates a deep anxiety over the integrity of selfhood. Jean, in *Les Météores*, passes out when his face is reflected in a triple mirror and he sees not himself, but his twin brother Paul, and through Paul the alterity which inhabits his own identity: 'un vide effroyable se

---

[37] On the paradigm, see Derrida, *La Vérité en peinture*, pp. 223–4; see also Kofman, *Mélancolie de l'art*, p. 32.

creusait en moi [. . .] je n'étais nulle part, je n'existais plus' (*M* 246).
In the short story 'Les Suaires de Véronique' Hector is '*vidé, épuisé,
ravagé*' (*CB* 152) by the photographs which Véronique takes of him.
The photographs are copies, but also a theft of his own substance:
'*dépouilles de moi-même*' (*CB* 152). He runs away from Véronique
in order to preserve the precarious integrity of his identity, but he
is finally destroyed by her art. However, in Tournier's fiction the
multiplication of images and the fragmentation of identity do not
give rise exclusively to anxiety and trauma. In 'Barberousse ou le
portrait du roi' art plays a conciliatory role as it both reveals and
teaches acceptance of the divisibility of the self. At the same time,
the story illustrates most clearly the tension between the theory and
the function of art in Tournier's writing. Ahmed's aesthetics rely upon
the metaphysical rhetoric which influences the discussion of art in
all Tournier's texts; but the artist's account of his own activity fails
to explain the experience of art as it is described in the story. Ahmed
calls himself 'le peintre de la profondeur' (*G* 45); he claims to depict
the 'voix de l'âme' of his subject and the 'chant profond' of humanity
(*G* 47). He hopes to practise a good *mimesis* which requires the
presence of his model: 'j'ai besoin de votre présence pour faire un
vrai portrait de vous'(*G* 48). But subsequent events in the story will
disrupt the hierarchical oppositions (true/false, presence/absence)
which are at the heart of Ahmed's account of his art. Because of an
anxiety about the appearance of his body, Barberousse refuses to
pose for the artist. In the absence of his model, Ahmed covers his
canvas with 'esquisses', which do not consitute a 'vrai portrait' but
only the 'ébauche d'un portrait'; this portrait is 'fait de mémoire'
rather than through direct contemplation of the model (see *G* 48).
Nevertheless, it is this rough copy which Ahmed takes to Kerstine,
the Scandanavian weaver, who adds a *tactile* dimension to the visual
image. Kerstine's picture of Barberousse is a copy of a copy rather
than the 'vrai portrait' to which Ahmed aspires. It is nevertheless
her tapestry which liberates Barberousse from his inability to accept
his own body. In accordance with an ancient superstition, and despite
the physiological improbability, it is believed that his red hair and
beard are the marks of having been conceived during his mother's
menstrual period. Kerstine's portrait is the scene of a second birth,
which presents Barberousse with a non-identical twin, whom he
nevertheless recognizes as himself. He touches the portrait with his
cheek, 'Pour mieux goûter sa propre douceur' (*G* 53), savouring the

interplay of self and other rather than regretting an impossible atemporal self. His own image, distorted and transfigured by the double labour of copying which it has undergone, enables him to confront his facticity and assume his own sobriquet:

Alors Kheir ed Dîn accomplit un geste inouï dont la nouveauté remplit d'épouvante les courtisans qui l'accompagnaient: d'un mouvement brusque, il arracha la housse de soie verte qui culottait son menton, et il jeta par terre son vaste turban. Puis il secoua sa tête comme un fauve qui veut faire bouffer sa crinière.
— Barberousse! rugit-il. Je m'appelle le sultan Barberousse! (*G* 53)

The theme of art in Tournier's fiction is, then, fractured by internal contradiction. Two distinct impulses seem to be pulling the texts in opposite directions: on the one hand, the nostalgia for a definitive identity captured and made eternal in the work of art; and, on the other hand, the affirmation of the alterity of the self as revealed through the proliferation of images. Both impulses entail the refusal of mourning: one through the belief in eternal essences unaltered by time, one through the acceptance of time and alteration. Tournier's fiction is at its least nostalgic and its most affirmative when it shows how the proliferation of images, copies, and doubles can be experienced without trauma. However, the tension between nostalgia and affirmation is essential to Tournier's writing, and his texts never fully espouse the traditional aesthetic positions which they seem to be adopting. Balthazar says that, for him, the portrait acquires 'une plus grande valeur, une valeur comme absolue, dès lors qu'il avait perdu son terme de référence' (*GMB* 69). Tournier's texts are like the portrait without a referent: the paintings of Urs Kraus, Assour, and Ahmed are imaginary objects which do not pre-exist the fictional descriptions of them. Even when Tournier's writing seems to affirm the priority of the model over the copy, it implicitly privileges its own discourse and claims for itself the absolute status of a copy without a model.

Despite the traditionalism of Tournier's philosophical allegiances and despite the idealism of what seem to be his aesthetic positions, moments in his texts suggest a surprising affinity to the post-Nietzschean philosophies of suspicion which have dominated the French intellectual scene in recent years. This affinity may be shown, for example, by his provocative preference for the copy and his subversion of the notion of originality.[38] When Tiffauges visits the Louvre in *Le Roi des aulnes*, he finds himself amongst statues which are copies of absent originals, which are themselves copies of long-dead models (*RA* 96–7). The reader of Tournier's texts is in a similar position. Tournier perpetually rewrites the works of his literary predecessors, or even his own novels, which then appear in 'new versions'.[39] Copying is not necessarily the 'bêtise' which seems the final hopeless resource of Flaubert's Bouvard and Pécuchet. Tournier's aesthetic endeavour is to reconcile imitation and repetition with originality and creation. The Original Text is always already written, but the labour of rewriting—represented in *La Goutte d'or* by calligraphy—offers a means of escaping the harsh necessity of belatedness: 'Le calligraphe, qui dans la solitude de sa cellule prend possession du désert en le peuplant de signes, échappe à la misère du passé, à l'angoisse de l'avenir et à la tyrannie des autres hommes. Il dialogue seul avec Dieu dans un climat d'éternité' (*G* 235).

(iv) *Writing*

Tournier's fifth novel, *La Goutte d'or* (1985), is his most sustained treatment of the potentially malicious force of the image. The image steals a fragment of its subject's identity (see *G* 25), arouses and frustrates sexual desire (see *G* 190–1), subverts the distinction between reality and illusion (see *G* 210–11) and encourages a morbid fascination with the past which is equated with a form of death-wish (see *G* 234–5). Above all else, however, *La Goutte d'or* is a novel about writing. In terms of Tournier's development as a novelist, *La Goutte d'or* is significant in that it represents a renewed reflection upon his own activity as author and constitutes his clearest statement of commitment to writing and to narrative and to their independence from philosophical, historical, or pedagogical constraints. We have already seen how, in 'La Reine blonde', writing is depicted as a

---

[38] On the subversion of the hierarchy of model and copy, see, for example, Derrida, *La Dissémination*, pp. 234, 248; Deleuze, *Différence et répétition*, pp. 91–5, and *Logique du sens*, pp. 292–307. See also ch. 3, sec. (i).

[39] The two principal examples of this are *Vendredi ou la vie sauvage*, a second version of *Vendredi ou les limbes du Pacifique*, and *Les Rois Mages*, taken from *Gaspard, Melchior et Balthazar*. See also 'La Fin de Robinson Crusoé', in *Le Coq de bruyère*, which gives an alternative ending to *Vendredi ou les limbes du Pacifique*, and *Gilles et Jeanne*, which can be regarded as a rewriting of *Le Roi des aulnes*.

transformation of and defence against frustrated desire. Indeed, the incorporation of the stories of Barberousse and 'La Reine blonde' into *La Goutte d'or* draws attention as much to the act of narration as to the content of the narrative; and, at the end of the novel, writing is presented as a strategy of self-liberation rather than a truth-dependent activity.

In *La Goutte d'or* Tournier's characters are engaged in a process of self-mystification which corrodes their ability to distinguish between reality and fiction (see, for example, G 197–9). Sigisbert de Beaufond makes a brief but revealing appearance in the novel. He recounts a story which he claims to have heard from Alexandre Bernard, the pilot of a plane which crashed in the Sahara in 1920: 'Il m'a fait le récit de ce drame. Écoute bien ça, Idriss, c'est une épopée vraie!' (G 152). As he recounts this 'true' story, Beaufond assumes the role of its original narrator, using the first person to describe incidents which he never experienced. He tells of his/Bernard's attempted suicide, and shows Idriss the imaginary scars on his wrists which should authenticate his story:

Il tendit ses poignets à Idriss.
— Tu vois ces traits blancs sur la peau. Ce sont les cicatrices!
— Non, avoua Idriss honnêtement, je ne vois rien.
— C'est trop mal éclairé ici, expliqua Sigisbert.
Puis, après un moment de silence, il reprit le fil de son rêve. (G 156–7)

The 'épopée vraie' has become the 'rêve' of a narrator who is indifferent to the veracity of his narrative. Beaufond shows Idriss his wrists in order to prove the truth of his story, but the act of legitimation does not take place. Significantly, Tournier does not leave matters there. At the end of *La Goutte d'or* he adds a postscript in which he refers to his own meeting with Alexandre Bernard, the pilot of the crashed plane. He assures the reader that 'tous les détails rapportés sont authentiques' (G 262). Beaufond is the deluded narrator of an aventure he never had, but Tournier insists that the scars which resulted from Beaufond's imaginary attempt at suicide could *actually* be seen on the wrists of Alexandre Bernard: 'Quand Sigisbert de Beaufond exhibe ses poignets pour montrer les cicatrices de sa tentative de suicide, Idriss ne voit évidemment rien. Ces cicatrices, je les ai vues sur les poignets de Bernard' (G 262). Tournier draws attention to the factual grounding of his text. But the theme of storytelling, by dint of the increasing emphasis placed upon it, has acquired a prominence unrelated to the empirical truthfulness or philosophical truth of what is described. The urge to narrate has, it seems, superseded the intellectual concerns of the *romancier–philosophe*.

La Goutte d'or is less evidently dependent on familiar literary and mythological models than any of Tournier's previous novels. Nevertheless, the self-referential aspect of the narrative is more pronounced than ever. Idriss is saved from the morbid fascination of the visual image by calligraphy, the copying and florid embellishment of texts composed by others. This inevitably recalls Tournier's own aesthetic quest for a mode of imitation which incorporates and also surpasses its model (see *VP* 52–3). Calligraphy represents the novelist's art, valued for its own sake rather than subordinated to notions of meaning and communication:

En vérité la main, telle une ballerine, doit danser légèrement sur le parchemin, et non peser comme un laboureur avec sa charrue.

La calligraphie a horreur du vide. La blancheur de la page l'attire, comme la dépression atmosphérique attire les vents et fait lever la tempête. Une tempête de signes qui viennent en nuées se poser sur la page, comme des oiseaux d'encre sur un champ de neige. Les signes noirs, rangés en cohortes belliqueuses, les becs dressés, les jabots enflés, les ailes recourbées, défilent de ligne en ligne, puis se rassemblent en corolles, en rosaces, en chœurs, selon une symétrie savante [. . .] les signes sont tous prisonniers de l'encre et de l'encrier. Le calame les en libère et les lâche sur la page. La calligraphie est libération. (G 233–4)

The title of *La Goutte d'or* is an allusion to the immigrant area of Paris. But the title is misleading, since the 'rue de la Goutte-d'or' plays little role in the novel (see G 202). In the text itself the 'goutte d'or' is a piece of jewellery, which Idriss first sees on the dancer Zett Zobeida. Idriss glimpses the possibility of his liberation from the force of the image in the abstract sign which has no external referent:

Tout semble contenu dans cet ovale légèrement renflé à sa base. Tout paraît exprimé dans le silence de cette bulle solitaire [. . .] A l'opposé des pendeloques qui imitent le ciel, la terre, les animaux du désert et les poissons de la mer, la bulle dorée ne veut rien dire qu'elle-même. C'est le signe pur, la forme absolue.

Que Zett Zobeida et sa goutte d'or soient l'émanation d'un monde sans image, l'antithèse et peut-être l'antidote de la femme platinée à l'appareil de photo, Idriss commença peut-être à le soupçonner ce soir-là. (G 35)

The 'goutte d'or' is 'le signe pur', and also, as Idriss learns on the ferry to Marseilles, a symbol of freedom (see G 18). Ultimately, it symbolizes the language of fiction, given absolute status because it is liberated from the logic of truth and falsehood and from the necessity of unambiguous meaning. Tournier's novel ends in the Place Vendôme when Idriss loses control of his hydraulic drill and sees the 'goutte d'or' in the window of a jeweller's shop. He has now become the novelist himself, clutching his pen and performing the frenetic and possibly insane dance of fiction in front of the symbol of his own terrible liberation from responsibility and seriousness: 'Sourd et aveugle, Idriss continue à danser devant la goutte d'or avec sa cavalière pneumatique' (G 257).

In La Goutte d'or Tournier gives his clearest account of the sexual and psychological anxieties which underlie the fear of the image and his own commitment to the written word. And the acceptance of writing as therapeutic process rather than pedagogical tool indicates a heightened understanding of his own relationship to language, which will be the subject of the final chapter of this study.

6

Silence, Language, and *Bavardage*

(i) *The Temptation of Silence*

Language is a persistent theme and problem in Tournier's writing. In *Vendredi ou les limbes du Pacifique* Crusoé seems close to abandoning language in favour of mystical silence. In *Le Roi des aulnes* Tiffauges feels possessed by a mysterious force as he composes his 'Écrits sinistres'. In *Les Météores* Paul Surin is obliged to choose between ordinary language, which can describe his experience to others, and a private language, which, after the departure of Jean, is intelligible only to himself. Each of these cases illustrates aspects of Tournier's own attitudes. Tournier is tempted by silence and fascinated by language; he oscillates between describing fiction as a means to a pedagogical and philosophical end and implying that it is an end in itself, radically unsuitable for any communicative role. The ambivalence of Tournier's relationship to language, and its consequences for his practice of writing, will be discussed in this final chapter.

The essay 'La Logosphère et les taciturnes' provides a useful starting-point.[1] Here, Tournier uses the word 'logosphère', coined by his philosophical mentor Gaston Bachelard, to refer firstly to the disembodied linguistic domain created and occupied by the radio, and then to language in general.[2] The small number of people who are regularly invited to speak on radio or television form what Tournier calls 'une société assez rare' or 'un club plutôt fermé' (p. 167). Throughout the essay Tournier clearly regards himself as one of these 'privilégiés' who comprise 'une sorte d'aristocratie de fait' (p. 168). He writes unambiguously and unapologetically from the perspective of someone who adheres to language: 'Nous autres, bavards intarissables et barbouilleurs de papier, nous, les logosphériques

[1] Michel Tournier, 'La Logosphère et les taciturnes'. Page references will be given in the text.

[2] For Bachelard, *logosphère* has only the first of these meanings; see Gaston Bachelard, 'Rêverie et radio', in *Le Droit de rêver*, pp. 216–32.

[. . .] Résolument installé dans la logosphère [. . .] Nous autres bavards [. . .] moi qui appartiens si totalement à la logosphère par goût, vocation et profession' (pp. 169, 170, 174, 176). Nevertheless, Tournier's essay describes the fascination which the garrulous subject feels for the pre- or non-verbal: 'D'ailleurs il existe en pleine logosphère une admiration latente pour ce qui se trouve irréductiblement situé à l'extérieur, hors d'atteinte des mots' (p. 174). Tournier shares what Sartre calls 'la hantise du silence';[3] and, although he never seriously considers the possibility of abandoning language, he exhibits a degree of envy for the 'taciturne', who is able to retain his innocence and freedom by covering his actions in a mantle of silence:

Si la logosphère est le domaine des convenances et des lois, la pragmasphère des taciturnes demeure un paradis avant la faute. Quelle faute? La parole, qui fait éclater la pragmasphère individuelle dans la logosphère collective. Tais-toi et fais ce que tu veux. Parle et conforme-toi à la règle commune. Il faut choisir entre ces formules. (p. 175)

The final words of Tournier's essay return to the notion of silence as a 'paradis avant la faute': 'Nous autres verbaux, verbeux et verbalisant, nous devons apprendre à trouver ou à retrouver le vert paradis du silence, et l'amitié muette et fidèle des taciturnes' (p. 176).

Throughout 'La Logosphère et les taciturnes' Tournier indicates his mistrust of language and its uncontrolled proliferation. The writer is characterized as someone who 'rêve d'élargir la logosphère aux dimensions du monde entier' (p. 171). For such a writer, reality and language are intimately related: 'On dirait que pour lui rien n'existe vraiment sans une traduction verbale adéquate' (p. 171). Once language has acquired this authority over reality, it takes control of the speaking subject: 'Nous autres bavards, nous sommes terriblement tenus, bridés, terrorisés par les innombrables fils de nos bavardages' (pp. 174–5). The 'logosphériques' are 'Ivres de paroles' (p. 172), and they allow language to replace action: 'Leur agitation bavarde s'aggrave à mesure que le monde réel — la pragmasphère — devient d'année en année plus pauvre' (p. 172). The 'monde irréel des mots et des images' (p. 173) supplants reality, and language becomes independent of the need to communicate: 'Or, on voit en même temps la logosphère se gonfler d'année en année. On parle, on lit, on regarde

---

[3] On 'la hantise du silence', see Jean-Paul Sartre, *Situations*, i. 103.

de plus en plus. Il en résulte une terrible disette de matière à information' (p. 172).

The donkey–narrator of the Nativity in *Gaspard, Melchior et Balthazar*, himself a 'bavard' (*GMB* 155), illustrates Tournier's ambivalence towards language. Both author and narrator must check their pleasure in the music of words in order to prevent language from getting carried away with itself: 'Qu'est-ce qu'un mulet? C'est une monture sobre, sûre et solide (emporté par les qualificatifs en s, je pourrais ajouter silencieux, scrupuleux, studieux, mais je sais que je dois surveiller mon goût excessif pour les mots)' (*GMB* 159). However, the donkey fails to exercise the control which he deems necessary, since he *does* add the 'qualificatifs en s' which he knows he should omit. Tournier shares the donkey's excessive, even potentially dangerous fascination with language;[4] and he defends his 'logophilia'[5] by showing that silence also has its dangers. In 'Le Logosphère et les taciturnes' he implicitly distinguishes between different kinds of silence; the absence of language may correspond to an Edenic state of innocence or it may be the sign that speech has been *repressed*. Tournier refers to people who desperately seek to liberate 'un discours visiblement refoulé depuis des années' (p. 168). If repressed, language acquires a dangerous potency: 'La parole accumulée dans le for intérieur et jamais proférée devient un poison dangereux qui contribue à coup sûr à la violence, au suicide, à la drogue et à la folie' (p. 169).[6] *Bavardage*, on the other hand, may have 'une certaine vertu thérapeutique': 'Les cris et les imprécations déchargent le malheur, l'objectivent, en font un spectacle pour tous, qui perd ainsi sa virulence à l'égard du principal intéressé. Les taciturnes, qui gardent tout dans leur cœur, meurent de chagrin sans doute plus souvent que les logosphériques' (p. 175).

Crusoé's experience of language in *Vendredi ou les limbes du Pacifique* reproduces much of the ambivalence shown by Tournier

---

[4] In an interview given when *Gaspard, Melchior et Balthazar* was first published, Tournier explicitly drew attention to the similarity between himself and the donkey of his novel: 'Je suis comme l'âne de mon livre [. . .] je dois surveiller mon goût excessif pour les mots' ('Saint Tournier, Priez pour nous!', interview with Gilles Pudlowski, p. 36).

[5] The term 'logophilia' is taken from Michel Pierssens, *La Tour de Babil*. For discussion, see Jean-Jacques Lecercle, *Philosophy through the Looking Glass*, pp. 15–46.

[6] See also *VP* 230, where Tournier refers to immigrant workers as 'ce peuple basané réduit au plus absolu silence' and warns of the danger involved in suppressing 'la voix de cette foule muette'.

in 'La Logosphère et les taciturnes'. Writing is described as 'cet acte sacré' which saves Crusoé from 'l'abîme de la bestialité où il avait sombré' (*V* 39); and Crusoé regards the loss of language as 'cette suprême déchéance' (*V* 46). On the other hand, he realizes that language—'une façon fondamentale de cet univers *peuplé*' (*V* 47)— can express the particular only in terms of the universal and so cannot communicate the singularity of individual experience. Dissatisfied with human speech, he begins to aspire to a fully literal language free from the falsification inherent in the use of concepts and metaphors: 'Il me vient des doutes sur le sens des mots qui ne désignent pas des choses concrètes. Je ne puis plus parler qu'*à la lettre*' (*V* 58).

The form of language to which Crusoé aspires is, Tournier's text suggests, a sacred idiom which speaks to the heart of the human subject. Crusoé believes in a 'parole intérieure' and 'La parole qui est en lui et qui ne l'a jamais trompé', which is opposed to 'les messages bavards que la société humaine lui transmet encore' (*V* 148). Defoe's Robinson Crusoe comes from a Protestant family with German origins; as Tournier's text indicates on several occasions, the protagonist of *Vendredi ou les limbes du Pacifique* has a Quaker background. This deviation from Tournier's principal source has an essential bearing on Crusoé's attitude to language and to the written text. For the Catholic Church, questions of doctrine may be resolved by recourse to the traditional authority of the Vatican; the Protestants rely more upon the Bible, believing that the truth of Christianity may be found in Holy Scripture (even if, in practice, this entails an infinite burden of exegesis, which never delivers a final Truth). The Quakers do not accept either the Church or the Bible as an ultimate authority on spiritual matters. Instead, they await a private revelation which comes directly from God. Crusoé's account of his mother's Quakerism illuminates his own experience of language:

Très attachée, comme le père, à la secte des Quakers, elle rejetait l'autorité des textes sacrés aussi bien que celle de l'Église papiste. Au grand scandale de ses voisins, elle considérait la Bible comme un livre dicté par Dieu certes, mais écrit de main humaine et grandement défiguré par les vicissitudes de l'histoire et les injures du temps. Combien plus pure et plus vivante que ces grimoires venus du fond des siècles était la source de sagesse qu'elle sentait jaillir au fond d'elle-même! Là, Dieu parlait directement à sa créature. Là, l'Esprit Saint lui dispensait sa lumière surnaturelle. (*V* 90)[7]

---

[7] However, see also V 146, where it is the Bible which is described as 'la source

Tournier's logocentric attitudes are given a clear reflection here. The Bible is a written text, and so 'défiguré', prone to distortion and misunderstanding, and hence unreliable as a source of truth; the true 'source de sagesse' is God's *spoken* word ('Là, Dieu parlait directement à sa créature'), both 'pure' and 'vivante', understood in the intimacy of the human heart without the mediation of fallen language.

Crusoé's 'parole intérieure' recalls the belief in a language of the soul described by Lamartine as 'la langue sans mots' or 'le verbe suprême, / Qu'aucune main de chair n'aura jamais écrit, / Que l'âme parle à l'âme et l'esprit à l'esprit'.[8] The aim of the poet or the inspired hermeneut is to find a means of translating what Tournier refers to in *Le Vol du vampire* as 'ce silence ineffable qui est le langage des anges' (*Vol* 357) into a human idiom. But the 'parole intérieure' and the ordinary language of society are not simply different languages, as, for example, French and English. They constitute two opposed *kinds* of communication, one inspired by God and the other divorced from all divine guarantee. Crusoé believes in the infallibility of 'La parole qui est en lui et qui ne l'a jamais trompé', but he remains perpetually uncertain as to what precisely it is *saying*. The language spoken to man by God may be misunderstood or simply incomprehensible in human terms. In *Les Météores* Tournier frequently returns to the theme of an infallible and universal idiom, which is also presented as the original language of mankind. But the text can never succeed in reproducing this idiom and, as we shall see in the next section of this chapter, ordinary language remains the fallible but indispensable tool of human understanding, as well as an essential defence against the horrifying prospect of absolute silence.

(ii) *Absolute and Ordinary Language*

According to a myth which was particularly influential during the Renaissance, Adam, the original name-giver, had a perfect knowledge

---

de toute sagesse'. This inconsistency perhaps reflects Tournier's own hesitation between a logocentric conception of the spoken word and his continuing faith in the force and value of the written text.

[8] Quotations taken from Alphonse de Lamartine, 'Pensées en voyage', in *Œuvres poétiques complètes*, pp. 554–5. See also Lamartine's poem 'Dieu', ibid. 71–5, where the poet distinguishes between ordinary human language and 'le langage inné de toute intelligence', which is 'éternel, sublime, universel, immense'. The latter is spoken by the soul, and also identified with the word of God, prayer, and poetry.

of all things.[9] The names he conferred on objects and animals were their true names, and his language was characterized by the perfect correspondence of word and referent. The attempt to recover the language of Adam, or at least to correct the imperfections of human language, forms part of man's effort to overcome his fallen condition. During the Renaissance, many scholars exerted their energy in the search for the truths hidden in language which are the surviving traces of the idiom spoken in Eden; and, paradoxically, the attempt to construct the language of Adam resulted in an unprecedented volume of verbose commentary. Thousands of pages are devoted to the discussion of an idiom which, if recovered, would make all further commentary surperfluous; and, at the heart of the Cratylist nostalgia of the Renaissance, we find a barely disguised logophilia.

The Greek historian Herodotus recounts a story which was to become a *topos* of Renaissance discussions of language and which can be used to illustrate the affinity between the linguistic speculations of sixteenth-century thinkers and elements to be found in Tournier's writing. An Egyptian king, anxious to know which is the oldest and most natural language, takes two infants and has them raised by people who never speak to them; after two years the children pronounce the word 'becos', meaning 'bread' in Phrygian.[10] The underlying assumption of this experiment is that the new-born child already knows the original language, here taken to be Phrygian, and that he forgets it only through contact with society. In his study of Renaissance myths of language Claude-Gilbert Dubois summarizes this belief: 'Si l'on évitait d'imposer à l'enfant le langage social issu de la corruption babélienne, la nature réapparaîtrait sous l'artifice, et l'on pourrait voir renaître sur les lèvres d'un enfant le langage de l'humanité dans son enfance.'[11] In a passage from *Les Météores* Paul echoes this belief when he describes the possible affinity between bestial and divine silence:

P.-S. — La parole humaine se situe à mi-chemin du mutisme des bêtes et du silence des dieux. Mais entre ce mutisme et ce silence, il existe peut-être une affinité, voire une promesse d'évolution que l'irruption de la parole oblitère à tout jamais. Le mutisme bestial du petit enfant s'épanouirait

---

[9] For a discussion of linguistic theory in the Renaissance, see Claude-Gilbert Dubois, *Mythe et langage au seizième siècle*, on which my account is based.

[10] The story is taken from Herodotus *Histories*, 2.2. 1–4. For discussion, see Dubois, *Mythe et langage*, pp. 21–2.

[11] Dubois, *Mythe et langage*, p. 57.

peut-être en silence divin si son apprentissage du tumulte social ne l'embarquait pas irrémédiablement dans une autre voie. (*M* 159)

Les Météores frequently alludes to the unrealized potential of language. The psycholinguist Doctor Larouet discovers that, although many of the 'débiles mentaux' of Sainte-Brigitte cannot speak, they are nevertheless sensitive to the use of symbols. He later observes that each of the children uses the same phonemes, and he formulates what he considers to be a bold hypothesis: 'C'était que tout être humain possède à l'origine tous les matériaux sonores de toutes les langues' (*M* 51). Because of their freedom from the influence of society, the 'débiles mentaux' still have access to the foundations of language: 'Il s'agissait non d'une langue, pensait Larouet, mais de la matrice de toutes les langues, d'un fonds linguistique universel et archaïque, d'une langue fossile demeurée vivante' (*M* 52). Sister Béatrice interprets Larouet's findings in an even bolder manner, and adds her own mystical twist: 'Bien plus encore que d'une langue, il s'agissait peut-être, pensait-elle, de *la langue originelle*, celle que parlaient entre eux au Paradis terrestre Adam, Eve, le Serpent et Jéhovah' (*M* 52). Just as the children of Adam and Eve could not understand 'la langue paradisiaque' of their parents, adults are incapable of understanding the language of the 'débiles mentaux':

De même si nous ne comprenons pas les échanges des débiles profonds, c'est que nos oreilles se sont fermées à cet idiome sacré en vertu d'une dégénérescence commencée par la perte du Paradis, couronnée par la grande confusion de la tour de Babel. Cette condition babélienne, c'était la condition actuelle de l'humanité divisée par des milliers de langues qu'aucun homme ne peut prétendre maîtriser dans leur totalité. Sœur Béatrice en revenait ainsi à cette Pentecôte qui constituait pour elle le miracle par excellence, la bénédiction suprême qu'annonçait la Bonne Nouvelle incarnée par le Christ. (*M* 52-3)[12]

The theme of an archaic idiom somehow preserved from the vicissitudes of time recurs on several occasions in *Les Météores*. Icelandic, for example, is described as 'très proche de la langue originelle apportée par les Vikings au IXe et Xe siècles [. . .] C'est un peu une langue fossile dont le danois, le suédois, le norvégien et même l'anglais sont sortis' (*M* 438). Alexandre echoes the Romantic

---

[12] Note the contrast between Sister Béatrice's belief that Pentecost represents 'la bénédiction suprême' with the description of the loss of language in *Vendredi ou les limbes du Pacifique* as 'cette suprême déchéance' (*V* 46).

theory of dreams as the recollection of an original language when he watches Daniel sleeping and speculates on the words which he overhears: 'Les paroles indistinctes qui s'échappaient parfois de ses lèvres appartenaient, pensais-je, à une langue secrète et universelle à la fois, la langue fossile que parlaient tous les hommes avant la civilisation' (*M* 257).[13] Typically, Tournier keeps a cautious distance from the views of his characters, aware, like Sister Béatrice, that such beliefs will be taken as 'une rêverie mystique de plus' (*M* 52). Moreover, internal differences between the various references to the 'langue fossile' make it difficult to unify them into a single myth. The author is presumably not trying to suggest, for example, that either the language spoken in Eden or the language of dreams can be identified with Icelandic. Nevertheless, Tournier is clearly attracted by the mythical power and sacred resonances of the Babel story, even if he refuses any unambiguous statement of belief in it. In *Le Vol du vampire* he discusses and rejects Leibniz's *caractéristique universelle* and the attempt to improve language by giving it a rational and mathematical basis. According to Tournier, such a system can only exacerbate the differential aspect of language and produce tautological truths rather than ' "vérités" renvoyant à une réalité extérieure considérée comme l'ultime critère' (*Vol* 279). Confronted with the problem of a fallen and fallible language, Tournier and his characters choose a mystical solution in preference to Leibnizian rationalism.

Sister Béatrice expresses the belief that Pentecost brings about the reversal of Babel (*M* 52-3, quoted above). When Thomas Koussek expands upon this view, he acknowledges the influence of Greek Orthodox theology on his thought, but he nevertheless diverges from his Orthodox authorities, who emphasize the continuing diversity of human languages after Pentecost.[14] Koussek is attempting to resolve a problem of interpretation which is raised by a discrepancy within the biblical account of the gift of tongues. On the one hand,

---

[13] On this theory in the writings of the German Romantic psychologist G. H. von Schubert, see Albert Béguin, *L'Âme romantique et le rêve*, p. 113.

[14] On the place of Pentecost in Orthodox theology, see Father Kallistos Ware, *The Orthodox Way*, pp. 125-6. Ware observes that the descent of the Holy Spirit 'reverses the effect of the tower of Babel' (p. 125), but he asserts that human languages remain diverse: 'At Pentecost the multiplicity of tongues was not abolished, but it ceased to be a cause of separation; each spoke as before in his own tongue, but by the power of the Spirit each could understand the others' (p. 126).

the apostles are described as speaking in various different languages; on the other hand, each of the onlookers, irrespective of nationality, *hears* the words of the apostles in his own language.[15] The dilemma of the theologians is to decide whether the miracle occurs in the *mouths* of the apostles or the *ears* of their audience. Koussek adopts a version of the former solution. He suggests that the apostles speak only one language, the divine *logos*, which all understand and which all mistakenly recognize as their own tongue:

Désormais les apôtres dispersés jusqu'aux confins de la terre deviennent nomades, et leur langue est intelligible à tous. Car la langue qu'ils parlent est une langue profonde, une langue lourde, c'est le logos divin dont les mots sont les semences des choses. Ces mots sont les choses en soi, les choses elles-mêmes, et non leur reflet plus ou moins partiel et menteur, comme le sont les mots du langage humain. Et parce que ce logos exprime le fonds commun de l'être et de l'humanité, les hommes de tous les pays le comprennent immédiatement si bien que, trompés par l'habitude ou l'inattention, ils croient entendre leur propre langue. Or les apôtres ne parlent pas toutes les langues du monde, mais une seule langue que personne d'autre ne parle, bien que tout le monde la comprenne. (*M* 137–8)

The most important variation on the theme of absolute language in *Les Météores* is the 'éolien' of the twins. The psychologist René Zazzo coined the term 'cryptophasie gémellaire' to describe the secret language often developed by twins in early childhood,[16] and by adopting the word 'cryptophasie' in *Les Météores* Tournier gives further evidence of his heavy reliance upon Zazzo's work. Paul implicitly accepts Zazzo's account of how cryptophasia is often accompanied by a marked retardation in the acquisition of ordinary language: 'il apparaît clairement que ce jargon gémellaire se développe aux dépens du langage normal et donc de l'intelligence sociale. Les statistiques établissent qu'à une cryptophasie riche, abondante, complexe, correspond un langage normal pauvre, rare et rudimentaire' (*M* 156). However, Paul diverges from Tournier's principal source when he describes the failure of psychologists to understand the language of twins: 'L'erreur de tous les psychologues qui se sont penchés sur l'énigme de la cryptophasie, c'est de l'avoir considérée

---

[15] See Acts 2: 1–13, quoted in shortened form in *M* 137.
[16] Zazzo first used the term 'cryptophasie gémellaire' in a conference to which he refers in *Les Jumeaux*, p. 345. On the relationship between cryptophasia and the slow intellectual and linguistic development of twins, see *Les Jumeaux*, pp. 340–423.

comme une langue ordinaire' (*M* 156). Paul's account of the words used in the 'éolien' (see *M* 157) suggests a very low level of linguistic development, as is shown, for example, by the absence of conceptual and abstract terms. But he insists that cryptophasia cannot be understood in terms of ordinary human language. In the 'éolien', implicit understanding far outweighs explicit statement:

Or dans l'éolien, *l'accident c'est le mot, l'essentiel, c'est le silence.* Voilà ce qui fait d'une langue gémellaire un phénomène absolument incomparable à toute autre formation linguistique [. . .] L'éolien part du silence de la communion viscérale [. . .] C'est un dialogue absolu [. . .] dialogue de silences, non de paroles [. . .] chacun de ses mots et de ses silences s'enracinait dans la masse viscérale commune où nous nous confondions [. . .] ce mutisme originel possédait des chances d'épanouissement exceptionelles, fabuleuses, divines [. . .] c'est ce silence foisonnant de significations que je cherche à retrouver, mieux, à porter à une perfection plus grande que celle déjà éblouissante qu'il avait atteinte le jour maudit. (*M* 156–9)

Jean's departure is, for Paul, a private re-enactment of the catas-trophe of Babel, which deprives him of the only other person capable of understanding the 'éolien' and which directly inaugurates his own activity as author: writing, for Paul and for Tournier, begins after the confusion of tongues. But Paul has not abandoned all hope of reacquiring a form of cryptophasia. In Iceland he considers what might happen to the 'éolien' after the loss of his only interlocutor: 'Mais quid de la *cryptophasie dépariée?* Parce qu'il a perdu son frère-pareil, le cryptophone sera-t-il réduit à l'alternative du silence absolu ou du langage défectueux des sans-pareil?' (*M* 443). Paul imagines a third possibility, which he describes as 'un langage universel, analogue à celui dont la Pentecôte dota les apôtres' (*M* 443), and which he will claim to have acquired in the final chapter of the novel (*M* 540–1). The 'silence foisonnant de significations' of the 'éolien' (*M* 159) is clearly *not* identical to the 'silence absolu' to which Paul refers in Iceland.[17] The 'éolien' and the universal language may consist largely of silence, but they are assimilable to other forms of human speech in as far as they have an expressive and communicative function (see *M* 154: 'Chacun exprimait simplement le sens de son arrachement au fonds commun'). The silence of cryptophasia is, then, an integral part of a language which is different perhaps by degree,

---

[17] On the different kinds of silence, see *V* 72 and *M* 190, 198, 224, 234.

but not by nature (see *M* 158), from the 'langage défectueux des sans-pareil'. Both Paul and Tournier remain committed to language because they recognize that 'silence absolu', which is the irreversible exclusion from discourse, may be more catastrophic than the inherent shortcomings of language iself. The 'hantise du silence' frightens as much as it entices.

In *Being and Time* Heidegger makes a distinction between *Rede* (discourse) and *Gerede* (idle talk, or in French *bavardage*) which parallels the distinction in *Les Météores* between the language of the twins and ordinary language.[18] *Rede* is authentic discourse which may in practice entail the absence of speech (*Schweigen*, keeping silent). *Gerede*, on the other hand, is everyday speech characterized by groundlessness (*Bodenlosigkeit*) and ambiguity (*Zweideutigkeit*). Authentic discourse degenerates into *Gerede* when speech is no longer grounded in understanding and when what is said acquires authority simply because it is said. *Rede* becomes contaminated by *Gerede*; and, once this has occurred, the groundlessness of *Gerede* becomes the precarious foundation of subsequent understanding:

The way in which things have been interpreted in idle talk [*Gerede*] has already established itself in Dasein [. . .] This everyday way in which things have been interpreted is one into which Dasein has grown in the first instance, with never a possibility of extrication. In it, out of it, and against it, all genuine understanding, interpreting and communicating, all re-discovering and appropriating anew, are performed. In no case is a Dasein untouched and unseduced by this way in which things have been interpreted, set before the open country of a 'world-in-itself', so that it just beholds what it encounters [. . .] Far from amounting to a 'not-Being' of Dasein, this uprooting is rather Dasein's most stubborn and most everyday 'Reality'.[19]

Gerede, with which writing (*Geschreibe*) is explicitly associated,[20] counfounds Heidegger's own nostalgia for the authentic and authenticating voice. An analogous tendency can be observed in Tournier's texts. In the first instance, *bavardage* is opposed to silence or absolute language as the negative pole of a hierarchical opposition. However,

---

[18] See Heidegger, *Sein und Zeit*, pp. 160–70, on which subsequent discussion in the text is based. On silence as a part of speech, see *Sein und Zeit*, p. 165: 'Nur im echten Reden ist eigentliches Schweigen möglich' ('Keeping silent authentically is only possible in genuine discoursing').
[19] Ibid. 169–70. The translation used is taken from the excellent and indispensable English translation of *Being and Time* by John Macquarrie and Edward Robinson.
[20] See Heidegger, *Sein und Zeit*, pp. 168–9.

the author himself is 'bavard', mistrusting language but unequivocally committed to it; and, as we shall see, far from being an accident or divine punishment which disfigures the authentic experience of language from the outside, *bavardage* is an essential part of the speaking (and writing) subject's commitment to discourse.

(iii) 'Le Fétichiste'

Tournier's characters repeatedly express the desire for a language in which accuracy of reference is assured: 'je ne puis parler qu'*à la lettre*', claims Crusoé (*V* 158); Tiffauges searches for a level of meaning at which 'le sens propre et le sens figuré se confondent' (*RA* 327); Koussek describes the divine *logos* in which words are 'les choses en soi, les choses elles-mêmes, et non leur reflet plus ou moins partiel et menteur' (*M* 137); and the Bedouin on the 'île de Dioscoride' scorn the 'parole vide, creuse, mensongère, sans valeur nutritive' (*GMB* 191) which mankind must speak after the Fall from Grace. However, alongside the fantasy of a language which shows everything is the more immediate desire for a language of dissimulation. In *Canada: Journal de voyage* Tournier seems to condemn the verbosity of the art critic, in which there is 'plus d'amitié bavarde que d'amour véritable' and which serves to mask the truth revealed by the artist.[21] Even so, as we saw in Chapter 5, Tournier himself clearly practises this form of 'amitié bavarde'. He both denounces and subscribes to a process of veiling which is identified with interpretation and, more generally, with writing and the use of language itself.

The role of language is to become what Tiffauges calls a 'miroir de vérité' (*RA* 24). However, even Tiffauges acknowledges that language may act as a beneficial screen between the self and a hostile reality. Forced to describe a humiliating experience for the amusement of Göring and his guests, he is protected by his imperfect knowledge of German: 'Cette exhibition eût été insupportable au Français, si la langue allemande n'avait dressé entre ces hommes et lui un écran translucide, mais non transparent' (*RA* 217). Later, in his 'Écrits sinistres', Tiffauges emphasizes the beneficial aspects of this linguistic screen, which affects both interpersonal relations and the subject's own self-image:

---

[21] See Tournier, *Canada: Journal de voyage*, pp. 128–9.

La distance — mêmé devenue infime — entre ma pensée et ma parole, quand je pense, parle ou rêve en allemand, présente des avantages indiscutables. D'abord, la langue, ainsi légèrement opaque, crée une sorte de mur entre mes interlocuteurs et moi, et me donne une assurance inattendue et fort bénéfique [. . .] Ceci s'ajoutant à la simplification qu'impose forcément à tout ce que je dis ma connaissance imparfaite de l'allemand fait de moi un homme beaucoup plus fruste, direct et brutal que le Tiffauges francophone. Métamorphose infiniment appréciable. . . pour moi du moins. (*RA* 288)

Martin, the protagonist of Tournier's one-act play 'Le Fétichiste', insists most urgently on the necessity of veiling; and, as we shall see, his fetishism illuminates Tournier's aesthetics and his use of language in general. For Martin, clothing rescues man from his essential and intolerable nudity: 'Un homme nu est une larve sans dignité, sans fonction, il n'a pas sa place dans la société. La nudité, c'est pire qu'indécent, c'est bestial' (*CB* 280). Clothes give individual identity a differential foundation which would otherwise be absent: 'l'habit fait l'homme! [. . .] Le vêtement, c'est l'âme humaine' (*CB* 280-1). Unable to tolerate nudity, and especially female nudity, Martin discovers his predilection for the ornament: 'Moi, mon destin, c'est. . . c'est. . . *(d'une voix imperceptible:)* le falbala. . . le falbala. . . ' (*CB* 283).

In an essay published in 1927 Freud explains how the fetish has an essentially ambiguous function: it represents the penis which, despite his knowledge to the contrary, the fetishist continues to believe his mother possesses or once possessed. Freud uses the term *Verleugnung* (disavowal) to describe the process by which the fetishist simultaneously denies and affirms something—his belief in the existence of the mother's penis and the fact that she has been castrated—which he nevertheless *knows* to be untrue.[22] This hesitation between denial and affirmation provides a key for understanding Tournier's play. Martin values *warm* clothes, which indicate the proximity of the unseen or half-seen human body. Nakedness is simultaneously hidden by the fetish and nevertheless implied by the warmth which it retains. The supreme fetish is the veil, because it both *conceals* and *suggests* the form of the human face. Martin loves neither the veil nor the face, but the indistinct image of the face when

---

[22] See Freud, 'Fetishism', in *The Standard Edition*, xxi. On *Verleugnung*, see Laplanche and Pontalis, *Vocabulaire de la psychanalyse*, entry under 'Déni (— de la réalité)', pp. 115–17.

seen through the veil: 'Comme c'est beau et troublant un visage de femme à travers l'ombre légère et tremblante d'une voilette!' (*CB* 283). The dual function of revealing and concealing, rather than a predilection for clothes themselves, is characteristic of Martin's fetishism. This is demonstrated when Martin becomes a pickpocket and begins to cherish what he calls 'le billet couvé': not money for its own sake, but money which conserves 'la chaleur humaine' bestowed by its recent owner (*CB* 289). Money acts as a sign of wealth, denoting the possession of wealth, but also, by its very nature as sign, suggesting the absence of what it denotes. Money, then, stands in the same relationship to wealth as clothes do to the human body: one suggests the other, but never entirely coincides with it. Neither has value on its own; neither the face nor the veil, neither wealth nor its sign, can satisfy Martin's perversion separately. Instead, he values the impalpable interplay of veil and face, or the transient warmth of the 'billet couvé'.

At the end of his monologue Martin indicates a relationship between fetishism and language which confirms that his 'perversion' is his love for the distance which separates the sign from the thing signified:

Le collant et le flottant [. . .] Je me suis toujours demandé ce qui a le plus de charme. Il y a deux écoles. Le collant bien sûr, ça épouse les formes, et en même temps, ça les tient, ça les affermit. Mais ça manque d'imagination. Ça ne parle pas. C'est sec, laconique, c'est pète-sec. Tandis que le flottant, le flou, c'est ça qui fait rêver! C'est bavard, c'est une improvisation continuelle, ça invite à glisser la main. (*CB* 300; see also *RA* 325)

'Le collant' suggests most closely the form of what it covers, but it is 'laconique'. Martin prefers 'le flottant', which, like *bavardage*, permits the imagination to thrive around the contours of a hidden object. The linguistic metaphors ('ça ne parle pas', 'C'est [. . .] laconique', 'C'est bavard') are not gratuitous; on the contrary, they relate directly to the aesthetic of *Le Coq de bruyère* as it is stated on the back cover of the original Gallimard edition of Tournier's text:

Comme des oiseaux dans les feuillages ou des crabes sous les rochers, des vérités sont en effet embusquées sous nos objets les plus familiers, tues sous la langue des gens que nous côtoyons chaque jour. Et ces vérités sont souvent subtiles, difficiles, parfois effrayantes, hideuses, magnifiques. C'est le rôle du métaphysicien de les exhiber dans leur terrible et incompréhensible nudité. C'est celui du conteur de les costumer selon leur vocation, de les faire danser sur la musique qui les habite.

The metaphysician attempts to reveal truths 'dans leur terrible et incompréhensible nudité'.[23] The role of the storyteller, on the other hand, is to 'costumer' and to 'faire danser', or, in the words of Lanza del Vasto quoted as an epigraph to Tournier's collection of stories, to throw a '*manteau d'images*' over the nudity of truth.[24]

In his discussions of literature Tournier repeatedly indicates his adherence to an aesthetic of dissumulation. In his account of the language of fiction he commends a position between the ideal transparency of the philosophical concept and the opacity of the poetic text (*VP* 200–1). In *Le Vol du vampire* he describes how the *conte* offers a 'milieu translucide, mais non transparent, comme une épaisseur glauque dans laquelle le lecteur voit se dessiner des figures qu'il ne parvient jamais à saisir tout à fait' (*Vol* 37; compare Tiffauges's remarks on the German language, *RA* 288, quoted above). The author's fetish is language, or more particularly the *bavardage* of fiction, which neither fully reveals nor totally hides and which therefore guarantees the tantalizing hiddenness of the text's hidden truth. Tournier's texts never disclaim their author's logophilia; and writing becomes a process of veiling which invites the reader to engage in a creative *rêverie* ('c'est ça qui fait rêver! C'est bavard, c'est une improvisation continuelle, ça invite à glisser la main', *CB*300), even if this detracts from the philosophical seriousness or pedagogical usefulness of the text. *Gerede*, despite Heidegger's mistrust, may be after all the characteristic discourse of modernity, or at least of modern literature; and Tournier's insistence upon his own traditionalism distracts from an unacknowledged sympathy for the self-interrogating and self-propagating practice which recent French theorists (Barthes, Derrida, Sollers, Kristeva) have called *écriture*. In Tournier's texts *bavardage* is both dismissed as trivialized discourse and accepted as essential to the poetic experience of language, which seeks images rather than truths. Writing becomes a play of masks which always refuses to uncover a final meaning

---

[23] Compare Nietzsche's condemnation of those indecent philosophers who strive to uncover the pudenda of truth; see, for example, the 'Vorrede' to *Jenseits von Gut und Böse*, in *Werke*, ii. 565.

[24] The epigraph to *Le Coq de bruyère* is taken from the first verse of Lanza del Vasto's poem 'Le Manteau d'images', in *Le Chiffre des choses*, p. 145. Tournier characteristically alters the meaning of the passage by quoting it out of context, since he uses Lanza del Vasto's poem to support his own aesthetic of dissimulation, whereas the poem itself privileges nudity.

or to deliver the hidden message which Tournier's texts seem to foreshadow.

However, whilst this interpretation of *bavardage* in the light of *Gerede* and *écriture* indicates the relevance of Tournier's texts to contemporary theories of writing, it overlooks a more traditional aspect of his enquiry into language. Tournier shares the interest of eighteenth-century theorists—Vico, Rousseau, and Herder, for example—in the origin of language; and, although he is clearly attracted to the myth of an inaugural divine *logos*,[25] his texts also describe how the source of human speech may be more intimate and physical.

(iv) *The Origins of Language*

In Tournier's fiction the questing subject perceives himself as the addressee of language rather than as its master or origin. Tiffauges claims to hear 'des paroles confuses murmurées à [ses] oreilles', which are 'la preuve réitérée que le ciel n'est pas vide' (*RA* 13). Joan of Arc, in *Gilles et Jeanne*, believes she hears the voices of saints, whereas Gilles de Rais perceives the presence of 'le Diable et sa cour', who, he says, 'murmurent à mes oreilles des choses obscures que je ne comprends pas et que je tremble de comprendre un jour' (*GJ* 19). The transcendent source of meaning and the need to distinguish between 'voix mauvaises' and 'voix bonnes' (see *GJ* 22) make the labour of interpretation all the more urgent: 'tout est signe [. . .] Mais signe de quoi? C'est mon éternelle question dans ce monde semé d'hiéroglyphes dont je n'ai pas la clé' (*RA* 103; see also *V* 49).

However, as we saw in Chapter 2, *Le Roi des aulnes* opposes Tiffauges's faith in the coherence of meaning to the Commander's apocalyptic vision of self-proliferating signs liberated from referential safeguards. The assumption that reality is meaningful does not guarantee the intelligibility of the world, and the messages which Tournier's characters discern may be ambiguous and polysemic rather than reassuringly unequivocal. Neither Tiffauges nor Gilles de Rais understands the voices which they claim to hear (see *RA* 13 and *GJ* 19), and their sincere quest for truth leads directly into criminal error. If, in Tournier's novels, 'le ciel n'est pas vide' (*RA* 13), God is playful or even dishonest, a baroque master of ornament, illusion,

---

[25] See, for example, Tournier, *Le Vagabond immobile*, p. 21.

travesty, and deception rather than a transcendent guarantor of meaning.[26]

Throughout Tournier's writing, language is characterized by a physical power which appears to be more essential than its conceptual meaning. Tournier defines the Heraclitean *logos* as 'la parole *lourde*';[27] and the 'logos divin' conferred on the apostles at Pentecost is, like its Heraclitean version, 'une langue profonde, une langue lourde' (*M* 137). The twins' 'éolien' is so-called 'par antiphrase sans doute' (*M* 159) since it is 'formé de paroles *lourdes*', which originate in the 'silence de la communion viscérale' (*M* 158). Paul describes it as 'un langage de plomb parce que chacun de ses mots et de ses silences s'enracinait dans la masse viscérale commune où nous nous confondions' (*M* 159). The etymologists amongst Tournier's characters search for the hidden truth of language. But Rachel, the 'être féminin' of Tiffauges's universe (*RA* 14), considers the effect of language on the interlocutor to be more important than its role in the acquisition of knowledge: 'pour elle la parole est toujours caresse ou agression, jamais miroir de vérité' (*RA* 24). The first reference to the 'éolien' in *Les Météores* describes the twins' language as 'cet échange de sons caressants' (*M* 12). Here also the word is a caress and its effect on the addressee is intimate and even sexual. Koussek describes the divine *logos* as a language 'dont les mots suffirent à engrosser Marie' (*M* 138). But, as Rachel knows, the sexual caress of language may turn into physical aggression. The 'éolien' is 'doué d'une force de pénétration effrayante'; and Jean deserts his brother in order to escape the 'pesanteur écrasante' of 'ce bombardement infaillible qui l'atteignait jusqu'à la moelle des os' (M 159). In Tournier's texts language has an awesome physical reality. It reaches down, too far perhaps, into the depths of the human body. At the end of *Les Météores* Paul claims to have learned a universal language which allows him to hear and understand 'la voix des choses'; yet he also concedes that 'la voix des choses' is 'comme la voix de ses propres humeurs' (*M* 540). In other words, what the crippled mystic perceives as the 'chant du monde' might be recognized by others as 'rumeur de sang, battement de cœur, râle, flatulence et

---

[26] See *V* 100: 'La nature avait-elle été modelée par un Dieu infiniment sage et majestueux, ou par un démiurge baroque poussé aux plus folles combinaisons par l'ange du bizarre?'

[27] Tournier, *Canada: Journal de voyage*, p. 107.

borborygme' (*M* 540). Paul projects the language of his own body on to the world: 'Ce qu'il y avait de plus intime devient universel' (*M* 541). As his own account suggests, his 'universal language' may be nothing other than vulgar flatulence.

The question of language, for Tournier, requires consideration of the speaking subject's relationship to his own body. In *Gaspard, Melchior et Balthazar* Balthazar describes how the tattoo unites word and flesh and makes it possible to 'incarner le signe': 'Il [le tatoué] appartient indéfectiblement à l'empire des signes, signaux et signatures. Sa peau est logos [. . .] le tatoué ne parle ni n'écrit: il est écriture et parole' (*GMB* 53). The tattoo is literally 'the Word made flesh'. Balthazar believes that this may be the restoration of the original unity of body and sign:

Oui, je ne serais pas surpris que le corps peint et sculpté des compagnons de Gaspard rappelât celui d'Adam dans son innocence originelle et sa relation intime avec le Verbe de Dieu. Cependant que nos corps lisses, blancs et besogneux correspondent à la chair punie, humiliée et exilée loin de Dieu qui est la nôtre depuis la chute de l'homme. . . (*GMB* 53-4)

Tournier's own discussion of tattoos in *Des clefs et des serrures* supports Balthazar's analysis.[28] For Tournier, the tattoo is a form of ornament compatible with the state of nature, whereas clothing 'ne fait que consacrer le divorce entre le corps et la nature' (p. 131). The primitive state of humanity, described as 'ce paradis' (p. 135), is characterized by 'une profonde consubstantialité de la chair et de la terre' (p. 131): body, sign, and environment are united. Tournier's essay describes primitive tribesmen who transform their bodies into a silent poem: 'Le Nouaba fait de son corps un grimoire. Il s'identifie à son propre chef-d'œuvre pictural et sculptural. Ici le verbe s'intègre totalement à la chair. Chaque corps est un poème muet et non écrit' (p. 135). Tournier refers to the work of the anthropologist Marcel Jousse, who distinguishes between the Greek tradition of the written sign and the Palestinian *oral* tradition, which involves, in Tournier's words, 'non seulement la voix, mais tout le corps, parce que ce discours n'est autre que la vérité mimée du cosmos' (p. 134). Jousse describes man as the 'Anthropos mimeur',

---

[28] See Tournier, *Des clefs et des serrures*, pp. 131–5. Page references will be given in the text.

who uses his body as *'un langage gestuel, spontané, universel'*;[29] and the term 'corporage' is used to designate the language of the body which gives a complete expression of the human subject's interaction with the universe.[30] Tournier draws on Jousse's work to support his own reflection 'sur la relation du signe et du corps humain dont il émane forcément' (p.134). The sign originates in the human body; but it is progressively alienated from 'sa source corporelle' (p.134) as civilization translates the primitive body-text into the spoken word and 'texts' in the more familiar sense. The growing disjunction between body and sign is described as both a cultural process and, more importantly, a vital stage in Christian history. In a passage which recalls Koussek's Trinitarian beliefs in *Les Météores*, Tournier describes how the Word must abandon the body of Christ in order to prepare the advent of the Paraclete:

C'est le sens de la Passion du Christ. Le corps de l'enseigneur ayant délivré son message, vidé de son contenu de vérité, peut être dégradé, privé de ses vêtements et des attributs de sa dignité, couvert d'oripeaux dérisoires, d'injures et de crachats. Le corps du Christ, déserté par la Parole au profit du Saint-Esprit et des apôtres, est couvert de plaies non parlantes, de scarifications dépourvues de toute valeur calligraphique. (p.135)

Tournier's account is characteristically ambivalent. On the one hand, the desertion of Christ by the Word seems to entail the humiliation and degradation of the flesh. On the other hand, the separation of the sign from its corporeal source is seen as a necessary fall from origins, which ensures the possibility of human and spiritual progress.

Like Antonin Artaud or Louis Wolfson, Tournier perceives language as an intimate part of the human body.[31] But he agrees with Marcel Jousse that *corporage* tends to become *langage*,[32] even if this entails the loss of man's original relationship with nature and the cosmos. Despite the nostalgia for origins which pervades his texts, Tournier suggests that this loss may be ultimately beneficial. The

---

[29] Marcel Jousse, *L'Anthropologie du geste*, p. 43.   [30] See ibid. 114.

[31] On Artaud and Wolfson, and the relationship between language and the body, see Jean-Jacques Lecercle, *Philosophy through the Looking Glass*, especially pp. 39–41. For Louis Wolfson's remarkable account of his 'linguistic illness', see *Le Schizo et les langues*.

[32] On the transition from *corporage* to *langage*, see Jousse, *L'Anthropologie du geste*, p. 114.

urge for self-expression pre-exists and motivates the acquisition of an adequate *means* of expression; and the demand for access to the order of signification is signalled by the cry, or even the *silent* cry, of agony and desolation which Tournier's characters perceive. At low tide on the beach near the Pierres Sonnantes, Jean is sensitive to 'un *cri* silencieux d'abandon et de frustration qui montait des sols marins découverts', and he is 'mobilisé par l'appel silencieux de ces mille et mille bouches assoiffées' (*M* 153). Tiffauges, persecuted by his teachers at Saint-Christophe, expresses his revolt in a silent cry: 'Le refus d'exister montait en moi comme une clameur silencieuse. C'était un cri secret, un hurlement étouffé qui sortait de mon cœur pour se confondre avec la vibration des choses immobiles' (*RA* 34; see also *RA* 45). In *Les Météores* Alexandre's account of how Briffaut loses an ear begins with a scream of pain: 'Le cri a éclaté au centre du roncier [. . .] C'est alors que le cri a retenti, un rugissement de douleur et de colère, une plainte furieuse, véhémente, pleine de menaces meurtrières' (*M* 210–11). After Martine's rape, Tiffauges hears 'un hurlement déchirant [. . .] un cri de bête blessée, une déchirure de l'air qui [le] pétrifia' (*RA* 132); and throughout *Le Roi des aulnes* he is haunted by 'un certain cri [. . .] qui l'avait percé comme un coup de lance' (*RA* 222) and which he believes to be the 'son fondamental de son destin' (*RA* 389):

j'ai été soudain cloué sur place par un long cri [. . .] C'était une note gutturale, d'une pureté incomparable, longtemps soutenue, comme un appel venu du plus profond du corps, puis s'achevant dans une série de modulations ensemble joyeuses et pathétiques. (*RA* 105)

C'est alors que le *cri* s'éleva [. . .] Cette longue plainte gutturale et modulée, pleine d'harmoniques, certains d'une étrange allégresse, d'autres exhalant la plus intolérable douleur, elle n'avait cessé de retentir depuis son enfance souffreteuse dans les couloirs glacés de Saint-Christophe jusqu'au fond de la forêt de Rominten où elle saluait la mort des grands cerfs. (*RA* 388)

The cry, described as 'ce chant transcendant' (*RA* 388–9), contains elements of 'allégresse' and 'douleur' (*RA* 388), and gives an impression of 'rigueur' and 'plénitude', 'équilibre' and 'débordement' (*RA* 105). It is not intelligible in any familiar sense of the word, since it consists of too many opposed qualities. Nevertheless, non-signifying sound is the origin and condition of intelligibility. This is illustrated by Tiffauges's 'brame', another version of the cry, which has a physical origin in the depths of the body: 'C'est comme un rot profond et prolongé qui semble monter de mes entrailles et qui fait longuement vibrer mon cou. En lui s'exhale tout l'ennui de vivre et toute l'angoisse de mourir' (*RA* 51). The 'brame' signals the rejection of silence, as it strains to 'make sense', to transform anguish into sound and then meaning. It both expresses and attempts to overcome Tiffauges's suffering: 'C'est à la fois une mimique de désespoir et une sorte de rite pour surmonter le désespoir' (*RA* 51).

In the final chapter of *Les Météores* Paul has been excluded from the community of language: 'Je ne suis plus qu'un cri, qu'une douleur [. . .] j'ai hurlé silencieusement [. . .] car il y a beau temps que mes paroles et mes cris ne parviennent plus à mon entourage' (*M* 525–6). Paul explicitly relates the necessity of confronting and surmounting pain to the acquisition of language. He realizes that he must 'Apprendre à nager dans la souffrance':

> Je sais cela depuis peu. Depuis que la souffrance massive et homogène comme la nuit noire se nuance, se différencie. Ce n'est plus le grondement sourd et assourdissant qui assomme. Ce n'est pas encore un langage. C'est une gamme de cris, de stridences, de coups sonores, de susurrements, de cliquetis. Ces mille et mille voix de la souffrance ne doivent plus être étouffées par le bâillon anesthésique. Apprendre à parler. (*M* 527).

'Apprendre à nager dans la souffrance [. . .] Apprendre à parler': verbal repetition suggests the equivalence of these two processes. Pain is described as sound ('une gamme de cris') which does not yet constitute an articulated language ('Ce n'est pas encore un langage'). Paul wants to learn to speak in order to give voice to his suffering, but also to overcome the intolerable immediacy of pain. The function of language is to express (ex-press, squeeze out), and thereby to surmount its origin in the violent mutilation of the body.

In *Le Vent Paraclet* Tournier recounts an episode from his childhood which illuminates the relationship between language and suffering and which gives an important illustration of the veiling function of writing. Like Michel Leiris in *L'Âge d'homme*,[33] Tournier emphasizes the enduring trauma caused by the brutal removal of his tonsils when he was a child: 'Mais quarante-cinq ans plus tard, j'en porte encore les traces et je reste incapable d'évoquer cette scène de sang-froid' (*VP* 16). He is left with 'une incurable méfiance à l'égard de mes semblables, même les plus proches, même les plus chers'

---

[33] See Michel Leiris, *L'Âge d'homme*, pp. 104–5, for the description of an experience which bears a striking resemblance to Tournier's account of the removal of his tonsils in *Le Vent Paraclet*.

(*VP* 16). Characteristically, however, Tournier subsumes the private trauma into a general meditation: 'Cette sanglante mésaventure dont s'éclabousse mon enfance comme d'un grand soleil rouge, je n'ai pas fini de la ruminer et d'en tirer toute sorte de questions, d'idées, d'hypothèses' (*VP* 17). This leads into a series of reflections on initiation and its cultural significance. Having briefly described a supposedly formative episode from his childhood, Tournier uses the general meditation as a means of diverting attention away from the particular experience. However, the discussion of initiation also *returns* to the problem of the scream and its role as a mode of entry into society: 'L'initiation d'un enfant se fait par un double mouvement: entrée dans la société — principalement des hommes — éloignement du giron maternel. En somme, passage d'un état biologique à un statut social. Et cela ne va jamais sans larmes ni cris' (*VP* 17).

Even when talking of his own childhood, Tournier's intentions are not primarily autobiographical. If anything, he is attempting to surmount the autobiographical through a movement of generalization— the philosophical gesture *par excellence*—which distracts author and reader from the intensity of personal suffering. Therefore it covertly counteracts the force of the trauma it purports to describe. In the account of his experience Tournier adopts an allegorical mode of writing which gives the incident a significance beyond its purely personal repercussions. This allegorical mode is first suggested by the use of upper case in the words 'Agression' and 'Attentat' with which the author introduces the anecdote ('il y avait eu l'Agression, l'Attentat', *VP* 15). Later, Tournier reveals that the surgeon who performed the operation is called 'Bourgeois' ('cet équarrisseur s'appelait Bourgeois', *VP* 16). The possibly true detail acquires, in this account, a significance which goes beyond its factual veracity. The whole episode can be read as an allegory of the child's initiation into bourgeois society. This coincides with both a violent atack on the child and the acquisition of language. Throughout the passage Tournier repeatedly uses the words 'enfant' and 'enfance':[34] always attentive to etymology, he knows that the infant is literally *in-fans*,

---

[34] See *VP* 15–18: 'un crime qui a ensanglanté mon enfance [. . .] J'étais un enfant hypernerveux [. . .] un enfant de quatre ans [. . .] Cette sanglante mésaventure dont s'éclabousse mon enfance [. . .] L'enfance nous est donnée comme un chaos brûlant [. . .] L'un des aspects paradoxaux de l'enfant [. . .] L'initiation d'un enfant [. . .] la liste des supplices infligés à l'enfant.'

unable to speak. Claude Lévi-Strauss taught Tournier one of the truisms of structuralist thought when he drew his attention to the inseparability and coextensivity of language and society (see *Vol* 387). The infant has no memory (see *M* 174: 'Il ne parle pas encore, il ne se souviendra de rien') and no social standing. According to Tournier, the operation which he describes was performed 'à l'aube de [sa] petite préhistoire personnelle' (*VP* 15). The 'aube' is neither fully light nor fully dark, but an intermediary period during which darkness becomes light. Here it represents the transitional process, which Tournier describes as a single event, through which consciousness and language are acquired. The surgeon attacks and disfigures the child's tonsils, which are metonymically related to the organs of speech. This disfiguration also signals the infant's entry into society; and, as Tournier says, 'cela ne va jamais sans larmes ni cris' (*VP* 17).

Tournier concludes from his experience that adulthood must become a never-complete gloss on infancy: 'L'enfance nous est donnée comme un chaos brûlant, et nous n'avons pas trop de tout le reste de notre vie pour tenter de le mettre en ordre et de nous l'expliquer' (*VP* 17). The chaos of the non-linguistic may be transformed into order through explanation and commentary. In *Le Vent Paraclet* Tournier recalls, describes, and gives meaning to a painful episode from his childhood; and the adult uses language in an attempt to come to terms with his own pre-verbal trauma.

By way of frontispiece to *Le Vent Paraclet*, Tournier describes 'Un enfant en larmes caché par l'œuvre qu'il porte' (*VP* 9). Later, he refers to 'le parti littéraire que chacun — moi tout le premier — peut tirer de ses plaies et bosses'; and he describes the artist's profession as 'un métier qui lui permet de mettre en musique ses propres pleurs' (*VP* 23). The literary consequences of this aesthetic are more interesting than any biographical misfortune to which Tournier may allude. The suffering of the non-speaker (*in-fans*) is described and surmounted by the intellectualized *bavardage* of his later speaking and writing self. Literature and, at least in Tournier's use of it, theory become the essential components of a necessary generalized fetishism which aims to renarrate chaos in the mode of order. In Tournier's writing, then, we find the ambivalences of an author who knows that 'Nous parlons trop',[35] but who will continue to speak and

---

[35] Tournier, *Vendredi ou la vie sauvage*, p. 114: 'Nous parlons trop. Il n'est pas toujours bon de parler. Dans ma tribu, chez les Araucans, plus on est sage, moins

write; who knows that he must 'surveiller [son] goût excessif pour les mots' (*GMB* 159), but who will inevitably allow his love for language to exceed the strict constraints of unequivocal meaning; who knows that, if someone 'brise le silence', then 'il rompt quelque chose, irrémédiablement' (*M* 175), but who remains irreversibly committed to his own logophilia.

Alexandre, the scandalous uncle of *Les Météores*, often expresses the most provocative aspects of Tournier's modernity which the author himself sometimes seems unwilling to accept. On the subject of language, he gives an important insight into Tournier's own practice. He is the most playful of Tournier's etymologists, and he makes a mockery of the search for the *etymon* by taking it too seriously. Through the etymologies of 'prolétaire', 'chien', and 'fesse', he discovers why proletarians are prolific, dogs are cynical, and buttocks should be singular rather than plural (*M* 125, 193, and 196). In one passage Alexandre gives what is perhaps the most revealing account of language to be found anywhere in Tournier's fiction. Surveying the rubbish tip which is also the negative image of an affluent but suicidal society, he realizes that 'la gadoue est un amas de *griffes*' (*M* 300). These 'griffes' are authenticating marks separated from the object which they are supposed to authenticate. In this passage Tournier indicates his own fascination for a language which has outlived its communicative purpose; and the derisory nature of a referential text which has ceased to refer is also what gives it an absolute quality in the eyes of both dandy and author:

Car ces griffes sont bavardes, et même prolixes, déclamatoires, exaltantes. Elles proclament les qualités brillantes, les vertus incomparables, les avantages décisifs d'un objet ou d'une matière — pour en détailler ensuite le mode d'emploi. Et comme cet objet, cette matière n'existent plus, cette possession se referme sur le vide, cette déclamation éclate dans le néant, devenant ainsi absolues et dérisoires.

Amas de griffes et de célébrations, vide, dérision et absolu — je reconnais bien là, dans ces traits de mon milieu naturel, les constantes de mon esprit et de mon cœur. (*M* 300)

on parle. Plus on parle, moins on est respecté. Les animaux les plus bavards sont les singes et, parmi les hommes, ce sont les petits enfants et les vieilles femmes qui parlent le plus.'

Concluding Remarks
Between Synthesis and Scarcity

Tournier describes his literary project as the ambitious combination of philosophy and fiction. Even so, he has frequently expressed dissatisfaction with his first novel, *Vendredi ou les limbes du Pacifique*, on the grounds that it is too *overtly* philosophical.[1] He insists that philosophy should provide 'une infrastructure métaphysique invisible'[2] rather than an established set of themes and ideas, and thereby he suggests that the philosophical significance of his work cannot be separated from questions of literary expression and context. These concluding pages will indicate some of the ways in which philosophical perceptions underlie the construction and composition of Tournier's fiction; and, more particularly, I shall indicate how the figure of the nomad has a special importance in Tournier's combination of philosophy and literature.

'La Famille Adam', the first story in *Le Coq de bruyère*, recapitulates some of Tournier's favourite themes and gives a concise version of the cycle of plenitude, loss, and reconciliation which plays an important role in much of his writing. A hermaphrodite creator makes man in his/her own image, but subsequently divides him/her into complementary and antagonistic halves: male and female, nomad and sedentary. Unity is forfeit, but the ensuing period of strife and conflict comes to an end when, in the final lines of the story, Jehovah is reunited with the rebellious sedentary Cain. Plenitude gives way to duality, which is in turn overcome, if only imaginatively, by this improbable reconciliation. The nostalgia for lost paradises recurs throughout Tournier's fiction. In *Gaspard, Melchior et Balthazar* the Bedouin chief Rabbi Rizza, whom Taor encounters on the 'île de Dioscoride', recalls an Edenic state when 'Le corps et l'âme étaient coulés d'un seul bloc' (*GMB* 191). However, the Bedouin chief realizes that 'La chute de l'homme a cassé la vérité en deux morceaux'

---

[1] See, for example, 'Vers la concision et la limpidité', interview with Jean-Marie Magnan, p. 16.
[2] Tournier, *Des clefs et des serrures*, p. 193.

(*GMB* 191). After the Fall, as Paul observes in *Les Météores*, 'Le propre de l'homme est la séparation de l'âme et du corps' (*M* 525). Tournier's fiction describes and participates in the quest for lost unity and a state of totality from which no experience, even (as *Gilles et Jeanne* indicates) the experience of Evil, is excluded. In *Le Roi des aulnes* the nostalgia for totality is illustrated by Tiffauges's description of the original Adam, a hermaphrodite in a state of permanent and total orgasm: 'perpétuellement en proie à des transports amoureux d'une perfection inouïe' (*RA* 25). This arouses 'je ne sais quelle nostalgie atavique d'une vie surhumaine, placée par sa plénitude même au-dessus des vicissitudes du temps et du vieillissement' (*RA* 26). Tiffauges's interpretation of Genesis offers a typical example of Tournier's provocative intellectual *bricolage*, as unorthodox biblical exegesis is combined with Platonic and Romantic myths of an original hermaphrodite.[3] For Tiffauges, the Fall is unity become trinity:

> Car s'il y a dans la Genèse une *chute de l'homme*, ce n'est pas dans l'épisode de la pomme — qui marque une promotion au contraire, l'accession à la connaissance du bien et du mal — mais dans cette dislocation qui brisa en trois l'Adam originel, faisant choir de l'homme la femme, puis l'enfant, créant d'un coup ces trois malheureux, l'enfant éternel orphelin, la femme esseulée, apeurée, toujours à la recherche d'un protecteur, l'homme léger, alerte, mais comme un roi qu'on a dépouillé de tous ses attributs pour le soumettre à des travaux serviles. (*RA* 26)

It is important to observe that the apparent plenitude of origins described in Tournier's texts is in fact already threatened by the spectre of dissatisfaction. Tiffauges's fantasy of return ('Remonter la pente, restaurer l'Adam originel', *RA* 26) is qualified by his realization that 'la solitude impliquée par l'hermaphrodisme n'est pas bonne' (*RA* 25). In consequence, Tiffauges chooses the sublimated sexuality of *phorie* rather than the solitary self-gratification of the hermaphrodite. In 'La Famille Adam' the original Adam 'n'était pas d'accord avec lui-même' and he explains to his Creator that 'Il y a deux êtres en moi' (*CB* 12). The linguistic dualisms male/female and nomad/sedentary are not simply the errors of a fallen language. The opposition corresponds to an ontological dualism which is all the more acute when antagonistic elements coexist within the same subject.

---

[3] Tournier himself relates the creation of Eve to the dislocation of the Platonic hermaphrodite in 'Des éclairs dans la nuit du cœur'.

All Tournier's fiction bears witness to the urge for reconciliation. The most simple expression of this is in the story 'La Mère Noël', which, in two pages, describes the unification of male and female, clerical and radical, Christian and pagan, when a female Father Christmas gives his/her breast to the Child Jesus (CB 27–9). But the reconciliation of opposites is not just the restitution of an archaic unity. The tripartite scheme of plenitude, loss, and eventual restoration is prospective rather than simply nostalgic. In terms which recur throughout Tournier's writing, the *donné* must be rectified by the *construit*. Exiled from Eden, Cain 'reconstituait à force de travail et d'intelligence ce qu'Adam avait perdu par sa bêtise!' (CB 15). Nostalgia for a lost paradise is combined with hope for the future correction of what made the Fall possible, achieved through a long and uncertain labour of construction. Even Paul Surin, the most nostalgic of all Tournier's characters, realizes in the course of his *voyage initiatique* that his journey enriches him and enables him to achieve a state which surpasses his relationship with Jean (see *M* 436). The final words of 'La Famille Adam' promise that, once consolidated, the reconciliation of Jehovah and Cain, God and man, nomad and sedentary, will never be disrupted by a second Fall: 'Le petit-fils serra le grand-père sur son cœur. Puis il s'agenouilla pour se faire pardonner et bénir. Ensuite Jéhovah — toujours un peu grognant pour la forme — fut solennellement intronisé dans le temple d'Hénoch qu'il ne quitta plus désormais' (CB 17).

The fallen and self-divided state of humanity is revealed and described with the aid of binary oppositions. Despite his nostalgia for unity, Tournier does not reject the use of dichotomies. On the contrary, in *Le Vol du vampire* he defends 'l'*alternative* [qui] — de Kierkegaard à Bergson — constitue un instrument d'analyse précieux et efficace' (*Vol* 212). The author and thinker may compensate for the imperfection of the linguistic tools at his disposal by the finesse with which he handles them: 'La "dichotomie" ne doit pas être maniée comme une hache de bûcheron, mais nuancée au contraire, jusqu'à l'effacement' (*Vol* 212). This 'effacement' of dichotomies is the surmounting of their inherent inadequacies rather than their abandonment. If the 'clefs binaires' are 'tempérées par ce qu'il faut de scepticisme et d'esprit ludique', they may still make an important contribution to the process of understanding (*Vol* 213). In *Le Roi des aulnes* Tiffauges asserts that the 'bonheur'/'malheur' dichotomy is inapplicable in his case, and later he advocates 'ignorance de l'alternative pureté-impureté' (*RA* 82 and 85). But neither Tiffauges nor Tournier aims to abolish binary thinking. Tiffauges replaces the purity/impurity opposition with his own distinction between innocence and purity (*RA* 85); and he prefers the Spinozistic terms 'joie' and 'tristesse' to 'bonheur' and 'malheur': 'Moi, je suis l'homme de la tristesse et de la joie. Alternative tout opposée à l'alternative malheur–bonheur' (*RA* 82).

The nomad/sedentary distinction which recurs throughout Tournier's writing illustrates his attitude to binary oppositions in general. In *Le Roi des aulnes* Tiffauges describes the relationship between Cain and Abel as an atavistic and archetypal conflict: 'La querelle d'Abel et de Caïn se poursuit de génération en génération depuis l'origine des temps jusqu'à nos jours, comme l'opposition atavique des nomades et des sédentaires, ou plus précisément comme la persécution acharnée dont les nomades sont victimes de la part des sédentaires' (*RA* 40). The linguistic opposition corresponds to a real historical and mythical distinction, but this does not exclude the possibility of mixed states. On the contrary, Tiffauges realizes that the spread of the sedentary life-style is the result of a historical process which corresponds to the nomad's own profound desires:

Après des siècles de cueillette, l'homme a inventé l'agriculture. Après des siècles de chasse, il a découvert l'élevage. Lassé de courir les steppes glacées, je rêve de vergers clos où les plus beaux fruits s'offriraient d'eux-mêmes à ma main, je rêve de vastes troupeaux dociles et disponibles, enfermés dans des étables tièdes et fumantes où il ferait bon dormir avec eux l'hiver. . . (*RA* 125–6)

Willingly or unwillingly, the nomad is fascinated and influenced by sedentary values. In 'L'Aire du Muguet' the lorry-driver Pierre is brought to grief by his 'nostalgies de cul-terreux' (*CB* 255), whilst his companion Gaston successfully domesticates the nomadic life-style by importing the comforts of home life into the cabin of his articulated lorry (see *CB* 239–42). The opposition between nomad and sedentary is qualified by a variety of mixed states, expressed by apparently paradoxical formulations, which are, however, never simply self-negating. Gaspard's followers are 'nomades sédentarisés' (*GMB* 34); Tiffauges is a 'faux sédentaire' (*RA* 41) because he temporarily suppresses his nomadic inclinations; Balthazar is a 'voyageur sédentaire' (*GMB* 69) because he travels in luxury and comfort; and Tournier describes himself as a 'vagabond immobile',[4] torn between the twin fascinations of nomadism and the sedentary life, profiting greatly from travel despite the complaints of 'un certain grincheux sédentaire qui est en [lui]' (VP 262).

The confusion of absolute distinctions between nomad and sedentary and the variety of mixed states do not entail a generalized collapse of oppositions. On this point, Tournier's writing invites comparison with the work of Deleuze and Guattari, particularly given their shared interest in the nomad/sedentary dichotomy. Deleuze and Guattari recognize that the nomad is always partially or potentially comparable to the sedentary: 'il n'y a pas de pur nomade, il y a toujours et déjà un campement où il s'agit de stocker, si peu que ce soit, d'inscrire et de répartir, de se marier et de se nourrir.'[5] They acknowledge the 'présupposition réciproque' of binary opposites and the existence of 'mélanges de fait', but they nevertheless insist upon 'la nécessité de la distinction la plus rigoureuse'.[6] For Deleuze and Guattari, the nomad must be preserved from recuperation within a sedentary system of values. Tournier, on the other hand, regards the possibility of describing mixed states ('faux sédentaire', 'nomades sédentarisés', 'voyageur sédentaire', 'vagabond immobile') as a triumph of the intellect over binary oppositions. He attempts to overcome the limitations of the dichotomy by rejecting absolute barriers between opposites; and so the nomad in his texts is never entirely independent of the sedentary order. Tiffauges execrates, but nevertheless maintains an uneasy dependence upon, what he calls the 'magma boueux qui s'appelle l'Ordre établi' (RA 83). The Bedouin of the 'île de Dioscoride' in Gaspard, Melchior et Balthazar seem alien to the values of their sedentary visitors: 'Tout ici disait la force, la vitesse, une avidité d'autant plus redoutable qu'elle s'accompagnait d'un absolu mépris pour les richesses et leurs douceurs' (GMB 192). Even so, they spend their lives in anticipation of the same revolution which will transform the life of Taor (see GMB 191). According to Koussek in Les Météores after the descent of the Paraclete the apostles are 'dispersés jusqu'aux confins du monde' and

---

[4] Tournier uses this phrase in the title of a selection of aphorisms and observations published together with drawings by Jean-Max Toubeau, Le Vagabond immobile.
[5] Deleuze and Guattari, L'Anti-Œdipe, p. 174.
[6] See, for example, Deleuze and Guattari, Mille plateaux, pp. 476-7, 510; see also ibid. 31 on the dichotomy as 'l'ennemi tout à fait nécessaire, le meuble que nous ne cessons pas de déplacer'.

they 'deviennent nomades'; but their nomadism is sustained by the 'logos divin' which they have learned to speak (*M* 137). Nomad and sedentary participate in the same spiritual drama and serve the same transcendent *logos*.

Deleuze and Guattari insist upon the distinction between nomad and migrant: 'Le nomade n'est pas du tout le migrant; car le migrant va principalement d'un point à un autre, même si cet autre est incertain, imprévu ou mal localisé.'[7] The migrant's journey is always the purposeful movement from one place to another, whereas the nomad travels without destination. Tournier makes no such distinction, and his nomads are frequently what Deleuze and Guattari would call migrants, since their journeys have, or retrospectively acquire, destination and motivation. Tiffauges describes wandering labourers, who constitute 'une masse fluctuante importante, et en principe mal-pensante, parce que déracinée'; but these wanderers 'se fixent dans des villes où ils forment la population prolétarienne des grandes cités industrielles' (*RA* 40–1). In *La Goutte d'or* Idriss is one of 'ceux qui doivent partir' (*G* 114) and he obeys 'un vieil atavisme nomade' (*G* 65); but his journey has a destination (Paris) and a purpose (to recover a photograph). The kings in *Gaspard, Melchior, et Balthazar* set out with vague or uncertain projects, but their disparate concerns are united as they travel to Bethlehem with a single quest—to find the new king. Balthazar puns on the word 'sens', which is both 'meaning' and 'direction', when he refers to 'le sens de notre voyage' (*GMB* 47). Meaning *is* direction. Once the journey acquires a destination, it falls easily into the categories of purpose and finality.[8]

In 'La Famille Adam' Tournier indicates his awareness that writing is a sedentary activity: '[Abel] était fier que ses enfants [. . .] ne sussent ni lire ni écrire, car il n'y a pas d'école pour les nomades' (*CB* 15). Despite the important role which the theme of oral narration plays in his most recent novels, *Gaspard, Melchior et Balthazar* and *La Goutte d'or*, Tournier himself remains committed to the art of writing, and in his texts nomadism is consistently interpreted from a sedentary perspective. Paul's interpretation of his nomadic brother's

---

[7] Ibid. 471.

[8] Compare Deleuze, *Logique du sens*, p. 93: 'Or le bon sens se dit d'une direction: il est sens unique, il exprime l'exigence d'un ordre d'après lequel il faut choisir une direction et s'en tenir à elle.'

experience of space in *Les Météores* gives a clear illustration of how, in Tournier's fiction, the writer and sedentary attempts to explain nomadism from his own viewpoint and thereby to assert the undiminished authority of his own modes of understanding over an essentially alien experience:

C'est pourquoi la réaction de Jean à ce pays est parfaitement compréhensible, logique, rationnelle. Il a répondu à l'espace canadien à la canadienne. En faisant ce qu'il pouvait pour *couvrir* cette terre [. . .] Jean-le-Cardeur est devenu ici Jean-l'Arpenteur. Arpenter, c'est *habiller intelligemment* une terre à l'aide de la chaîne, du jalon, de la fiche plombée, du graphomètre. Par l'arpentage, une terre cesse proprement d'être *immense*, c'est-à-dire sans mesure. Elle est mesurée et donc assimilée par l'intelligence malgré ses courbes, ses dénivellations, ses zones impénétrables — taillis et marécages — et prête à l'abornement et à l'enregistrement cadastral. (*M* 495)

The key phrases in Paul's account are '*habiller intelligemment*' and 'assimilée par l'intelligence'. The sedentary cannot tolerate space unless it is subdivided and mastered by human intelligence. He constructs technical instruments and a technical vocabulary in order to bring the alterity of space under the control of reason. For Paul, space is an inconvenience. Despite his interest in Urs Kraus's theory of 'espace riche', he cannot accept the notion of movement as a process of perpetual becoming. He attempts to enclose and overcome space rather than to experience its richness. Deleuze and Guattari illuminate this tendency in Paul's and Tournier's writing with their account of how the State attempts to impose order on to the open spaces:

Une des tâches fondamentales de l'État, c'est de strier l'espace sur lequel il règne, ou de se servir des espaces lisses comme d'un moyen de communication au service d'un espace strié. Non seulement vaincre le nomadisme, mais contrôler les migrations [. . .] c'est une affaire vitale pour chaque État. L'État en effet ne se sépare pas, partout où il le peut, d'un procès de capture sur des flux de toutes sortes, de populations, de marchandises ou de commerce, d'argent ou de capitaux, etc. Encore faut-il des trajets fixes, aux directions bien déterminées, qui limitent la vitesse, qui règlent les circulations, qui relativisent le mouvement, qui mesurent dans leurs détails les mouvements relatifs des sujets et des objets.[9]

It will be clear by now that the figure of the nomad, for Tournier and for Deleuze and Guattari, has philosophical as well as social

---

[9] Deleuze and Guattari, *Mille plateaux*, p. 479.

and anthropological significance. In *Différence et répétition* Deleuze describes his adherence to what he calls an 'anti-hégélianisme généralisé';[10] and, in his later work with Guattari, the nomad provides an important illustration of contemporary resistance to Hegel's metaphysics and politics. The nomad is not *opposed* to sedentary values and the sedentary state, on a political or intellectual level, he is simply and irreducibly *different*. This irreducible difference makes him absolutely irrecuperable to the categories of sedentary thought, and thereby upsets the dialectical process which aims to surmount antitheses. Despite the existence of 'mélanges de fait', the nomad perpetually resists synthesis. Tournier's treatment of the relationship between nomad and sedentary, on the other hand, bears witness to the urge for synthesis which informs all his writing. This is illustrated in political terms by Melchior's experience of poverty in *Gaspard, Melchior et Balthazar*. The dispossessed prince comes into contact with 'sédentaires [. . .] hostiles aux voyageurs sans statut bien défini' (*GMB* 83); but he envisages a new social order in which oppositions are subsumed and annulled: 'Ces réflexions [. . .] me faisaient découvrir [. . .] qu'un ordre social s'instaurera peut-être un jour, où il n'y aura plus de place ni pour un roi, ni pour un bandit, ni pour un mendiant' (*GMB* 87).

In *Le Vent Paraclet* Tournier acknowledges the influence of Hegel in a provocative statement of his aesthetic project: 'Comment faire sortir un roman de Ponson du Terrail de la machine à écrire de Hegel?' (*VP* 175). The clearest evidence of this debt is provided by the treatment of opposites in *Vendredi ou les limbes du Pacifique*. The relationship between Crusoé and Vendredi recalls the Hegelian dialectic of master and slave, as Vendredi takes the initiative from Crusoé and the master becomes dependent upon the slave.[11] Hegel uses the verb *aufheben*, which can mean both 'to preserve' and 'to abolish', to describe the dialectical surmounting of antitheses. In *Le Vent Paraclet* Tournier refers to the 'allure dialectique' of *Vendredi* (*VP* 226), and, after the explosion which destroys the 'île administrée', Crusoé believes that he has achieved the simultaneous preservation, abolition, and overcoming of opposites promised by

---

[10] Deleuze, *Différence et répétition*, p. 1. On the influence of Hegel and the difficulties involved in escaping it, see also Michel Foucault, *L'Ordre du discours*, pp. 74–7; 'toute notre époque, que ce soit par la logique ou par l'épistémologie, que ce soit par Marx ou par Nietzsche, essaie d'échapper à Hegel' (p. 74).

[11] See ch. 1 n. 3.

Hegel. Crusoé realizes that freedom need not be understood as the negation of order: 'La liberté de Vendredi [. . .] n'était pas que la négation de l'ordre effacé' (V 156). Order is effaced, but also preserved, as Vendredi's freedom is governed by 'une unité cachée, un principe implicite' (V 156). Crusoé also believes that the dialectic of master and slave has been transcended: he is unable to tell whether Vendredi is a 'chien fidèle' or a 'maître [. . .] impérieux' because 'il avait dépassé dans ses relations avec Vendredi le stade de ces mesquines alternatives' (V 156). Crusoé makes the same point when he describes how he and Vendredi have learned to overcome sexual difference: 'En vérité, au suprême degré où nous avons accédé, Vendredi et moi, la différence de sexe est dépassée' (V 185).

The words 'dépasser' and 'dépassement' recur frequently in Tournier's texts, describing the self-creation and self-overcoming in which his characters are engaged. But an important tendency in his writing insists that becoming is not anarchic, since it is directed towards a specific though perhaps unknown goal. In *Le Roi des aulnes* the narrator gives what can almost be regarded as a definition of the Hegelian dialectic, which also illuminates the structure of the novel; a strict teleology governs the process of *dépassement* as it governs the composition of Tournier's texts:

Tiffauges avait toujours pensé que la valeur fatidique de chacune des étapes de son cheminement ne serait pleinement attestée que si, tout en étant dépassée et transcendée, elle se trouvait en même temps conservée dans l'étape suivante. Il était donc anxieux que les acquisitions qu'il avait faites à Rominten trouvassent leur accomplissement à Kaltenborn. Il fut exaucé dès le mois d'octobre. (*RA* 278)

In the above passage, however, it is important to observe how the narrator is careful to attribute the Hegelian rhetoric to Tiffauges ('Tiffauges avait toujours pensé que. . . ') rather than adopting it in his own voice. In the final section of *Le Roi des aulnes* a series of *inversions malignes* demonstrates the extent to which Tiffauges has misunderstood his own situation and frustrates his anticipation of ultimate enlightenment. Tournier conceives of the inversion in terms of a 'change of sign' (plus becomes minus or minus becomes plus), which involves neither the suppressing nor the surpassing essential to the Hegelian dialectic.[12] Tournier's texts adopt a rhetoric which

---

[12] For Tournier's conception of the inversion as a process which is opposed to the Hegelian dialectic, see *Vol* 231, where Tournier refers to the qualities which Gide

suggests the influence of Hegel, but the promise of totalizing synthesis is never unambiguously fulfilled. Opposites are juxtaposed without synthesis, as Tournier indicates in his discussion of *phorie* in *Le Vent Paraclet*: 'Servir et asservir, aimer et tuer. Cette terrible dialectique est la constante de nombre d'êtres humains' (*VP* 122). The 'terrible dialectique' of *phorie* depends precisely upon the absence of dialectical synthesis. 'Servir' and 'asservir', 'aimer' and 'tuer' remain in conflict despite their paradoxical coexistence.[13] In a largely sympathetic article, the East German critic Christa Bevernis has described how Tournier remains caught within bourgeois ideology and fails to indicate the possibility that historical conflicts may be surmounted and superseded.[14] However much his texts may express the desire for synthesis, they never escape the vicious circle of thesis and antithesis. This failure might be regarded as his success when seen from the perspective of the Nietzschean and anti-Hegelian current in contemporary French thought. But Tournier is neither a committed Hegelian nor a joyful Nietzschean. His writing oscillates between assertive dogmatism and anxious self-interrogation and never unequivocally embraces the success or failure of the Hegelian scheme.

Tournier's most radical theme is the self-inflicted hermeneutic blindness which impedes his characters in their search for knowledge. The interpretation of nomadism provides a particularly instructive illustration of this blindness. Tournier's narrators attempt to make the nomad compatible with sedentary modes of thought, but it is also clear that the nomad is indifferent to the notions of direction and destination which are essential to the sedentary hermeneut:

Pour ces hommes qui sont tous des nomades sédentarisés — et malheureux de l'être — , partir trouve sa justification en soi-même. Peu importe la destination. Je crois qu'ils n'ont compris qu'une chose: nous irions loin, donc nous partions pour longtemps. Ils n'en demandaient pas davantage pour jubiler. (*GMB* 34)

---

inherited from his mother: 'Hérédité détestée et détestable qu'il ne surmonte ni se supprime, mais à laquelle il fait subir une inversion bénigne.' On inversion as a change of sign, see *RA* 351–2.

[13] Compare also Paul Surin's account of the dispersion and corrosion caused by the 'processus dialectique' in *M* 365–6.

[14] See Christa Bevernis, 'Zum Bild des Menschen im französischen Gegenwartsroman: Michel Tournier—J. M. G. Le Clézio—Georges Perec, Schreibweisen und Sehweisen'.

— Et veux-tu que je te dise une chose? Eh bien si tu lui demandais où il va et ce qu'il compte y faire, il ne te répondrait pas. Ou alors il inventerait une histoire à dormir debout. Parce qu'en réalité, un: il ne sait pas où il va, deux: il n'a pas l'intention d'y faire quoi que ce soit. C'est ça un Toubou, ça se déplace par principe, sans but et sans raison. Le vagabondage total, quoi! (*G* 79)

The Toubou whom Idriss encounters briefly in *La Goutte d'or* is an object of suspicion and fear because he seems recalcitrant to the notions upon which sedentary understanding relies. He combines contrary characteristics in a manner which disrupts the logic of non-contradiction and which inevitably makes him appear the enemy of civilized values:

[Idriss] connaissait l'exécrable réputation de ces nomades noirs du Tibesti que la sédentarisation avait décimés, dispersés et transformés en vagabonds ou en aventuriers du désert. On les disait paresseux mais infatigables, ivrognes et goinfres, mais d'une sobriété surhumaine dans leurs déplacements, taciturnes, mais mythomanes dès qu'ils profèrent une parole, farouchement solitaires, mais voleurs, violeurs et meurtriers dès qu'ils sont en société. (*G* 76)

Le Toubou, lui, paraissait en lutte ouverte ou masquée avec tous ses semblables [. . .] C'était un fauve. Non, ce n'était pas un fauve. Aucune bête ne s'entoure d'une pareille solitude, aucune bête ne se comporte avec autant d'hostile indifférence à l'égard de ses semblables. (*G* 82-3)

The sedentary regards travel as a necessary evil and space as an inconvenience which separates points of departure and arrival. For the nomad, on the other hand, perpetual departure forms part of an existential project. In *Les Météores* Jean describes his own nomadism as 'un goût de rupture et de solitude, de départ sans destination avouée' (*M* 362). Urs Kraus shares Jean's passion for departure: 'il faut être fou pour quitter cela. Pourtant je vais partir! Je pars toujours!' (*M* 474). Kraus's notion of 'espace riche' underlines the essential equation between travelling and becoming:

— Ma vie a changé le jour où j'ai compris que la situation d'un être ou d'un objet dans l'espace n'était pas indifférente, mais mettait au contraire en cause sa nature même. Bref qu'*il n'y a pas de translation sans altération* [. . .] L'espace est devenu une substance pleine, épaisse, riche de qualités et d'attributs. Et les choses des îlots découpés dans cette substance, faits *de* cette substance, mobiles certes mais à condition que toutes les relations de leur substance avec la substance extérieure accompagnent et enregistrent le mouvement. (*M* 475, 478)

Movement through rich space alters the substance of the traveller. The nomad's journey is without *sens*—either direction or meaning; and the lack of ultimate destination ensures the absence of finality in the process of becoming.

Nomadism is also the thematic trace of an anarchic impulse, the 'rappel au désordre',[15] which is at the core of Tournier's creative urge. The composition and philosophical significance of his texts can never be entirely explained by his claim to write 'traditional' novels and his admiration for the work of Plato, Leibniz, Spinoza, and Kant. The work of art itself has neither the purposiveness nor the utility which characterize the sedentary notion of travel. Movement without certain destination becomes, in Tournier's writing, a metaphor for creativity in aesthetic, philosophical, and practical spheres, as Gaspard explains in *Gaspard, Melchior et Balthazar*: 'Le poète l'a dit:[16] l'eau qui stagne immobile et sans vie devient saumâtre et boueuse. Au contraire, l'eau vive et chantante reste pure et limpide. Ainsi l'âme de l'homme sédentaire est un vase où fermentent des griefs indéfiniment remâchés. De celle du voyageur jaillissent en flots purs des idées neuves et des actions imprévues' (*GMB* 33-4).

As a novelist, Tournier is more interested in creative delusion than sterile insight, and he is fascinated by the disjunction between the beautiful coherence of intellectual constructions and the chaos which they inevitably fail to comprehend. His principal characters (Crusoé in *Vendredi ou les limbes du Pacifique*, Tiffauges in *Le Roi des aulnes*, Paul Surin in *Les Météores*) stake their faith in the coherence and intelligibility of experience. They enter into self-legitimating spirals of interpretation which seek to exclude the human reality of doubt. At the end of each of Tournier's novels we are left to decide whether the protagonist has arrived at a higher level of truth or succumbed to his self-created blindness. The model for this is, as we have seen, the final sentence of Flaubert's 'Un cœur simple', where the transfiguration of a stuffed parrot is offered either as a sign of Félicité's sainthood or as proof of her senility. However, Tournier's protagonists are less benign than Félicité, and their endeavour to find

---

[15] See *Vol* 32, where myth is described as 'un rappel au désordre', and *VP* 191, where, in a discussion of Bergson's analysis of 'le rire', Tournier refers to laughter as 'un rappel au désordre qui est vie, remise en question permanente de l'ordre d'hier'.

[16] A note given in the text indicates that the poet in question is Muhammad Asad (*GMB* 273). On Muhammad Asad, see also Tournier, *Petites Proses*, pp. 62-4.

meaning in chaos frequently threatens to lead them into criminal territory. *Le Roi des aulnes*, most notably, describes the stages by which an ineffectual garage mechanic is transformed into a contemporary version of Gilles de Rais. The search for order and coherence, whatever its human cost, is consistently presented as a human need which takes absolute priority over ethical considerations. It motivates Tiffauges's complicity with the Nazi regime and is also reflected in the formal precision which governs the structure and composition of all Tournier's fiction.

Tournier has no Fascist sympathies, despite the suspicions of at least one critic.[17] However, it is true that, in his writing, the simultaneous demands for creative freedom and aesthetic order coexist uneasily. This unease is explained in 'Les Malheurs de Sophie', the final chapter of *Le Vent Paraclet*, as the sign of Tournier's ambiguous attitude to what he perceives to be his own historical situation. He prefers the coherence of philosophical systems to the anti-systematic modes of philosophizing which have dominated the French intellectual scene in recent years. His highest philosophical ideal is 'sagesse', which he defines as the combination of knowledge, action, and morality (*VP* 276). He believes that the greatest illustration of this is to be found in Spinoza's *Ethics*, where reason and virtue appear as inseparable. Spinoza's 'préceptes admirables' are the 'déduction géométrique' of his premises rather than 'fragments d'une pensée vagabonde' (*VP* 277). However, Tournier recognizes that the 'soleil simple et nu de la sagesse' (*VP* 281) has been shattered — 'brisé en mille morceaux' (*VP* 281) — by Rousseau's eulogy of instinct, Newtonian physics, and Kant's demonstration of the limits of understanding (*VP* 277–80). Romanticism confirms the demise of the ideals exemplified by Spinoza (see *VP* 275), and modernity is characterized by a 'triple dégénérescence': 'La sagesse morte s'est décomposée en science physico-mathématique, morale formelle et information utilitaire' (*VP* 280).

As in his fiction, Tournier compares a lost ideal with contemporary indigence, but he complicates the scheme by the ambivalence of his own sympathies. He laments the demise of the ideal of wisdom, but concludes that 'Il faut en prendre son parti' (*VP* 287); and, only a few pages after his rejection of 'pensée vagabonde', he describes himself, the artist, in unmistakably nomadic terms. He insists that

[17] See ch. 2 n. 27.

'Les œuvres sont les fruits du désert et ne s'épanouissent que dans l'aridité' (*VP* 287); and, in order to be able to write and create, the artist requires '[ses] steppes familières où souffle le vent sec et glacé de l'idée pure' (*VP* 287). Earlier, Tournier referred to Spinoza's recommendation that the wise man should live in a community rather than in solitude (see *VP* 277); but now he argues that 'On ne peut séparer création et solitude' (*VP* 286). The creator and thinker must choose 'le mince bagage du voyageur à pied de préférence aux vastes et tièdes dortoirs des grandes familles spirituelles' (*VP* 287). Isolated from God and from man, 'entre un ciel rigoureux et une terre ingrate' (*VP* 287-8), the nomad develops a philosophy in accordance with his situation: 'on peut se faire une philosophie de disette, une sagesse de subsistance, un vade-mecum de va-nu-pieds' (*VP* 288). This 'philosophy of scarcity' ('philosophie de disette') entails Tournier's half-reluctant break with his masters in metaphysics. He refers to an 'atomisation de l'absolu' (*VP* 290) which resituates the transcendent within the banal and the metaphysical within the physical: the nomad discovers the absolute nowhere other than in his own proximity. Tournier describes a 'visage ravissant' seen in a crowded train, and the nomad finds a secret oasis in the middle of the human desert: 'Dans cette atmosphère close et empuantie, j'ai trouvé cette infime et vivante oasis. Je me délecte secrètement. Je m'en mets plein la vue. Au milieu de tous ces indigents, je suis riche comme Crésus' (*VP* 290).

In 'Les Malheurs de Sophie' Tournier renounces his most profound desires for the coherence of reality and the unity of knowledge. This renunciation is never definitive, and it will be repeated in the experience of each of his characters and each of his texts. Tournier's writing is situated uneasily between order and chaos. An urgent demand for structure competes with the 'rappel au désordre' which is the artist's call to creative freedom, and Tournier's defence of the 'traditional novel' is a fraught disavowal of the tensions within his own fiction. Despite the fantasy of an infallible mode of communication which his texts frequently describe, Tournier is aware that the language of fiction is an ambiguous and potentially non-communicative idiom. He is both fascinated and repelled by the possibility that his texts should become *écriture* and not *sens*. This tension can be seen in his simultaneous identification with both nomad and sedentary, when the former values the journey and the latter only the destination. Nietzsche described intellectual and spiritual nomadism ('ein geistiges

Nomadentum') as his highest ideal.[18] One of the central concerns of recent philosophical debate in France, itself strongly influenced by Nietzsche's writing, has been to repudiate the totalizing synthesis promised by Hegel. Tournier's dilemma is his inability to make a definitive choice between Hegel and Nietzsche, between the warm comfort of synthesis and the cold wind of scarcity. This indecision is, I would suggest, what makes Tournier's work so relevant to the predicament of the contemporary reader. Between *sens* and *écriture*, truth and dissemination, structure and freedom, it is perhaps not possible to choose.

[18] See Nietzsche, *Werke*, i. 817. On Nietzsche and 'nomadic thought', see Deleuze, 'Pensée nomade', in P. Boudot *et al.*, *Nietzsche aujourd'hui?*, i; see also Deleuze and Guattari's 'Traité de nomadologie', in *Mille plateaux*, pp. 434–527. For an account of the 'nomadization' of thought in France, which, bizarrely, does not mention the work of Deleuze and Guattari, see Dominique Grisoni, 'Ouverture', in Grisoni (ed.), *Politiques de la philosophie*, pp. 20–7.

Bibliography

1. *Tournier*

(i) PRINCIPAL WORKS

Vendredi ou les limbes du Pacifique (Paris, Gallimard, 1967).
Le Roi des aulnes (Paris, Gallimard, 1970).
Vendredi ou la vie sauvage (Paris, Flammarion, 1971). (The edition used is the Gallimard 'Folio Junior' edition of 1977.)
Les Météores (Paris, Gallimard, 1975).
Le Vent Paraclet (Paris, Gallimard, 1977).
Canada: Journal de voyage (photographs by Edouard Boubat) (Ottawa, Les Éditions la Presse, 1977). (This has also been published with different photographs and a postscript as *Journal de voyage au Canada* (Paris, Robert Laffont, 1984).)
Le Coq de bruyère (Paris, Gallimard, 1978).
Des clefs et des serrures: Images et proses (Paris, Chêne/Hachette, 1979).
Pierrot ou les secrets de la nuit (Paris, Gallimard, 1979).
Gaspard, Melchior et Balthazar (Paris, Gallimard, 1980).
Le Vol du vampire: Notes de lecture (Paris, Mercure de France, 1981).
Vues de dos (Photographs by Edouard Boubat) (Paris, Gallimard, 1981).
Gilles et Jeanne (Paris, Gallimard, 1983).
Les Rois Mages (Paris, Gallimard, 1983). (The edition used is the 'Folio Junior' edition of 1985.)
Le Vagabond immobile (drawings by Jean-Max Toubeau) (Paris, Gallimard, 1984).
La Goutte d'or (Paris, Gallimard, 1985).
Petites Proses (Folio 1768) (Paris, Gallimard, 1986).

In recent years Tournier has made numerous contributions to the press and literary journals and given a large number of interviews. The following lists include only those articles and interviews which have proved useful in the preparation of this study.

(ii) ARTICLES

'Des éclairs dans la nuit du cœur', *Les Nouvelles littéraires*, 26 Nov. 1970, pp. 1, 6.
'La Dimension mythologique', *La Nouvelle Revue Française*, 238 (1972), 124–9.

'Les Voyages initiatiques', *La Nouvelle Critique*, NS 105 (1977), 106–7 (discussion of Marcel Brion, *L'Allemagne romantique* iii. *Le Voyage initiatique*).

'Lettre-préface', in Manfred S. Fischer, *Probleme internationaler Literaturrezeption: Michel Tourniers „Le Roi des aulnes" im deutsch-französischen Kontext* (Bonn, Bouvier/Grundmann, 1977), 7–9.

'La Logosphère et les taciturnes', *Sud*, 'Hors Série' (1980), 167–77.

'Gustave et Marguerite', *Sud*, 55 (1984), 68–77 (on Flaubert's *Salammbô* and Marguerite Youcenar's *Mémoires d'Hadrien*).

'Les Mots sous les mots', *Le Débat*, 33 (1985), 95–109.

(iii) INTERVIEWS

'Plaidoyer pour un ogre: Entretien avec Michel Tournier', with Quentin Ritzen, *Les Nouvelles littéraires*, 26 Nov. 1970, p. 6.

'Une logique contre vents et marées: Entretien avec Michel Tournier', with Alain Poirson, *La Nouvelle Critique*, NS 105 (1977), 47–50.

'Je suis comme la pie voleuse', in Jean-Louis de Rambures, *Comment travaillent les écrivains* (Paris, Flammarion, 1978), 163–7.

'Dix-huit questions à Michel Tournier', with Jean-Jacques Brochier, *Magazine littéraire*, 138 (June 1978), 11–13.

'An Interview with Michel Tournier', with Penny Hueston, *Meanjin*, 38 (1979), 400–5.

'Entretien avec Michel Tournier', with Daniel Bougnoux and André Clavel, *Silex*, 14 (1979), 12–16.

'Une conversation avec Michel Tournier', with Alison Browning, *Cadmos*, 11 (1980), 5–15.

'Saint Tournier, Priez pour nous!', with Gilles Pudlowski, *Les Nouvelles littéraires*, 6 Nov. 1980, p. 36.

'Un dialogue avec Michel Tournier', conversation with René Zazzo, in *Le Paradoxe des jumeaux* (Paris, Stock/Laurence Pernoud, 1984).

'Rencontre avec Michel Tournier', with Alain Sanzio, Katy Barasc, and Jean-Pierre Joecker, *Masques: Revue des Homosexualités*, 23 (1984), 8–26.

'Tournier face aux lycéens', with various schoolchildren, *Magazine littéraire*, 226 (Jan. 1986), 20–5.

'Vers la concision et la limpidité', with Jean-Marie Magnan, *La Quinzaine littéraire*, 1 Feb. 1986, p. 16.

'Michel Tournier en questions', in Serge Koster, *Michel Tournier* (Paris, Henri Veyrier, 1986), 149–58.

2. Tournier: Critical Works

(i) BOOKS

BEVAN, D. G., *Michel Tournier* (Amsterdam, Rodopi, 1986).
CLOONAN, WILLIAM, *Michel Tournier* (Twayne's World Authors Series; Boston, Twayne, 1985).
FISCHER, MANFRED S., *Probleme internationaler Literaturrezeption: Michel Tourniers „Le Roi des aulnes" im deutsch-französischen Kontext* (Bonn, Bouvier/Grundmann, 1977).
JAY, SALIM, *Idriss, Michel Tournier et les autres* (Paris, Éditions de la Différence, 1986).
KOSTER, SERGE, *Michel Tournier* (Paris, Henri Veyrier, 1986).
SALKIN SBIROLI, LYNN, *Michel Tournier: Le Séduction du jeu* (Geneva–Paris, Slatkine, 1987).
STIRN, FRANÇOIS, *Tournier: Vendredi ou les limbes du Pacifique* (Profil d'une œuvre; Paris, Hatier, 1983).
YAICHE, FRANCIS, *"Vendredi ou la vie sauvage" de Michel Tournier* (Lectoguide; Paris, Éditions Pédagogie Moderne-Bordas, 1981).

(ii) ARTICLES AND LONGER STUDIES WHICH DISCUSS TOURNIER'S WORK

AMÉRY, JEAN, 'Ästhetizismus der Barbarei: Über Michel Tourniers Roman „Der Erlkönig"', *Merkur*, 297 (1973), 73–9.
BAROCHE, CHRISTIANE, 'Michel Tournier ou l'espace conquis', *Critique*, 342 (1975), 178–84.
BEVERNIS, CHRISTA, 'Michel Tournier: L'œuvre et son message', *Philologica Pragensia*, 26 (1983), 197–203.
—— 'Zum Bild des Menschen im französischen Gegenwartsroman: Michel Tournier—J. M. G. Le Clézio—Georges Perec, Schreibweisen und Sehweisen', *Weimarer Beiträge*, 31 (1985), 1589–613.
BOLZAN, LOREDANA, 'Les Météores o la retorica binaria', *Saggi e ricerche di letteratura francese*, 23 (1984), 9–37.
BONNEFIS, PHILIPPE, 'L'Excentrique du texte', in Jean Descottignies (ed.), *Les Sujets de l'écriture* (Lille, Presses Universitaires de Lille, 1981), 23–39.
BOSQUET, ALAIN, 'Tournier et les mythes renouvelés', *La Nouvelle Revue française*, 270 (1975), 82–6.
BOUGNOUX, DANIEL, 'Des métaphores à la phorie', *Critique*, 301 (1972), 527–43.
BROGNIET, ÉRIC, 'Michel Tournier: De l'initiation au salut', *Marginales*, 204 (1982), 10–18.

CAZELLES, BRIGITTE, and JOHNSON, PHYLLIS, 'L'Orientation d'Abel Tiffauges dans *Le Roi des aulnes*', *Rocky Mountain Review*, 29 (1975), 166–71.

CESBRON, GEORGES, 'Notes sur l'imagination terrienne du corps dans *Vendredi ou les limbes du Pacifique* de Michel Tournier', *Revue de l'Université de Bruxelles*, 3–4 (1979), 357–65.

CHABOT, JACQUES, 'Un frère jumeau du monde: Michel Tournier', *Études*, 345 (1977), 49–71.

CLAVEL, ANDRÉ, 'Un nouveau cynique: Tournier le jardinier', *Critique*, 361–2 (1977), 609–15.

CLOONAN, WILLIAM, 'The Artist Conscious and Unconscious in *Le Roi des aulnes*', *Kentucky Romance Quarterly*, 29 (1982), 191–200.

DAVIS, COLIN, 'Art and the Refusal of Mourning: The Aesthetics of Michel Tournier', *Paragraph*, 10 (1987), 29–44.

—— 'Identity and the Search for Understanding in Michel Tournier's *Les Météores*', *French Forum*, 12 (1987), 347–56.

——'Michel Tournier's *Vendredi ou les limbes du Pacifique*: A Novel of Beginnings', *Neophilologus* (forthcoming).

——'Michel Tournier between Synthesis and Scarcity', *French Studies* (forthcoming).

DELEUZE, GILLES, 'Michel Tournier et le monde sans autrui', in *Logique du sens* (Paris, Minuit, 1969), 350–72 (first published in *Critique*, 241 (1967), 503–25, and also published as a postface to the 'Folio' edition of *Vendredi ou les limbes du Pacifique*).

ENDERLÉ, MARCELLE, 'L'Espace dans *Le Nain Rouge*, nouvelle de Michel Tournier', *Littératures*, 5 (1982), 111–16.

FERNANDEZ, MARIE-HENRIETTE, 'Bessons et sorors germaine', *Littératures*, 9–10 (1984), 23–9.

FUMAROLI, MARC, 'Michel Tournier et l'esprit d'enfance', *Commentaire*, 3 (1980), 638–43.

GARNEAU, JOSEPH, 'Réflexions sur Michel Tournier', *French Review*, 58 (1985), 682–91.

GENETTE, GÉRARD, *Palimpsestes: La Littérature au second degré* (Paris, Seuil, 1982), 418–25.

IDOUX, MARIE-JOSEPH, '*Vendredi ou les limbes du Pacifique* de Michel Tournier', *Recherches sur l'imaginaire*, 8 (1982), 159–68.

——*Incidences*, NS 2–3, no. 2–3 (1979) (Collection of essays on 'Les Suaires de Véronique').

JARDINE, ALICE, 'Woman in Limbo: Deleuze and His Br(others)', *SubStance*, 44–5 (1984), 46–60.

LAUREILLARD, RÉMI, 'Le Porte-enfant', *Les Temps modernes*, 292 (1970), 916–28.

LEMOINE-LUCCIONI, EUGÉNIE, *Partage des femmes* (Paris, Seuil, 1976), 125–50.

LUCCIONI, GENNIE, 'Michel Tournier: *Vendredi ou les limbes du Pacifique*', *Esprit*, 35 (1967), 1041–5.

MACLEAN, MAIRI, 'Human Relations in the Novels of Tournier: Polarity and Transcendence', *Forum for Modern Language Studies*, 23 (1987), 241–52.

——*Magazine littéraire*, 138 (June 1978) (dossier on Tournier).

——*Magazine littéraire*, 226 (Jan. 1986) (dossier on Tournier).

MAGNAN, JEAN-MARIE, 'La Boue. Mais l'âme', *Sud*, 17 (1975), 105–10.

——'*Le Vent Paraclet* ou le rire d'enfance des philosophes', *Sud*, 22–3 (1978), 254–8.

——'Un passionnant roman sur la vie des livres: *Le Vol du vampire* de Michel Tournier', *Sud*, 43 (1982), 196–200.

MANSUY, MICHEL, 'Trois chercheurs de paradis: Bosco, Tournier, Cayrol', *Travaux de linguistique et de littérature*, 16 (1978), 211–32.

MAURY, PIERRE, 'Michel Tournier ou la perversion du mythe', *Revue générale* (Jan. 1977), 15–33.

MERLLIÉ, FRANÇOISE, 'Histoires de barbes: Petite métaphysique de la barbe dans l'œuvre de Tournier, de Barbe-Bleue à Barberousse', *Magazine littéraire*, 226 (Jan. 1986), 29–35.

——'La Reine blonde: De Méduse à la Muse, ou comment les mots délivrent de l'image', *Sud*, 61 (1986), 14–29.

MONÈS, PHILLIPE DE, 'Abel Tiffauges et la vocation maternelle de l'homme', postface to the 'Folio' edition of *Le Roi des aulnes* (1975), 585–600.

MORITA-CLÉMENT, MARIE-AGNÈS, *L'Image de l'Allemagne dans le roman français de 1945 à nos jours* (Nagoya (Japan), Presses Universitaires de Nagoya, 1985), 245–66.

NETTELBECK, COLIN, 'The Return of the Ogre: Michel Tournier's *Gilles et Jeanne*', *Scripsi*, 2/4 (1984), 43–50.

O'HEARNE, D. J., 'Michel Tournier: Symbols and Stories', *Scripsi*, 2/4 (1984), 13–22.

PETIT, SUSAN, 'The Bible as Inspiration in Tournier's *Vendredi ou les limbes du Pacifique*', *French Forum*, 9 (1984), 343–54.

——'*Gilles et Jeanne*: Tournier's *Le Roi des aulnes* Revisited', *Romanic Review*, 56 (1985), 307–15.

——'Salvation, the Flesh and God in Michel Tournier's *Gaspard, Melchior et Balthazar*', *Orbis litterarum*, 41 (1986), 53–65.

PIETRA, RÉGINE, 'Génétique et modèles culturels du Robinson valéryen', *Littérature*, 56 (1984), 75–91.

POIRIER, JACQUES, *Approche de. . . Le Roi des aulnes (Michel Tournier)* (Dijon, Éditions de l'Aleï, 1983).

——*Approche de. . . Vendredi ou les limbes du Pacifique (Michel Tournier)* (Dijon, Éditions de l'Aleï, 1985). (This and the preceding item are short pamphlets published under separate cover.)

POULET, ROBERT, 'Michel Tournier, romancier hors série', *Écrits de Paris*, 350 (1975), 93–101.

PRÉVOST, CLAUDE, 'Les Ogres de l'Histoire (Sur *Le Roi des aulnes*, roman de Michel Tournier)', in *Littérature, politique, idéologie* (Paris, Éditions sociales, 1973), 247–52.

PURDY, ANTHONY, '*Les Météores* de Michel Tournier: Une perspective hétérologique', *Littérature*, 40 (1980), 34–43.

——'From Defoe's *Crusoe* to Tournier's *Vendredi*: The Metamorphosis of a Myth', *Canadian Review of Comparative Literature / Revue Canadienne de Littérature Comparée*, 11 (1984), 216–35.

REDFERN, W. D., 'Approximating Man: Michel Tournier and Play in Language', *Modern Language Review*, 80 (1985), 304–19.

SANKEY, MARGARET, 'Meaning through Intertextuality: Isomorphism of Defoe's *Robinson Crusoe* and Tournier's *Vendredi ou les limbes du Pacifique*', *Australian Journal of French Studies*, 18 (1981), 77–88.

SAUBER, MARIANNE, L'Ogre et les symboles', *Europe*, 501 (1971), 158–62.

SHATTUCK, ROGER, 'Locating Michel Tournier', in *The Innocent Eye: On Modern Literature and the Arts* (New York, Farrar Straus Giroux, 1984), 205–18.

SMITH, STEPHEN, 'Toward a Literature of Utopia', in George Stambolian and Elaine Marks (eds.), *Homosexuality and French Literature: Cultural Contexts / Critical Texts* (London, Cornell University Press, 1979), 341–52.

STRICKLAND, GEOFFREY, '*Gaspard, Melchior et Balthazar* by Michel Tournier', *Cambridge Quarterly*, 10 (1982), 238–41.

——*Sud*, 'Hors Série' (1980) (issue devoted to Tournier).

——*Sud*, 61 (1986) (issue devoted to Tournier).

TAAT, MIEKE, 'Et si le roi était nu? — Michel Tournier, romancier mythologue', *Rapports: Het Franse Boek*, 52 (1982), 49–58.

VIERNE, SIMONE, *Rite, roman, initiation* (Grenoble, Presses Universitaires de Grenoble, 1979).

WAELTI-WALTERS, J., 'Autonomy and Metamorphosis', *Romanic Review*, 73 (1982), 505–14.

WHITE, J. J., 'Signs of Disturbance: The Semiological Import of some Recent Fiction by Michel Tournier and Peter Handke', *Journal of European Studies*, 4 (1974), 223–54.

WORTON, MICHAEL J., 'Myth Reference in *Le Roi des aulnes*', *Stanford French Review*, 6 (1982), 299–310.

——'Écrire et ré-écrire: Le projet de Tournier', *Sud*, 61 (1986), 52–69.

——'Intertextuality: To inter Textuality or to resurrect it', in David Kelley and Isabelle Llasera (eds.), *Crossreferences: Modern French Theory and the Practice of Criticism* (Leeds, Society for French Studies, 1986), 14–23.

——'Use and Abuse of Metaphor in Tournier's "Le Vol du vampire"', *Paragraph*, 10 (1987), 13–28.

YORK, R. A., 'Thematic Construction in *Le Roi des aulnes*', *Orbis litterarum*, 36 (1981), 76–91.

3. *Other Works Consulted*

ABRAMS, M. H., *The Mirror and the Lamp: Romantic Theory and the Critical Tradition* (New York, OUP, 1953).

ANOUILH, JEAN, *L'Alouette*, ed. Merlin Thomas and Simon Lee (London, Methuen, 1956).

ARISTOTLE, *Metaphysics*, trans. John Warrington (rev. edn.; London, J. M. Dent, 1961).

BACHELARD, GASTON, *Le Droit de rêver* (Paris, PUF, 1970).

BARTHES, ROLAND, *S/Z* (Points; Paris, Seuil, 1970).

——*Le Bruissement de la langue* (Paris, Seuil, 1984).

BATAILLE, GEORGES, *Le Procès de Gilles de Rais*, documents introduced by Georges Bataille, trans. Pierre Klossowski (Paris, Le Club français du livre, 1959).

——*L'Expérience intérieure*, in *Œuvres complètes*, v (Paris, Gallimard, 1973).

BAUDELAIRE, CHARLES, *Œuvres complètes* ed. Claude Pichois (Bibliothèque de la Pléiade; 2 vols.; Paris, Gallimard, 1975-6).

BÉGUIN, ALBERT, *L'Âme romantique et le rêve* (Paris, Corti, 1939).

BLANCHOT, MAURICE, *La Part du feu* (Paris, Gallimard, 1949).

BLOOM, HAROLD, *The Anxiety of Influence: A Theory of Poetry* (New York, OUP, 1973).

——*A Map of Misreading* (New York, OUP, 1975).

BRION, MARCEL, *L'Allemagne romantique*, iii. *Le Voyage initiatique* (Paris, Albin Michel, 1977).

BUNGAY, STEPHEN, *Beauty and Truth: A Study of Hegel's Aesthetics* (Oxford, OUP, 1984).

CAMUS, ALBERT, *L'Homme révolté* (Idées; Paris, Gallimard, 1951).

CASANOVA, JACQUES (GIACOMO), *Histoire de ma vie* (12 vols.; Wiesbaden/Paris, Brockhaus/Plon, 1960-2).

CLAUDEL, PAUL, 'Du sens figuré de l'Écriture', in *Œuvres complètes de Paul Claudel*, xxi (Paris, Gallimard, 1963).

——*Le Soulier de satin*, in *Théâtre*, ii, ed. Jacques Madaule and Jacques Petit (Bibliothèque de la Pléiade; Paris, Gallimard, 1965).

COLERIDGE, SAMUEL, *Samuel Taylor Coleridge*, ed. H. J. Jackson (Oxford, OUP, 1985).

CULLER, JONATHAN, *The Pursuit of Signs: Semiotics, Literature, Deconstruction* (London, Routledge and Kegan Paul, 1981).

DELEUZE, GILLES, *Le Bergsonisme* (2nd edn.; Paris, PUF, 1968).

——*Logique du sens* (Paris, Minuit, 1969).

DELEUZE, GILLES, 'Pensée nomade', in P. Boudot et al., Nietzsche aujourd'hui? (10/18; Paris, Union Générale d'Éditions, 1973), i. 159–90.

——Différence et répétition (2nd edn.; Paris, PUF, 1972).

——Spinoza: Philosophie pratique (2nd edn.; Paris, Minuit, 1981).

——and GUATTARI, FÉLIX, Capitalisme et schizophrénie, i. L'Anti-Œdipe (Paris, Minuit, 1972).

——and——Capitalisme et schizophrénie, ii. Mille plateaux (Paris, Minuit, 1980).

DE MAN, PAUL, Blindness and Insight: Essays in the Rhetoric of Contemporary Criticism (2nd edn.; London, Methuen, 1983).

DERRIDA, JACQUES, De la grammatologie (Paris, Minuit, 1967).

——L'Écriture et la différence (Points; Paris, Seuil, 1967).

——La Dissémination (Paris, Seuil, 1972).

——Marges de la philosophie (Paris, Minuit, 1972).

——Positions (Paris, Minuit, 1972).

——'Economimesis', in S. Agacinski et al., Mimesis des articulations (Paris, Flammarion, 1975), 55–93.

——La Vérité en peinture (Paris, Flammarion, 1978).

DESCARTES, RENÉ, Œuvres et lettres, ed. André Bridoux (Bibliothèque de la Pléiade; Paris, Gallimard, 1953).

DUBOIS, CLAUDE-GILBERT, Mythe et langage au seizième siècle (Bordeaux, Ducros, 1970).

FAUCON, BERNARD, Les Grandes Vacances (Paris, Herscher, 1980).

FLAUBERT, GUSTAVE, Madame Bovary (Livre de Poche; Paris, Librairie Générale Française, 1972).

——Trois Contes (Folio; Paris, Gallimard, 1973).

FOUCAULT, MICHEL, Les Mots et les choses: Une archéologie des sciences humaines (Paris, Gallimard, 1966).

——L'Ordre du discours (Paris, Gallimard, 1971).

FREUD, SIGMUND, The Standard Edition of the Complete Psychological Works of Sigmund Freud, ed. James Strachey (24 vols.; London, Hogarth Press and the Institute of Psycho-Analysis, 1953–74).

GADAMER, HANS-GEORG, Kleine Schriften, i. Philosophie, Hermeneutik (Tübingen, J. C. B. Mohr (Paul Siebeck), 1967).

——Wahrheit und Methode: Grundzüge einer philosophischen Hermeneutik (4th edn.; Tübingen, J. C. B. Mohr (Paul Siebeck), 1975).

GIDE, ANDRÉ, Romans, récits et soties, œuvres lyriques (Bibliothèque de la Pléiade; Paris, Gallimard, 1958).

GILSON, ÉTIENNE, La Théologie mystique de Saint Bernard (Paris, Vrin, 1934).

GIRAUDOUX, JEAN, Suzanne et le Pacifique, ed. Roy Lewis (London, University of London Press, 1964).

GOMBRICH, E. H., The Story of Art (11th edn.; London, Phaidon, 1966).

GRISONI, DOMINIQUE, 'Ouverture', in Dominique Grisoni (ed.), *Politiques de la philosophie* (Paris, Bernard Grasset, 1976), 9–27.

HEGEL, FRIEDRICH, *Vorlesungen über die Aesthetik*, in *Werke in zwanzig Bänden*, xiii–xv (Frankfurt am Main, Suhrkamp, 1970).

HEIDEGGER, MARTIN, *Holzwege* (Frankfurt am Main, Klostermann, 1950).

——*Unterwegs zur Sprache* (Tübingen, Neske, 1959).

——*Being and Time*, trans. John Macquarrie and Edward Robinson (Oxford, Basil Blackwell, 1978).

——*Sein und Zeit* (15th edn.; Tübingen, Max Niemeyer Verlag, 1979).

HOMER, *The Odyssey*, trans. E. V. Rieu (Harmondsworth, Penguin, 1946).

HUTIN, SERGE, *Les Gnostiques* (Que sais-je?; 2nd edn.; Paris, PUF, 1963).

HUYSMANS, JORIS-KARL, *A Rebours/Le Drageoir aux épices* (10/18; Paris, Union Générale d'Éditions, 1975).

JOUSSE, MARCEL, *L'Anthropologie du geste* (Paris, Gallimard, 1974).

KANT, IMMANUEL, *Kritik der Urteilskraft*, ed. Karl Vorländer (6th edn.; Hamburg, Felix Meiner, 1924).

KOFMAN, SARAH, *Quatre romans analytiques* (Paris, Galilée, 1973).

——*L'Énigme de la femme: La Femme dans les textes de Freud* (Paris, Galilée, 1980).

——*Mélancolie de l'art* (Paris, Galilée, 1985).

KRAUSS, WILHELMINE, *Das Doppelgängermotif in der Romantik: Studien zum romantischen Idealismus* (Berlin, Erich Ebering, 1930).

LACAN, JACQUES, *Écrits* (Paris, Seuil, 1966).

LAMARTINE, ALPHONSE DE, *Œuvres poétiques complètes* ed. Marius-François Guyard (Bibliothèque de la Pléiade; Paris, Gallimard, 1963).

LANZA DEL VASTO, JOSEPH JEAN, *Le Chiffre des choses* (4th edn.; Paris, Denoël, 1953).

LAPLANCHE, JEAN, *Vie et mort en psychanalyse* (Paris, Flammarion, 1970).

——and PONTALIS, J.-B., *Vocabulaire de la psychanalyse* (Paris, PUF, 1967).

LECERCLE, JEAN-JACQUES, *Philosophy through the Looking Glass: Language, Nonsense, Desire* (London, Hutchinson, 1985).

LEIRIS, MICHEL, *L'Âge d'homme* (Folio; Paris, Gallimard, 1939).

LICHTENBERG, CHRISTIAN FRIEDRICH, *Gesammelte Werke*, ed. Wilhelm Grenzmann (2 vols.; Frankfurt am Main, Halle, 1949).

LYOTARD, JEAN-FRANÇOIS, *Des Dispositifs pulsionnels* (10/18; Paris, Union Générale d'Éditions, 1973).

MUSIL, ROBERT, *Der Mann ohne Eigenschaften*, in *Gesammelte Werke*, i–v (Reinbek bei Hamburg, Rowohlt, 1978).

NIETZSCHE, FRIEDRICH, *Werke*, ed. Karl Schlechta (3 vols.; Munich, Carl Hanser, 1966).

NOVALIS, *Heinrich von Ofterdingen*, ed. Wolfgang Frühwald (Stuttgart, Reclam, 1965).

PEIRCE, CHARLES S., *Collected Papers,* ii. *Elements of Logic,* ed. Charles Hartshorne and Paul Weiss (Cambridge (USA), Harvard University Press, 1932).

PEREC, GEORGES, *Les Choses: Une histoire des années soixante* (J'ai lu; Paris, René Julliard, 1965).

PERRAULT, CHARLES, *Contes de Perrault,* ed. Gilbert Rouger (Paris, Garnier, 1967).

PIERSSENS, MICHEL, *La Tour de Babil* (Paris, Minuit, 1976).

PLATO, *The Collected Dialogues,* ed. Edith Hamilton and Huntingdon Cairns (various translators; Princeton, Princeton University Press, 1961).

PLOTINUS, *The Enneads,* trans. Stephen Mackenna, third edn., revised by B. S. Page (London, Faber and Faber, 1956).

REEVES, MARJORIE, *The Influence of Prophecy in the later Middle Ages: A Study in Joachimism* (Oxford, OUP, 1969).

RICŒUR, PAUL, *Finitude et culpabilité,* ii. *La Symbolique du mal* (Paris, Aubier-Montaigne, 1960).

—— *De l'interprétation: Essai sur Freud* (Paris, Seuil, 1965).

—— *Le Conflit des interprétations: Essais d'herméneutique* (Paris, Seuil, 1969).

—— *Temps et récit,* i (Paris, Seuil, 1983).

RIMBAUD, ARTHUR, *Œuvres,* ed. Suzanne Bernard (Paris, Garnier, 1960).

SARTRE, JEAN-PAUL, *L'Imaginaire: Psychologie phénoménologique de l'imagination* (Paris, Gallimard, 1940).

—— *L'Être et le Néant: Essai d'ontologie phénoménologique* (Paris, Gallimard, 1943).

—— *Situations,* i (Paris, Gallimard, 1947).

—— *Situations,* ii (Paris, Gallimard, 1948).

—— *Saint Genet, comédien et martyr* (Paris, Gallimard, 1952).

—— *La Transcendance de l'ego: Esquisse d'une description phénoménologique,* ed. Sylvie Le Bon (Paris, Vrin, 1972; first published 1936).

—— *La Nausée,* in *Œuvres romanesques,* ed. Michel Contat and Michel Rybalka (Bibliothèque de la Pléiade; Paris, Gallimard, 1981; first published 1938).

SAUSSURE, FERDINAND DE, *Cours de linguistique générale* (Paris, Payot, 1973).

SCHELLING, FRIEDRICH, *Sämmtliche Werke* (5 vols.; Stuttgart/Augsburg, Cotta, 1856–61).

SCHOPENHAUER, ARTHUR, *Die Welt als Wille und Vorstellung,* in *Sämmtliche Werke,* i (Stuttgart/Frankfurt am Main, Insel/Cotta, 1960).

SPINOZA, BARUCH DE, *Éthique,* trans. by Charles Appuhn, in *Œuvres,* iii (Paris, Garnier-Flammarion, 1965).

TYMMS, RALPH, *Doubles in Literary Psychology* (London, Bowes and Bowes, 1949).

BIBLIOGRAPHY 217

VALÉRY, PAUL, *Œuvres*, ed. Jean Hytier (Bibliothèque de la Pléiade; 2 vols.; Paris, Gallimard, 1957 and 1960).

WARE, FATHER KALLISTOS, *The Orthodox Way* (Oxford, Mowbray, 1979).

WOLFSON, LOUIS, *Le Schizo et les langues* (Paris, Gallimard, 1970).

ZAZZO, RENÉ, *Les Jumeaux: Le Couple et la personne* (2 vols. (with consecutive pagination); Paris, PUF, 1960).

ZOLA, ÉMILE, *Le Ventre de Paris* (Livre de Poche; Paris, Fasquelle, 1978).

Index